Assessment Case Studies:
Common Issues in Implementation with
Various Campus Approaches to Resolution

By the same author

*A Practitioner's Handbook for Institutional Effectiveness and Student
    Outcomes Assessment (3rd ed.)*
*The Departmental Guide and Record Book for Student Outcomes
    and Institutional Effectiveness (2nd ed.)*

Assessment Case Studies: Common Issues in Implementation with Various Campus Approaches to Resolution

James O. Nichols
Director, University Planning and Institutional Research
The University of Mississippi

AGATHON PRESS
NEW YORK

Library of Congress Cataloging-in-Publication Data
Nichols, James O. (James Oliver), 1941-
    Assessment case studies : common issues in
implementation with verious campus approaches to
resolution / James O. Nichols
        p.   cm.
    ISBN 0-87586-112-1
    1. Universities and colleges—United States—
Evaluation—Case Studies.   I. Title.
LB2331.63.N546   1996
378.73—dc20   95-40856
                                          CIP

*What infinitely small contribution has been made to the improvement of student learning at institutions of higher education by the family of publications (*A Practitioner's Handbook, The Departmental Guide, *and* Assessment Case Studies*), of which* Assessment Case Studies *is the latest, is the result of three forces' impact on my professional life. First, I learned to focus work to achieve longer-range ends from my beloved parents Jimmy and Lorraine Nichols. Second, my immediate family, Karen (my spouse), Patricia, Barbara, Elizabeth, and Jay (our children) were understanding and patient enough to allow me to develop my field of study as my hobby as well as my vocation. Finally, I am particularly grateful to Richard E. White, Richard R. Perry, and Robert Reiman, each of whom by their actions convinced me as a young professional that being of service to others was among life's greatest achievements.* Assessment Case Studies *is dedicated to each of these individuals.*

Jim Nichols

CONTENTS

PREFACE AND ACKNOWLEDGMENTS

This is the third book in a series begun in 1988 concerning the practical aspects of implementation of institutional effectiveness or educational outcomes assessment at institutions of higher education. Each of the books in the series has been progressively less theoretical and more based upon actual campus experiences than was its predecessor. This book has been the most enjoyable, frustrating, and yet most promising of the three. It has been "enjoyable" from the standpoint of witnessing the widespread initiation of assessment activities across our country and having the pleasure of working with eleven institutions conducting an in-depth analysis of their implementation experiences. It has been "frustrating" from the standpoint of recognizing, even more clearly than in the past, the difficulty the case study institutions have had with campus issues regarding implementation and the rather limited extent to which educational outcomes assessment has penetrated to the departmental level on several campuses. It is "promising" from the standpoint of the future of the field of assessment activities and the growing tendency toward greater in-depth implementation at institutions, leading to more departmental and program involvement by faculty in the use of assessment results to improve learning on our campuses.

The hard work of three separate groups of people clearly needs to be acknowledged. The most obvious is the work of those listed beside their institution in Chapter I, the case study contributors. Each of these individuals spent a considerable amount of time on his or her campus analyzing their implementation activities (using the agreed upon standardized format shown in Appendix A). It would have been much easier for these contributors to have merely "written the story" of their implementation experiences as a narrative; however, several have commented that participation in the case study forced them to review implementation and bring about further improvements on their campus. These case study contributors include:

Harriott D. Calhoun is Director of Institutional Research at Jefferson State Community College in Birmingham, Alabama. She is an active member in state, regional, and national associations related to institutional research, in which she has held elected/appointed positions. She currently serves on SACS Visiting Committees as a consultant and speaker on institutional planning, student outcomes, and assessment of institutional effectiveness.

Myrtes Dunn Green is Assistant to the President for Institutional Effectiveness at Stillman College in Tuscaloosa, Alabama. She has worked as an educational consultant in the areas of planning, assessment, and evaluation, as well as in proposal development. Her professional interests are in the area of planning and evaluation focusing on historically black colleges and universities.

Roseann Hogan serves as Director of Planning and Assessment for the Lexington Campus of the University of Kentucky. Previously she worked in a variety of institutions, including the University of Kentucky Community Colleges, Kentucky State University, and the University of Notre Dame.

Richard Middaugh is the Assistant Vice President for Information and Research at Daytona Beach Community College. From 1990 to 1994 he served as the Director of Institutional Research at Sam Houston State University. He is the former Associate Director of Institutional Research and Planning at the University of South Alabama and the former Research Manager for Hillsborough Community College.

Gerry Perkus has been the Director of Institutional Research at Collin County Community College since 1986. Previously he held a variety of administrative and teaching posts in Texas and the Northeast. His professional interests focus on strategic planning, program evaluation, and classroom research.

Julia (Judy) S. Rogers has been Director of Institutional Evaluation and Professor of Psychology at the University of Montevallo in Montevallo, Alabama since 1974, where she has presented papers and published in areas of cognitive development, assessment of college outcomes, program evaluation, and quality improvement.

Bobby Sharp is the Director of Institutional Research and Planning at Appalachian State University in Boone, North Carolina, where he also holds an academic appointment in the Department of Leadership and Educational Studies. Previously he served as Associate Director of University Planning and Institutional Research at the University of Mississippi and Director of Institutional Research at Mississippi University for Women.

Walter H. Timm, Jr. has been the Executive Vice President at Coastal Carolina Community College (CCCC) since 1989 and serves as President of the Community College Planning and Research Organization. During his tenure at CCCC he was the principal author and remains responsible for the "Desktop Audit," an innovative annual accountability, planning, and evaluation tool.

David Underwood is the Director of Assessment and Assistant Professor of Education at Clemson University and serves on the Executive Board of the South Carolina Higher Education Assessment Network. He is currently chairing a statewide committee to determine minimal graduation and retention rates for the State Postsecondary Review Program in South Carolina.

James Fredericks Volkwein is Director of Institutional Research and Associate Professor of Educational Administration and Policy Studies at the State University of New York in Albany. He has written more than 50 research reports, conference papers, journal articles, and book reviews and frequently serves as a consultant to campuses interested in designing and implem3enting outcomes assessment programs.

R. Dan Walleri is the Director of Research, Planning, and Computer Services at Mount Hood Community College. He has also served as President of the National Council for Research Planning and of the Pacific Northwest Association for Institutional Research and Planning. He is the author and co-author of articles on student outcomes, assessment, and institutional effectiveness.

In addition to these individuals, I am indebted to their institutions for their willingness to allow their implementation experiences to be candidly described for the benefit of others. Where these experiences have been less than successful, the institutions have been shielded from embarrassment and where successful, referenced by name. In particular, I am indebted to those institutions which provided permission to reproduce materials from their campus as a portion of the appendices to this document and, finally, to the additional institutions noted at the beginning of Appendix B that provided example statements of educational outcomes/ means of assessment for use in that Appendix.

Much less evident in most publications is the work done by those who support the author; in this case, Mrs. Harolyn Merritt, Miss Heidi Tickle, and Mrs. Katherine Adams. Preparation of the entire manuscript would have been impossible without Mrs. Merritt's careful attention to detail and willingness to work on what has been a time consuming project. All authors should be blessed with a secretary with a master's degree from Columbia University as well as a cheerful and forgiving disposition. Miss Heidi Tickle, a doctoral graduate assistant at The University of Mississippi, is primarily responsible for the examples shown in Appendix B (which will undoubtedly become a very "well worn" section of the book), and Mrs. Katherine Adams, who carefully reviewed the manuscript, contributed substantially to its coherence.

For all of the above assistance, I am very grateful and as this publication assists those in the process of implementation of educational outcomes assessment across the country, readers should bear in mind that more than fifteen professionals from a dozen campuses made this book possible.

Jim Nichols
Fall, 1994

Chapter I

INTRODUCTION

It is quite tempting to utilize the well-worn phrase "You've come a long way, baby" when discussing the development of the assessment movement in the last few years. Prior to the mid-1980s, the primary thrust toward assessment or measurement of student learning was restricted to the teacher education field in postsecondary education and to K-12 public education. Perhaps the only serious work regarding student outcomes assessment in higher education taking place during this period of time was that pioneering work by Peter Ewell published by the National Center for Higher Education Management Systems (NCHEMS). Regretfully these publications were considerably ahead of their time and to all extent and purposes fell on "deaf ears."

During the middle part of the 1980s, it was difficult to pick up a copy of the *Chronicle of Higher Education* without finding one call or another, such as: "To Strengthen Quality in Higher Education: Summary Recommendations of the National Commission on Higher Education Issues" (1982); "A Nation at Risk: The Imperative for Educational Reform" (1983); "To Reclaim a Legacy" (1984); and "Involvement in Learning: Realizing the Potential of American Higher Education" (1984) for the improvement of undergraduate education. These calls had essentially three things in common. They cited the need: (a) to focus efforts toward improvement on undergraduate education, (b) to study student learning (as opposed to teaching), and (c) for additional funding to accomplish both of the previous proposed actions.

The calls referenced above in the national studies listed were only partially adopted by then Secretary of Education William Bennett when he revised the regulations for federal recognition of accrediting agencies in which he identified four key elements that have to a great extent driven the assessment movement and particularly the institutional effectiveness aspect. In 1987, the federal regulations were revived to indicate that an accrediting association in order to receive federal recognition must:

- Determine whether an educational institution or program maintains clearly specified educational objectives consistent with its mission . . .;
- Verify that satisfaction of certificate and degree requirements by all students . . . who have demonstrated educational achievement as assessed and documented through appropriate measures;
- Determine that institutions or programs document the educational achievements of

their students . . . in verifiable and consistent ways, such as evaluation of senior theses, review of student portfolios, general educational assessment (e.g. standardized test results), graduate or professional school test results (graduate or professional school placements, job placement rates, licensing examination results, employer evaluations, and other recognized measures.

- Determine the extent to which institutions or programs systematically apply the information obtained through the measures described in this section to foster enhanced student achievement . . .

In the middle 1980s, the Commission on Colleges of the Southern Association of Colleges and Schools (SACS) in response to the criticism of several southern governors (most notably Governor Martinez of Florida) began movement toward a student outcomes or learning-based revision to their *Standards for Accreditation.* This revision was comprehensive in nature, incorporated the elements referenced by Bennett eventually in the change in federal regulations, and became known as institutional effectiveness. Effective in 1985-86, SACS' reaffirmation of accreditation as well as initial candidacy for accreditation was accomplished through the *Criteria for Accreditation* (which include educational outcomes assessment or institutional effectiveness) that have been even further strengthened since that time. Because of limited experience in implementation of educational outcomes assessment on campuses, SACS received a rather substantial grant from the Fund for the Improvement of Postsecondary Education for the development and publication of a "Resource Manual" on institutional effectiveness to guide SACS' institutions in compliance with the educational outcomes assessment (institutional effectiveness) aspects of the *Criteria for Accreditation.* This author along with a number of others, including Trudy Banta, John Harris and Michael Yost, met for a period of some 18 months in a number of two- to three-day sessions in order to pool their experience in implementation of student outcomes assessment, resulting in the publication in 1989 of the *Resource Manual on Institutional Effectiveness* by SACS.

What's changed since the early to mid-1980s? Only a small portion of institutions were even beginning to think of implementation of assessment activities in the early to mid-1980s, but in *Campus Trends, 1993,* Elaine El-Khawas reports that nationally 97% of the institutions responding to her annual questionnaire indicated one type or another of assessment activities underway. Comprehensive institutional implementation of student outcomes assessment was reported in separate studies conducted in 1991 by Johnson/Prus and Nichols/Wolff as taking place at approximately 25-30% of the institutions nationwide. This was confirmed in El-Khawas' 1993 report indicating "extensive" assessment activities at 43% of institutions responding nationwide.

Regional and professional accrediting associations continue to grow in emphasis concerning student outcomes assessment. Most of the SACS institutions have been through reaffirmation of their accreditation under the student outcomes assessment based *Criteria for Accreditation.* SACS is currently increasing the rigor expected of its member schools in regard to student outcomes assessment. SACS' current expectation is institution-wide documentable implementation showing use of assessment results to improve programming by institutions.

Assessment of "student academic achievement" is the driving force behind the Institutions of Higher Education, North Central Association of Colleges and Schools (NCA) accreditation procedures now in the early stages of implementation. Assessment of student academic achievement has been described as a "reinvigorating force" behind the whole NCA accreditation process.

Professional accrediting procedures continue to grow in their recognition of the importance of student outcomes assessment. Requirements for professional accreditation, teacher education through NCATE, business schools through AACSB, and allied health through NLN and other agencies all focus progressively more on the outcomes of student learning.

At the state level, virtually all state coordinating agencies or governing boards now require some form of outcomes assessment effort on the part of public institutions. During the early part of the assessment movement such central coordinating or governing boards showed remarkable restraint in not prescribing specific assessment procedures for institutional comparisons. However, over the last several years, Ewell has noted a steady erosion of this restraint and growth in prescribed means of assessment by state coordinating agencies or governing board for public colleges and universities.

What has remained constant during this period of growth in the assessment movement? Beyond much doubt, there remains a large degree of public cynicism regarding the value of higher education and the appropriateness of its priorities. As recently as this year, a "wingspread" report (*An American Imperative: Higher Expectations for Higher Education*, Johnson Foundation Inc., Racine, WI, 1993), by a distinguished group of public representatives cited the need for increased focus on undergraduate student learning in the nation's colleges and universities and concomitant de-emphasis on research, etc. Because of the limited pool of funds available and the competition for these funds by other public agencies, the charge that higher education needs to refocus its priorities on student learning has become a convenient excuse through which to deny or reduce funding provided to support higher education in many states.

The primary difference in the student outcomes assessment movement between the mid-1980s and the publication of this document is the growth in the number of institutions with specific and in-depth experience in implementation of such programs. Unlike earlier in the movement when the only institutions with in-depth experience in implementation were unique due to their nature, administrative commitment, or motivation for state funding, there now exist a number of institutions that have implemented institutional effectiveness or assessment of educational outcomes in a comprehensive manner across most disciplines to the point of using results to improve academic programming. Because of the relatively early emphasis by the Commission on Colleges of the Southern Association of Colleges and Schools, most institutions with such in-depth comprehensive experience in implementation of institutional effectiveness or educational outcomes assessment are located in the southern portion of the United States. While there are a number of institutions that at this time are making great strides toward implementation in a comprehensive manner across the country, those institutions that began early provide the basic source material for *Assessment Case Studies*. It should be noted that none of these institutions would describe themselves as fully implemented. Like all who have been in the field for some time, their implementation has "matured" only because they've been trying a little longer. Shown below are the major research universities, primarily four-year colleges and universities, and community colleges who have contributed to this case studies book and the contributors from each institution.

Major Research Universities
- Clemson University, David G. Underwood
- SUNY-Albany, J. Fredericks Volkwein
- University of Kentucky-Lexington Campus, Roseann R. Hogan

Primarily Four-Year Colleges and Universities
- Sam Houston State University, Richard W. Middaugh
- Appalachian State University, Bobby H. Sharp
- University of Montevallo, Julia S. Rogers
- Stillman College, Myrtes Dunn Green

Community Colleges
- Coastal Carolina Community College, Walter H. Timm, Jr.
- Collin County Community College, Gerald H. Perkus
- Mount Hood Community College, R. Dan Walleri
- Jefferson State Community College, Harriott D. Calhoun

These institutions represent a relatively reasonable cross-section of institutional types and size. They have had both similar and dissimilar experiences in implementation. Without exception, each of the institutions referenced has confirmed the importance of a carefully planned sequence of implementation activities. A number of the institutions (both 2-year and 4-year) have utilized successfully the generic or four-year model (as modified to fit their institution) described in *A Practitioner's Handbook for Institutional Effectiveness and Student Outcomes Assessment Implementation* to implement institutional effectiveness. In addition, the majority of these institutions have encountered similar issues in implementation of institutional effectiveness or assessment of educational outcomes on their campuses.

Because of their uniqueness of purpose, student body composition, campus politics, etc., these institutions have slightly different versions or "arrangements" (to use a musical metaphor) of the basic issues described in this publication. Likewise, approaches to handling the issues described and the relative degree of success experienced by each institution have varied based upon institutional circumstances. Nonetheless, there appear to be a consistent set of issues and approaches to solution of those issues which institutions have experienced in implementation of institutional effectiveness or assessment of educational outcomes. It is the purpose of this book to outline the issues most frequently encountered in implementation of assessment of student academic achievement, educational outcomes assessment, or institutional effectiveness and various approaches or solutions to those issues.

In order to provide a common framework with which to relate the implementation issues experienced by the institutions, the generic model or plan for implementation over four years, described in *A Practitioner's Handbook for Institutional Effectiveness and Student Outcomes Assessment Implementation* and shown in Figure 4 on page 24 of that publication, has been utilized as a framework for comparisons of issues and solutions. Institutions were asked to respond to the outline of issues shown in Appendix A regarding their implementation of educational outcomes assessment or institutional effectiveness. That outline was structured based upon the generic plan or model for implementation originated in *A*

Practitioner's Handbook and briefly described in the following chapter. In Chapters III-VI, the issues experienced in each stage of implementation are addressed. *First*, each issue is identified, as are its permutations from the generic model on different campuses taking part in the study. *Second,* methods for addressing the issue are discussed and their relative success described. *Third*, when appropriate, relatively unique aspects of the issue related to the institutional type (two-year or four-year institution, composition of the student body, etc.) are reviewed. Hence, readers need only identify the section of this publication relating to a particular issue to determine how the case study institutions approached solution to this issue rather than having to review the individual case study of each institution.

In addition to the case study material presented in the following chapters, Appendix B includes specific examples of educational outcomes for a wide variety of disciplines and a limited number of administrative departments. In many cases, institutions for whom the author has served as a consultant have commented upon the need for examples of how various disciplines approach the issue of identifying intended educational objectives and means of assessment. The examples provided come from both the case study institutions and a number of other institutions listed at the beginning of Appendix B. They are intended not as *models*, but as *examples* of the way various disciplines have identified intended educational outcomes and means of assessment. Some readers will find this the most useful aspect of this publication as they work with the individual academic departments on their campus.

There are certainly a multitude of terms used in the assessment community to identify essentially similar concepts. This is particularly so in relationship to program or departmental level assessment. *A Practitioner's Handbook* utilizes the terms, intended educational, research, and public service outcomes and administrative objectives. In most cases, this publication will continue that practice. It should be noted that intended educational outcomes in this publication are synonymous with intended student academic achievement (NCA terminology), expected educational results, (SACS terminology), and the more commonly used generic term, intended student outcomes.

This publication, as have been *A Practitioner's Handbook for Institutional Effectiveness and Student Outcomes Assessment Implementation* and *The Departmental Guide to Implementation of Student Outcomes Assessment and Institutional Effectiveness,* is decidedly practitioner oriented and is not intended as a scholarly publication. It represents the sharing of experiences among colleagues who have indeed been in "travail and heavy laden." Therefore, the reader may expect some "unburdening or cathartic release" as the contributors (as well as the author) attempt to help you, the readers, deal with the situations which you are likely to encounter during the journey through implementation of student outcomes assessment or institutional effectiveness. We have been more concerned with precautionary notes or comments concerning our experiences than "footnotes" and ask that you grant us a modest amount of "slack" in scholarship in order to focus on the intent of the publication.

Chapter II

ORGANIZATION OF IMPLEMENTATION ISSUES AROUND THE GENERIC MODEL

The generic model for implementation of institutional effectiveness or assessment of educational outcomes shown in Figure 1 on the following page was the result of discussions taking place among several of the experienced practitioners of institutional effectiveness identified by the Southern Association of Colleges and Schools in preparation of their *Resource Manual on Institutional Effectiveness* during the 1986-87 time period. The generic model was established, based upon the experience available at that time, to lay out a logical sequence of events through which an institution would progress in implementing the institutional effectiveness requirements of the Southern Association for Colleges and Schools. The model was structured to service both two- and four-year colleges in their implementation.

As other regional accrediting associations have more fully implemented their own assessment initiatives, the generic model has also been successful as a guide for assessment planning and implementation to meet the accreditation requirements developed by these associations. The original period of time established for implementation, four years, has proven in practice to be a reasonable estimate for campuses starting with little or no assessment activity, since this time frame allowed them to demonstrate comprehensive institution-wide use of assessment information for improvement of academic and institutional programming. For those institutions more advanced in their initial assessment activities, it has been possible for implementation to progress in a satisfactory manner in as little as two years. However, implementation in less than two years has usually led to pushing the process so hard as to cause overwhelming resistance from the faculty regarding the *nature* of the implemental process itself as well as the *substance* of outcomes assessment. Regardless of the time period used for implementation, the general sequence of events from refinement of the Statement of Purpose through Establishment of the Institutional Effectiveness Cycle has held up in practice across the country.

The case studies reviewed in this publication are organized around the generic model for implementation as described in Figure 1.

Figure 1

A Generic Model for Implementation of Institutional Effectiveness and Assessment Activities in Higher Education

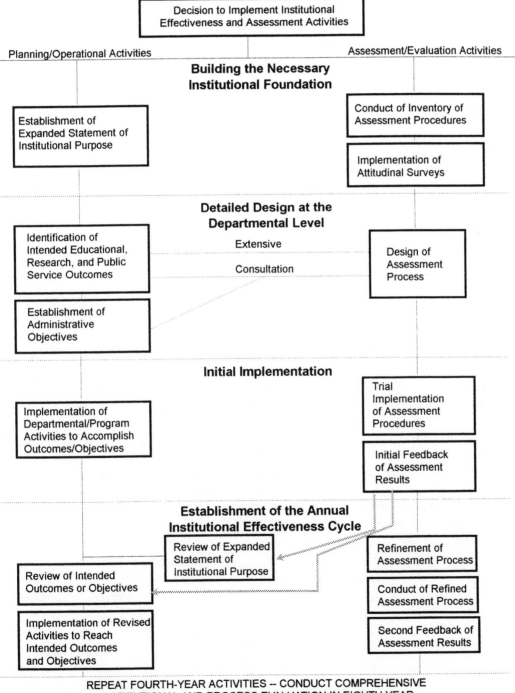

Figure 2. Generic Model Phases of Implementation

- Building the Necessary Institutional Level Foundation

- Detailed Design at the Departmental Level

- Initial Implementation

- Establishment of the Institutional Effectiveness Cycle

- Maintenance Over an Extended Period

Decision to Implement

While the requirement to implement institutional effectiveness or assessment activities may be more than abundantly apparent to those reading this publication, it has not always been so on every campus. Identification of the need for or *"awareness"* of the requirement for implementation is discussed beginning on page 11 and deals with the notion of readiness from the highest levels including the Chief Executive Officer through individual faculty members. While the need for implementation may be initiated by an external agency such as an accrediting association, the apparent benefit of or need for implementation at the departmental level by faculty members has frequently been found to be a significantly different matter.

Building the Institutional Foundation

During the first year or period of time identified in the generic model for implementation, a number of important issues are frequently experienced. Among the most important factors facilitating implementation of educational outcomes assessment across the country is the appointment of a single individual to coordinate the process. How is this initial leadership decision made? What type of background should this leader bring to the charge to guide implementation? What group is identified to support implementation? How is implementation structured and organized? Each of these key management questions in the initiation of the process are discussed in Chapter III and have a lasting impact on overall institutional implementation.

The condition of the institutional Statement of Purpose at the beginning of the implementation process is frequently and legitimately of great concern. Many such statements are found to be still of a *"mother, home, and country"* nature; they offend no one but succeed in accomplishing nothing. What steps were taken to revise the institutional Statement of Purpose? Which were successful and which were unsuccessful? These issues are also discussed in Chapter III.

There are few *"sure things"* in the assessment movement; however, one is that an inventory of the assessment procedure on a campus will reveal far more assessment taking place than those originally charged with implementation imagined. This chapter concludes by relating some of the experiences in that regard and how this inventory was subsequently used on the campus.

Detailed Design at the Department and Program Level

The bulk of the work and benefit in implementation of institutional effectiveness or assessment of educational outcomes is realized within the institution's academic departments and educational support or administrative units. Within those academic departments and units, the primary tasks are divided into (a) agreement upon statements of intended educational outcomes for the academic programs at the institution and administrative objectives for the institution's educational support and administrative units; (b) establishment of appropriate procedures and criteria for the assessment of the accomplishment of intended educational outcomes or administrative objectives; and (c) use of the results of the assessment activities to improve programs.

The single subject which this author has seen cause the greatest amount of controversy, "blood letting," etc., on campuses, is the identification of the intended educational outcomes for various degree programs. Faculty feel very strongly concerning their disciplines and frequently argue passionately about these topics. Among the issues reviewed in the case studies beginning in Chapter IV are the following:

- How were faculty involved?
- What was the role of the chair?
- How were these statements of intended educational outcomes tied or related to the institutional Statement of Purpose?
- How long were academic departments given to develop such statements?
- Were criteria for successful programs identified?
- Were these statements required to be approved by an administrator on the campus?
- How many statements were identified for each degree program?

This rather long chapter reviews institutional experiences regarding issues/solutions in the identification of intended educational outcomes for general education as well as majors at institutions taking part in the case study.

In addition to academic departments and programs, many institutions have been required to identify administrative objectives for the educational support and administrative units on their campus. The case studies reviewed in this chapter also include institutional experiences in identification of these administrative objectives as well as the primary issues surrounding implementation in this area.

The design of the assessment process and the many issues involved therewith are also discussed in this chapter. These issues include:

- Choice of locally developed or standardized tests
- Use of attitudinal surveys
- Organization of assessment effort
- Motivation of students to seriously take part in assessment
- Assessment planning

While most of these issues require more or less unique solutions on different campuses, there clearly were many commonalities identified in the approached described by the case study institutions.

The Establishment of the Institutional Effectiveness Cycle

The ultimate goal of implementation of an institutional effectiveness or assessment program is its institutionalization into an ongoing cycle of activities leading to continuous improvement of the academic and administrative programs taking place. Issues such as the following are explored in Chapter V beginning on page 59:

- The types of institutional effectiveness or assessment cycles established on campuses in the case study
- Integration of the institutional effectiveness cycle into other institutional processes
- Problems encountered in establishment of the cycle

In addition, evaluation of the institutional effectiveness cycle as well as its continuation over a number of years are discussed.

The end result of implementation is a cycle of institutional effectiveness/assessment activities as described in the generic model and adapted to each campus which fosters the use of assessment results to improve academic programming. At the close of this chapter, issues such as the following are reviewed: Who will analyze the data? Will there be a clearinghouse for assessment data? Is there a need for a "use of assessment results" statement? To whom will assessment results be distributed? How will the use of assessment results be documented?

The generic model presented in this chapter serves as a useful framework for exploring all of the issues identified above. However, it can hardly be described as inclusive of all of the assessment issues which have been identified by the case study institutions. Chapter III explores additional issues brought forward by the case study institutions as well as final comments concerning the various institutional experiences with implementation of institutional effectiveness or assessment activities on their campuses.

ISSUES AND SOLUTIONS SURROUNDING INITIATION OF INSTITUTIONAL EFFECTIVENESS OR ASSESSMENT OF EDUCATIONAL OUTCOMES— BUILDING THE FOUNDATION

The old adage "as the twig is bent, the tree will grow" has oftentimes proven accurate in implementation of institutional effectiveness or assessment of educational outcomes on a campus. Four major issues are frequently encountered in this initial period of implementation. The solution to these issues will have a lasting impact throughout implementation on most campuses. These issues include:

(1) Communicating an awareness of the need for implementation and motivation of the faculty
(2) Organization of the institutional team to coordinate and support implementation
(3) Establishing a suitable statement of institutional purpose
(4) Determination of the status of existing assessment activities on the campus

Each of these issues will be addressed in turn.

Communicating an Awareness of the Need for Implementation and Motivation of the Faculty

Initial Awareness—Of the eleven institutions taking part in the case study, initial institutional level attention to the need for implementation was primarily attributable to regional accreditation in nine of the cases. This initial awareness related to regional accreditation resulted from: the publication by the regional accrediting association of outcomes assessment requirements, the anticipated visit of a reaffirmation team from the regional accrediting association, or, in one case, response to criticism from a reaffirmation visitation team.

In two cases, the University of Kentucky and Stillman College, changes of leadership created conditions receptive to the regional accrediting association's initiative regarding student outcomes assessment. In the case of the University of Kentucky-Lexington Campus, the appointment of a new Chancellor brought to the position "...exciting, new ideas, energy, and most importantly, the effectiveness climate, a data-oriented approach to decision making," which had a significant impact upon the degree of acceptance of the regional accrediting association's mandate. At Stillman College, the implementation of strategic planning type activities focusing upon clearly articulated goals and priorities by the Chief Executive Officer appointed in 1982 fostered a climate in which response to the regional accreditation association's assessment initiative was rooted.

At the University of Montevallo, revision of the general education program at the institution in the early 1980s included incorporation of an assessment or evaluation component. Thus when regional accreditation initiatives were expanded to include the requirement for assessment of educational outcomes, a portion of the campus was already engaged in the process, naturally leading to its expansion across the campus.

In the case of two other institutions, Mt. Hood Community College and the State University of New York-Albany, regional accrediting played little if any part in implementation of assessment activities. At Mt. Hood Community College, implementation grew from a statewide concern regarding student attrition rates and was focused at Mt. Hood on the establishment of a Student Success Task Force. This effort was reinforced by Mt. Hood's joining the Kellogg/NCHEMS Student Outcomes Project designed to improve management's utilization of student outcomes data in decision making. Of all of the institutions, Mt. Hood's initiation of outcomes assessment is probably the case which can be most described as comprehensive self-initiation for the sake of improving student retention/learning or *intrinsic* institutional motivation for implementation.

At the State University of New York at Albany, assessment activities began in the late 1960s and early 1970s as a portion of that institution's systematic evaluation of all graduate and undergraduate programs. These activities were extended into the late 1970s based upon a series of cohort studies of student experiences at the institution and was assisted in the 1980s by Albany's participation in the Kellogg/NCHEMS funded program concerning the utilization of assessment results in decision making previously referenced at Mt. Hood Community College. Albany's interest in assessment is well represented in its 1990 Assessment Panel Report approved by the faculty senate structure and focusing on the impact of degree programs on students. It is important to observe that while the work done at SUNY-Albany has in many cases been utilized to satisfy external requirements (regional accreditation, system administration, granting agency requirements) the assessment work which has taken place preceded the external stimuli which came later.

The General Campus "Climate" for Implementation—Circumstances surrounding implementation on case study campuses ranged from relatively positive to absolutely negative dependent upon the institution's motivation for initial implementation and other factors. At Stillman College, the University of Kentucky, and the University of Montevallo, the climate was positively influenced by other administrative and educational activities (strategic planning, data orientation of incoming administrators, previous general education assessment efforts) and many faculty on the campuses saw implementation as a logical next step or involvement by the faculty in a continuing change taking place at their institution. At SUNY-Albany, the climate for implementation was positively influenced by the involvement of the faculty governance structure in setting assessment policies and a long history of such activities at the institution. At Coastal Carolina Community College as well as Jefferson State Community College, the institutional administration's commitment to reaffirmation of accreditation and to the improvement of student learning, seem to have created a receptive climate for implementation.

At the other institutions represented in the case study, the climate was described as varying from ordinary skepticism to downright suspicion. Faculty at many of the institutions were skeptical regarding the long-range implications of institutional effectiveness or assessment of educational outcomes and questioned whether these activities would actually lead to improved student learning. Many faculty questioned the additional commitment of time on their part given the austerity with which their budgets were viewed. Perhaps the most difficult environment within which to implement such activities occurred in one primarily four-year university and one community college at which implementation of institutional effectiveness or assessment activities was, in the eyes of many faculty, seen in connection with budget cuts, increases in faculty workload, and program review/termination which were of necessity taking place at the same time.

At roughly half of the case study institutions, the internal climate for implementation had been impacted by some type of state initiative regarding assessment of student learning for accountability purposes or other external stimulus. These state initiatives ranged from program review mandates (obviously intended to reduce or eliminate academic programs), through more potentially benign "report card" type legislative requirements in which the institutions were asked to provide substantial amounts of assessment data to the public, to the "cutting edge" legislation in South Carolina in which significant additional funding was provided for the institutions while requiring a considerable amount of assessment data be centrally reported. At Mt. Hood Community College, the adaptation of outcomes assessment types of measures into the Carl Perkins Act reporting played an important part in initiation and continuation of the process over a ten-year period. Perhaps the most positive external stimulus (other than reaffirmation of accreditation) to campus implementation was reported by Stillman College which earlier received a grant from the Kellogg Foundation through the United Negro College Fund that provided a strong strategic planning foundation upon which to build implementation of institutional effectiveness that was later funded by a substantial grant from the E. J. Lilly Foundation.

Identification of the Need to Implement—Initial awareness of the need to implement institutional effectiveness or educational outcomes assessment activities seems to have sprung relatively evenly from three sources at the case study institutions. The Chief Executive Officer (CEO) at roughly a third of the case study institutions was cited as the first individual on the campus to become aware of the need for implementation. This awareness in many cases came from the CEO's serving upon regional accreditation visiting teams or understanding of the importance of the change in regional accreditation requirements. Likewise, about a third of the institutions identified the Chief Academic Officer (CAO) as the initiating party on their campus. In addition to the awareness of the need to implement institutional effectiveness that resulted from service on regional accrediting teams, in several cases, Chief Academic Officers saw assessment activities as a way to genuinely improve student learning on their campus. The third general point of awareness of the need to implement came from the institutional staff and/or faculty engaged in the self-study process as part of regional accreditation. In one case, the initial awareness of the need was on the part of the faculty self-study committee rather than any representative of the administration of the institution who resisted implementation.

Communicating the Need and Motivating the Faculty—Without regard to the initial stimulus for implementation, the influence of external forces, or the identification of the need by any party or group on the campus, all case study institutions were challenged to communicate the need for implementation broadly upon the campus and to go about encouraging involvement by faculty and staff. The means through which the need for implementation of institutional effectiveness or student outcomes assessment was communicated throughout the institution varied significantly from campus to campus. In general, there were four means of communication utilized:

- Campus-Wide Meetings/Workshops
- Traditional Top/Down Communication
- Integration Into an Ongoing Institutional Activity
- Written Communication—"Send a Memo"

Direct verbal communication with the institutional faculty and staff was accomplished through a number of mechanisms, of which the most frequently utilized was the college-wide workshop or seminar. On one campus, the Chief Executive Officer devoted his annual "State of the College" address to the need for assessment activities to meet accreditation requirements and followed up this initial presentation in each of the succeeding several years with working sessions at the beginning of each fall semester to support and ascertain departmental progress in implementation. On another campus, workshops were conducted at the college and departmental level by institutional staff. At another institution, a representative of the regional accrediting association was asked to conduct a series of workshops to convince the staff that the regional accrediting association had no specific agenda in mind other than the faculty taking an active part in developing a program for assessment of educational outcomes. Finally, one institution established its first institutional research office and the new director (hired specifically to guide implementation) personally visited most of the institution's academic departments to explain the need to implement a program of institutional effectiveness or assessment of educational outcomes.

Several case study institutions integrated implementation of institutional effectiveness or educational outcomes assessment into existing task forces/committees which already had credibility on the campus. This was particularly true at Appalachian State University where a previously functioning Undergraduate Educational Goals Task Force was subdivided creating an institutional effectiveness committee making regular reports to the institution's academic/administrative structure while forwarding proposals to all faculty for comment. Similarly at Mt. Hood Community College, outcomes assessment implementation was initially integrated into the Student Success Task Force and communications facilitated by membership on the task force of representatives of all units in the institution, publication of the task force's activities, and the distribution of reports concerning assessment findings.

On two of the campuses within the case study group, it was reported that no other means of communication of the need for implementation or motivation other than "passing down the word" from the top and the attendance of various faculty and staff at professional meetings was accomplished. It must be pointed out, however, that due to the nature of these institutions' administrative functioning, this type of communication was effective in fulfilling the regional accrediting association's requirements and in one of the two cases, in motivating the faculty. These two institutions are excellent examples of fitting the means of communication to the "style" of administration practiced on the campus.

Among the least effective means for communication and motivation was that reported by one of the major research universities which "sent a memo" outlining the regional accrediting association's requirements from the Chair of the Self-Study Committee, a member of the faculty. On another small campus (not mature enough in its implementation yet to be included in the case study, but with whom the author is familiar), the appointment of a faculty assessment committee from whom the original communication alerting the faculty to the need for implementation emanated, appears to have been much more successful in motivating the faculty to take part in the process. This success is attributable to the relatively smaller size of the institution, addressing the need for program improvement rather than reaffirmation of accreditation in the correspondence and finally, follow-up by the committee members into discussions in each department concerning the content of the memorandum.

The Basis for Faculty Motivation—What was the basis for attempting to convince the rest of the institution that there was a need for a program of institutional effectiveness or assessment of educational outcomes? Beyond any question, the primary reason stated by the case study institutions as the "selling point" for implementation was the requirement for reaffirmation of regional accreditation. Nine of the eleven institutions taking part in the case study indicated that regional accreditation was the primary reason utilized to explain the need for implementation at their institution. At three of these institutions, regional accreditation and program improvement were cited equally as reasons that the campus should implement a program of student outcomes assessment. At three other institutions, satisfaction of an external accountability requirement was also cited as equal to regional accreditation as a motivation for campus implementation. It is significant to note that all of the nine institutions within the Southern Association of Colleges and Schools (SACS) cited regional accreditation as a primary reason for implementation. At two of these nine institutions, circumstances created a condition receptive to the regional accrediting association's initiative regarding student outcomes assessment. At the other institutions, program and service improvement in response to external requirements were frequently identified as the reason for faculty implementation.

The best example of a balanced approach using both the focus of institutional improvement and regional accreditation as a basis for motivating faculty was described in the case study material forwarded by the University of Montevallo.

"The primary basis for selling the assessment initiative was for program and instructional improvement. The first principle in the implementation document states: 'The purpose of assessment is for continuing improvement of all university functioning. Assessment is a means to an end, not an end in itself.' (p. 7, *A Proposal for the Measurement of Institutional Effectiveness at the University of Montevallo*.) Many of the people who had been involved in assessment before the SACS criteria were concerned that the external requirements would fundamentally change the reason we did assessments. Therefore, throughout the process we have worked to keep the focus on an internal desire to improve what we do, with the external requirements used mainly to urge those who otherwise did not seem already committed to improvement and to substantiate reporting requirements. Everyone is aware of the accreditation requirements, and sometimes they serve as a wedge to move stationary individuals, but mostly continuous improvement is our focus."

Clearly the best motivational situation existed for faculty "buy in" when faculty:

- Originated the process
- Did not feel threatened

• Were provided with a substantive role in shaping the process

Indication of the intent of the institution to use the results of the process in a formative manner early in the process was found to be a key to faculty motivation.

The Role of the Chief Executive Officer and Chief Academic Officer—The role of these key administrative officers in creating an initial awareness of the importance of implementation and motivating faculty, varied among the case study institutions from assuming a highly visible "driving force" role in implementation through benign neglect to an active and equally visible role in opposition to implementation. On one campus, the retiring Chief Academic Officer published in the campus newspaper the following: "If there is a threat to teaching at (name of the institution) in the immediate future, it may be from an over emphasis on assessment rather than an over emphasis on research.... There's the chance that we will not only throw out the baby with the bath water, but throw out the baby and keep the bath water simply because it is possible to measure how dirty it is.... There is much good that can result from assessment, but there is also much that can be used to the detriment of the university. It can result in an attempt to quantify the unquantifiable or worse to see only quantifiable things as valuable." In fairness to the administrator cited, it must be noted that a part of this response was directed at an externally mandated state requirement for assessment data for accountability purposes. Nonetheless, the impact on implementation by the faculty was a predictable absence of enthusiasm for the subject.

At some other case study institutions, the CEO's and CAO's actions can be described as ranging from bungling incompetence to passive indifference. In one institution's experience, this was illustrated by a failure to deal with basic apprehensions and concerns among the faculty regarding the intent of assessment activities (leading to charges of it representing "quantitative reductionism"), extreme decentralization in the process of implementation without any oversight, and administrative reluctance to ask the faculty to take part. All of these shortcomings were based upon a "failure of leadership to understand the dramatic changes this new requirement necessitated."

At most of the institutions in the case study, the Chief Executive Officer or Chief Academic Officer were described as truly the "driving force" behind implementation. The Chief Executive Officer was cited in many reports as creating the environment necessary for implementation by his/her public pronouncements regarding the importance of the issue at institution-wide seminars and workshops; appointment of an administrative officer widely respected on the campus to manage implementation; provision of the necessary funding for implementation; and, in one particularly laudable and highly visible case, use of the resulting data to review and improve academic programs.

On one of the campuses in the case study, the Chief Executive Officer had served on the regional accrediting body's review committee for institutions experiencing substantive difficulties in reaffirmation of accreditation. In that capacity, he had witnessed numerous institutional Chief Executive Officers "grovel" in front of their contemporaries to ask for "forgiveness" and the opportunity to continue in an accredited status while more fully complying with the regional accrediting association's requirements regarding institutional effectiveness. He then returned to his own campus, gathered his senior administrators, and communicated in very clear and unmistakable terms that if he was required to appear before such a committee and go through a similar humiliation, they were all going with him and would all suffer the consequences equally. A sense of awareness was achieved and communicated quickly throughout the campus; however, it is important to observe that it was accomplished positively based upon both regional accreditation and program improvement justifications.

In cases where the Chief Academic Officer served as the driving force behind implementation, more of a tendency was reported for the CAO to take on some of the operational responsibilities for seeing that implementation took place. In other cases, the CAO and CEO were clearly seen as committed to the process, but remaining somewhat distant from it and counting on an administrator specifically designated to carry through with implementation.

Regretfully, there does appear to be a difference concerning the role played by the CEO and CAO in the institutional case studies by type of institution. Among the case study institutions, community colleges reported closer involvement with and concern for implementation by Chief Executive and Chief Academic Officers. These administrators communicated widely on their campuses a sense of awareness of the importance of the process. This active role in communication diminished (though clearly not disappeared) in certain of the examples from primarily four-year colleges and universities, though sufficient commitment remained to support the process. However, at larger research universities, the majority (two out of three) of the institutions reporting indicated the least amount of support for implementation from the institution's central administrative structure. Why? It is this author's belief that this relative lack of support for implementation to meet regional accreditation requirements by the CEO's and CAO's at major research universities (MRU's) flowed from: lesser involvement of administrators at major research universities with the regional accreditation processes; the feeling that institutions of this type were "untouchable" in the regional accreditation process; and a general focus on research more than student learning. It is the author's observation that this condition also exists at many MRU's he has visited.

Summarizing the Case Study Experiences—What generalizations can be drawn from the case study institutions experiences concerning communication of the importance of implementation widely on the campus and motivating the faculty? The following actions were apparently related to _ineffective_ attempts to communicate the need for or the awareness of the importance of implementation and motivation of the faculty to actively engage therein:

- Communication of the need for implementation primarily in a written form by the institution's leadership or self-study apparatus.
- Active opposition to implementation by either the Chief Executive or the Chief Academic Officer.
- Intrusion into the implementation process by state agencies intent upon gaining assessment information for accountability purposes—leading to faculty resistance or focus upon "playing the game" to satisfy external requirements.
- Failure to deal with the attitudes or potential misconceptions of assessment by a portion of the faculty.
- Lack of follow through with institutional commitments to support faculty implementation.
- Failure to recognize that implementation will cause a substantive change in operations in the academic sector of the institution.
- Sole or exclusive reliance on regional accreditation as a means for creating a sense of motivation.

Regarding this last point, one institution indicated "regional accreditation may encourage compliant behavior, but will not cause the essential commitment to the process. Wielding regional accreditation as a club will produce results that may look good, but will not cause significant improvement in the institutions' programs and services."

On the other hand, the following actions were reported to have *significantly aided* communication and creation of a commitment to implementation by faculty on case study campuses:

- Genuine and highly visible support by the Chief Executive and Chief Academic Officer.
- Explanation of the reason for implementation as regional accreditation as well as internal improvement of academic programs.
- Communication of their support by the Chief Executive and Chief Academic Officer verbally in campus-wide presentations, workshops, etc., as well as smaller group discussion sessions emphasizing empowerment of the faculty to make the process work for the improvement of the institution's academic programs.
- Building the process of implementation into ongoing and successful existing activities (Student Success Task Force, Undergraduate Goals Task Force, etc.) that already had credibility among the faculty.
- Provision of resources to lead and assist the faculty in their implementation efforts.
- Sustenance of the motivation for faculty involvement by avoiding administrative intrusiveness and maturation of the process in relationship to faculty development efforts at the institution.

While none of the above circumstances are guaranteed to result in an awareness of and motivation to take part in implementation among the faculty, clearly there are some lessons to be learned from those institutional experiences reported.

Organization of the Institutional Team to Coordinate and Support Implementation

Few decisions more substantially impact ultimate implementation on campuses than the appointment of the party responsible for coordinating implementation and the nature of the committee chosen to assist that party.

Who gets the call to lead implementation?—Clearly one of the most important issues having substantive and significant impact on implementation is institutional choice of the party identified as responsible for coordinating that implementation. Among the case study institutions, four reported that an administrator with the title of Director of Institutional Research or Director of Institutional Research and Planning, as having been designated as the sole or (in two cases), one of two persons on campus with the responsibility for implementation. At one of the institutions, an Office of Academic Research with many of the responsibilities of a traditional institutional research component was established to lead assessment activities. The institution's Chief Academic Officer was identified as the coordinator on two campuses as was the Assistant/Associate Chief Academic Officer on two others, while an institutional administrator with the title of Executive Vice President on one campus and Associate Vice President for Institutional Advancement lead implementation activities on two other campuses. On two or three of the case study campuses (depending on definitional differences), responsibility was shared among two administrators, in both cases, the Director of Institutional Research and an Associate/Assistant Vice President.

On two campuses, no individual was designated to assume or coordinate leadership responsibility. In one case, a self-study committee was identified to take such a responsibility and in the other case, units subordinate to the institutional level were charged with the responsibility for implementation and hence, no overall coordination was effected.

On all the campuses, the party or parties charged with implementing reported either to the Chief Executive or Chief Academic Officer. By a slight majority, the Chief Executive Officer was the party to whom most coordinators reported. It is this author's belief that this was primarily due to the SACS comprehensive approach to institutional effectiveness which spans all institutional functions, including those outside of academic affairs. On many campuses within other regions of the country (particularly in the North Central Association of Colleges), the party responsible for implementation most frequently reports within the academic sector of the institution.

At two of the case study institutions, it was relatively obvious that faculty had been "promoted" into responsibility for implementation, while at two others, the institution had gone "outside" to employ a party with the specific skills required for implementation. In both of these cases of outside employment, the institution chose an experienced administrator who had served in either an institutional research or assessment capacity at another institution and possessed the type of psychometric background necessary to support implementation from a technical point of view. However, with only one other exception, administrators and faculty given responsibility for coordination did not describe themselves in technical terms, but rather as having degrees in higher education, sociology, english, psychology, etc. Institutions did not find it generally necessary to identify internal candidates with particularly strong quantitative credentials to lead the implementation process.

In many cases, it appeared from the case study reports that the coordinator was chosen based upon: their willingness to assume the responsibility, their "knowing more about it than anybody else" or the desire to increase their "visibility" on the campus as a reward for previous service. In some cases, faculty with previous experience in assessment and credibility among the faculty naturally "grew" into the campus leadership role.

At every institution in the case study, one type or another of assessment committee was established. Their general purposes ranged from oversight of the assessment process ·creating a sense of legitimacy concerning the process among the faculty to actually doing or supporting a part of the assessment work. Their specific charges included: none at all (much time exhausted trying to figure out what they should be doing); absolute control of the process (by a committee of 25); setting of assessment policy; detailed design of assessment activities; and conduct of assessment operations.

Among the roles frequently assigned to the assessment committee was the establishment of an overall framework or set of principles upon which the institution would base its assessment procedures. The institutional effectiveness assessment principles established by Appalachian State University and shown below are typical of these types of statements and in the case study, have been described as "quite worthwhile over the long term" by that institution.

- The faculty will be responsible for setting and assessing educational goals.

- The focus of assessment is improvement of the educational process and outcomes at Appalachian.
- For purposes of institutional effectiveness assessment, the unit of study is the program rather than the individual student or faculty member.
- Assessment activities will be conducted as unobtrusively as possible. Existing points of contact will be used extensively.
- Single measures are not as effective as multiple measures. Depending upon a single test or type of information may be a reasonable way to begin assessing, but it is not the approach we should have in the long run.
- Assessing a large number of goals is not as effective as multiple measures of important goals.
- Assessment results will be reported in the aggregate and used for the improvement and development of programs. Unit plans will include assessment results and information on their uses.

The assessment committees appointed ranged in size from a high of 25 through the smallest size working committees of between three and five members. Their composition was normally heavily faculty dominated to convey a sense of control of the process by the faculty with a seasoning of administrators at the assistant/associate vice president level and resource staff, many of whom came from the institutional research community. Those committees which tended to be more successful were at institutions which decided to adapt an existing or otherwise functioning committee to the purpose of institutional effectiveness coordination. The next most successful type of committees were those established specifically for institutional effectiveness or assessment coordination apart from any connection with the institutional self-study. The least successful type of committees were those specifically associated with the self-study process who in most cases were disbanded after the institution's reaffirmation visitation to leave the campus without significant leadership in continuing assessment activities.

In summary, the most successful organization for implementation appeared to have been characterized by:

- Appointment of an individual clearly charged with the responsibility for coordination of overall implementation.
- Appointment or adaptation of an institutional effectiveness or educational outcomes assessment committee separate from the accreditation self-study process for the purpose of advising the coordinator regarding policy-level issues and communications with the faculty.
- Composition of assessment committee predominantly by faculty from across all disciplines at the institution.
- Establishment of the assessment committee as a standing committee of the institution not subject to discontinuance.

Status of the Existing Institutional Statement of Purpose

At nine of the eleven case study institutions, the Statement of Purpose at the time that implementation of institutional effectiveness or assessment of educational outcomes began was either completely revised or substantially modified. Typical of the comments used to describe statements in existence on the case study campuses at the beginning of the process are the following:

- "All Purpose Mission…could have been any mission statement for virtually any community college in the United States."
- "Did not seem to express a vision of the future, ideals to be achieved, or a set of standards of high performance."
- "Did not establish criteria for evaluating the achievement of objectives."
- "Was too general and did not allow for a clear understanding of expected outcomes."
- "Grandiose statements of student expectations."
- "Did not contain statements specific enough to form a basis for the evaluation of effectiveness in achieving the mission."
- "Not comprehensive enough to include all components of the college."

At the one case study institution beginning the implementation process "in reaction to "rather than anticipation of the reaffirmation visit," a freshly drafted statement of institutional purpose in which "list specific purposes and global outcomes" was found acceptable as a basis for implementing institutional effectiveness throughout the institution. At the other case study institution not changing its Statement of Purpose, the existing Statement of Mission and Goals (revised in 1978) was described as serving reasonably well as a guideline for institutional effectiveness efforts though "not without its ambiguities."

Actions to Modify Existing Statements of Purpose—Actions ranging from major reconsideration of the institution's purpose to minor adjustment of existing institutional statements took place at case study institutions. It is worthy to note that those two institutions at which the greatest revision to the statement of purpose was evidenced were not engaged in the process of implementation for the sake of reaffirmation of accreditation. At Mt. Hood Community College in 1989, a commitment was made to review and revise the mission statement. This was accomplished through two campus-wide forums. The first forum was built around the AAJC document "Building Communities" which contains 63 recommendations for the community college of the 21st century. Participants identified six major themes important to the work of Mt. Hood. High on the list was a commitment to excellence in teaching as the hallmark of the community college. With these six major themes as a foundation, the forum groups went on to draft portions of a mission statement reflecting these themes. Several months later, the second forum was held and the various drafts were honed down to one new mission statement. From that point the new mission statement moved through the various levels of the college and ultimately was approved by the Board of Trustees. The intent of shaping a new mission was to give a new sense of direction to college planning—to weave the fabric of the process from the stated mission to the final measurement of institutional practices in fulfillment of the mission. The mission was made the centerpiece of the strategic planning initiative and planners were encouraged to explicitly state how their plans supported the institutional purpose. All of these efforts were based upon the assumption that the first and foremost indicator of institutional effectiveness was fulfillment of purpose, the college mission or purpose.

At the State University of New York, the statement of purpose or mission played a strong role in their development of the assessment process over a period of years. The early part of their development of assessment activities took place under the influence of necessary program evaluation and priority setting activities that resulted in a mission statement in 1977 that charted a plan for SUNY-Albany's development as a major research university. The current statement of purpose or mission (dated 1992) provides a clear agenda for evaluating campus and student development, particularly in terms of student diversity and undergraduate learning.

Less far reaching revisions to their statement of purpose were undertaken at the other seven institutions finding it necessary to adjust or change their statement of purpose for implementation of institutional effectiveness. Most case study institutions modified their statement of purpose in conjunction with the self-study process in preparation for reaffirmation of accreditation, while some recognized its importance to the institutional effectiveness effort and began modification of their statement of purpose prior to the self-study process.

At some colleges, separate ad hoc committees were established to review and revise the statement of purpose while at other colleges existing groups were utilized. In most cases, portions of the existing statement of purpose were maintained for both political and continuity purposes and lists of goals, purposes, etc., were added to provide operational guidance for institutional effectiveness implementation.

At two of the institutions in the case study while revision of the statement of institutional purpose did take place in conjunction with the self-study process, the result did not aid implementation of institutional effectiveness or educational outcomes assessment. On one campus, the assessment committee recognized the inadequacies of the existing statement of purpose and a "turf battle" erupted resulting in the assessment committee being effectively precluded from input into the statement of purpose revision process. On another campus, revision of the statement of purpose took place as part of the self-study process without consideration of the statement's implication for institutional effectiveness or educational outcomes assessment. In both cases, these actions resulted in a statement of purpose more global or vague, and hence, less useful (but more politically acceptable) than the statement it replaced.

In summary, the experiences regarding the statement of purpose at case study institutions indicated that:

- Most institutions will find it necessary to alter their existing statement of institutional purpose to make it functional for implementation of institutional effectiveness or educational outcomes assessment activities.

- On most campuses, alteration will take the form of addition of more concrete and specific goals to an already existing statement of mission or philosophy, while on a limited number of campuses, a complete rethinking of the institution's purpose may be in order.

- While on some smaller campuses the "committee of the whole" approach to governance and input into the statement of purpose may succeed, the revision of the statement of purpose is most frequently accomplished by a cross constituency representative group of institutional employees representing the faculty and staff as well as potentially the institution's students and external constituents.

- The revision to the existing statement of purpose should be specifically attuned to the needs for institutional effectiveness and take place well in advance of the need to address this issue as part of the institutional self-study connected with reaffirmation of accreditation.

Incorporated in this volume as Appendix C are the Statements of Purpose for Mt. Hood Community College, The University of Montevallo, and The University of Mississippi. They vary considerably in length, level of detail, and content. However, each of these Statements of Purpose has provided a level of guidance or leadership within which implementation of institutional effectiveness or assessment of educational outcomes has been accomplished.

Inventorying Existing Means of Assessment

Conducting the Inventory—The majority, but by no means all, of the case study institutions conducted an inventory of assessment activities existing on their campuses at the time implementation began. This inventory was conducted through a variety of means, but primarily took place by asking academic and administrative departments to submit a description of the means of assessment which they felt were currently being utilized to reflect the effectiveness of their programming. At the University of Montevallo, this inventory has been annualized through yearly assessment reports from all departments.

Use of the Inventory—The uses of the inventory of existing means of assessment reported by the case study institutions varied more than the means for collecting the information. All of the case study institutions reported use of the inventory to inform the assessment committee of the current level of assessment activity taking place on the campus and to identify "gaps" or "deficiencies" in existing operations. Three other uses were described.

The inventory of existing assessment activities was also utilized in relation to state accountability initiatives as well as reaffirmation of accreditation efforts. At several of the institutions involved with implementation for not only the reaffirmation of regional accreditation and program improvement, but to satisfy state accountability initiatives, the inventory of existing assessment procedures represented a "quick and dirty" means through which to provide evidence to the state authority that assessment was already taking place on the campuses. Several of the other institutions were implementing institutional effectiveness or assessment of educational outcomes activities parallel to their self-study process and found the inventory of existing assessment practices useful in writing the self-study to describe their current activities.

While not frequently articulated in the case studies, the inventory served in some cases as a substantial aid in convincing reluctant faculty that assessment activities were already an ongoing part of some disciplines on their campus. One of the major research universities concluded in their case study report that "instructions and examples of the types of activities to include (in the inventory) turned out to be quite helpful to the departments because it was their first concrete evidence to them that they could think in more expanded terms of what assessment included. The exercise helped overcome some of the preconceptions that assessment meant quantitative testing."

On one campus in the case study, a major outcome of the inventory was the realization that "…very little formal evaluation was being conducted in programs and services on the campus. For instance, the inventory revealed that much relevant assessment data was already being collected by the Office of Institutional Research's various surveys and studies, but that there were not, as yet, a formal instructional review process." While on another campus, results of the inventory were used as a benchmark from which to measure future assessment activities.

Awareness of the need for implementation, organization of the campus to accomplish this task, adjustment or revision of the institutional statement of purpose, and inventory of existing means of assessment all play an essential role in building the necessary institutional foundation for implementation of institutional effectiveness or assessment of educational outcomes. However, the real work takes place within the institution's academic and educational support units. The case study institutions reported many issues and various solutions to these department based issues which are described in the following chapter.

Chapter IV

ISSUES AND SOLUTIONS SURROUNDING INITIATION OF INSTITUTIONAL EFFECTIVENESS OR EDUCATIONAL OUTCOMES ASSESSMENT— DETAILED DESIGN AT THE DEPARTMENTAL/ PROGRAM LEVEL

On campuses implementing institutional effectiveness or educational outcomes assessment, there are two levels of activities. The first level of activity is institutional in nature and involves establishing the foundation (coordination, expertise, resources, etc.) upon which the actual work of implementation takes place. This activity was described in Chapter III. The second level of work is among the faculty and staff within the institution's academic and educational support units. The following chapter deals with a number of issues and solutions in implementation at that level. It is subdivided into sections regarding:

- Origination of statements of intended educational outcomes (academic achievement, expected results, etc.) for academic programs and general education.
- Identification of administrative and educational support objectives.
- Designing the educational assessment process.
- Use of assessment results to improve programming.

Origination of Statements of Intended Educational Outcomes (Student Academic Achievement, Expected Results, etc.) for Academic Programs and General Education

In implementation of the institutional effectiveness paradigm described in detail on pages 7 through 11 of *A Practitioner's Handbook*, faculty in the institution's academic departments are expected to identify what they intend for students to think, know, and do upon completion of the institution's academic programs, to include general education and where appropriate remedial education/developmental programming. It is identification of this "think, know, and do" at the departmental level where most faculty at an institution become involved with implementation.

How are faculty involved?—The manner of faculty involvement in identification of intended educational outcomes varied significantly between the case study institutions and within many of the case study institutions themselves.

At some of the smaller institutions, a more centralized approached was found useful.

In these cases, the institutions' existing governance style might be described as a "committee of the whole" approach to academic policy making. Typical of these institutions was the holding of an institutional level workshop at which all faculty members would be informed of the requirement for identifying intended educational outcomes and means of assessment followed by a series of departmental level "committee of the whole" discussions resulting in identification of intended educational outcomes for each degree program.

More common among the case study institutions was what might be described as a decentralized model of implementation leading through the department chair to the faculty in each department. Among the different departments, many various approaches to gaining faculty involvement were reported. The committee of the whole approach was frequently utilized to involve all faculty in identification of intended educational outcomes for each program. Just as frequently, a faculty subcommittee within the department held responsibility for originating statements of intended educational outcomes for consideration by the entire department. Somewhat less frequently was the identification of one person to draft the statements of intended educational outcomes for each program for ultimate consideration by the department faculty as a whole. While there seem to be little consistency in faculty organizational patterns to address this issue, the size of the department and the relative perceived expertise of its individual faculty appeared to have had a bearing on the manner in which the faculty organized themselves to approach this issue.

All case study institutions involved the departmental faculty at least in the review of statements of intended educational outcomes for each program. On some campuses, this was accomplished by "consensus" of the departmental faculty, while on other campuses, what amounted to almost a "sign off" by individual faculty members on the statements of intended educational outcomes was required.

Two particularly interesting examples of faculty involvement were reported among the case study institutions. At Coastal Carolina Community College, because of its relatively smaller size, faculty involvement frequently became a one-on-one discussion between a faculty member in the discipline and the individual in charge of coordination of the implementation process for the institution. This type of direct relationship between the faculty at the departmental level and leadership in the implementation process was most likely to occur at relatively smaller institutions. At Mt. Hood Community College, the results of faculty involvement in identification of intended student outcomes and means of assessment were eventually published in a formal document titled "Mission to Measurement" which illustrated to all on the campus the extent to which the institution as a whole had taken part.

The Role of the Department Chair—Not unexpectedly, on the majority of case study campuses, the departmental chair or head was charged with responsibility for leadership of implementation among the faculty. In most cases the charge to the departmental chair went substantially beyond "coming up with" statements of intended educational outcomes and included specific directives to involve faculty within the department in arriving at these statements.

The role of the departmental chair in implementation is for some an uncomfortable one. Departmental chairs frequently acquire an image or sense of authority within their department as they conduct necessary administrative operations. In this case, the departmental chair should function as "first among equals" in relationship to the other members of the faculty for this set of requirements involves not administrative matters, but the curriculum which is jointly the responsibility of all faculty. The departmental chair can without appearing to "abuse" his/her authority, gather information concerning the process, schedule meetings, serve as the department secretary, and other similar, less assertive type of functions. However, the chair should avoid expressing too early in the process his/her beliefs regarding intended educational outcomes for fear of dominating or prejudicing the discussion.

Departmental chairs in the case study sought to minimize their own role in this issue in several ways. On a number of campuses, departmental chairs chose to appoint faculty subcommittees who assumed leadership within their department in the identification of intended educational outcomes. On other campuses, an assessment coordinator was selected from among the faculty in the department for liaison with the institutional level leadership of assessment activities.

On two campuses in the case study, the role of the department chair was relative unique. At Sam Houston State University, "measurable goals and outcomes that are agreed upon by faculty consensus are approved by the department chair." In this example, the department chair acts separately from the faculty in an approval capacity. At Clemson University, the departmental chair had major responsibility for initiating assessment activities within the department and appointing an assessment committee; however, once that committee was appointed, the department chair's role was effectively eliminated and the assessment committee member appointed by the chair related with the overall university assessment committee, part of the institution's self-study process.

Several of the campuses reporting in the case study indicated that the turnover in department chairs during the implementation process was a significant impediment. One institution went as far as reporting that one could easily correlate those departments showing the least amount of progress in assessment in the major with those exhibiting the greatest amount of change in departmental leadership during the period. Through whatever means deemed appropriate, continuing education of departmental chairs regarding their responsibility for implementation is essential to facilitation of implementation.

Many faculty on the campus will see implementation of assessment activities through the eyes of their department chair. If the department chair plays his/her role as described in the case study material from Coastal Carolina Community College as "...leader, motivator, resource, and conduit of information...," then the likelihood of successful implementation is improved. If on the other hand, the department chair perceives implementation as "yet another burden," then the faculty's willingness to take part in the process and the likelihood of success are significantly diminished. As noted in the response from the University of Montevallo, "From the outset, department chairs have been probably the most important key in implementing...."

Providing Guidance for Departmental Implementation—At the case study institutions, the guidance provided to the institution's academic departments concerning the nature of their statements of intended educational outcomes came from administrators, self-study directors, primarily faculty committees, consultants, and publications. Administrators involved in providing this guidance were frequently titled Director of Institutional Research; however, associate deans and vice presidents also provided this guidance for departmental implementation.

On some campuses, such as Mt. Hood Community College, an existing committee, the Strategic Planning Committee, provided guidance to departments and examples of implementation. While on other campuses, such as Jefferson State Community College, an instructional outcomes steering committee was appointed for this purpose.

The use of the self-study director to provide guidance for departmental identification of intended educational outcomes met with mixed results. At Appalachian State University, the chair of the self-study took a personal interest in this subject and provided excellent departmental leadership and guidance. While at one of the major research universities, "guidance" was provided by the self-study chair by merely forwarding the regional accreditation associations very general requirements. The result was predictable apathy.

Two particularly interesting and unique providers of guidance for departmental implementation were identified among the case study institutions. At Jefferson State Community College, an instructional design specialist played a major role in assisting the departments and individual faculty with framing their statements of intended educational outcomes. This member of the professional staff was able to facilitate the process in a particularly "non-threatening" manner within the institution's academic departments. At Sam Houston State University and at Jefferson State Community College, the appointment of an assessment liaison faculty member to receive training and relate with the overall institutional assessment committee served a useful purpose in each department's identification of intended educational outcomes.

On some of the campuses in the case study, it was felt that the use of a consultant to provide initial departmental leadership was the best option open. This approach provided the necessary expertise while avoiding the campus "political baggage" accumulated by faculty and staff at any institution. In order for this approach to be effective, it was necessary that someone be identified on the campus to sustain the implementation process following the consultant's departure.

Initial guidance concerning departmental implementation took a number of forms. On many campuses, departmental level workshops for faculty involved in implementation were held by the administrators leading implementation or representatives of faculty committees. On some campuses, locally developed publications, such as the *Institutional Effectiveness Handbook* published at Collin County Community College, were provided to the departments to guide implementation, while on other campuses, documents from the assessment literature, such as *The Departmental Guide to Implementation of Student Outcomes Assessment and Institutional Effectiveness* were used to provide faculty with examples and guidance. In most cases, both written and follow-up guidance of an individual nature were provided to departments identifying intended educational outcomes.

On almost half of the campuses in the case study, academic departments preparing statements of intended educational outcomes provided them to an individual or group to review in draft prior to their finalization by the department. The nature of this review ranged from "assistance in narrowing down," to "make sure measurement was possible," to "adjustments in format and style." In most cases, this "peer review" type of consideration of the initial drafts was conducted by what was seen as a "neutral party," including a subcommittee of the institutional effectiveness committee, the instructional design specialist, the chair of the self-study, or an external consultant. In only one case, was the review of the draft statements of intended educational outcomes accomplished by a line administrator at the institution.

In general, reviewing the draft statements of intended educational outcomes put forward by the academic departments was reported as a very positive step which substantively improved the ultimate statements. While the decisions regarding the nature of these statements remained with the faculty, the opportunity to have an independent peer review: (a) refined faculty thinking in many cases, (b) assured an outcomes orientation, (c) provided consistency of format, and (d) served as an alert for the need and conduit for providing additional assistance to faculty unfamiliar with the process.

Linkage of Programmatic Statements to the Institutional Level—Among the case study institutions, the linkage of statements of intended educational outcomes developed at the department or program level to the statement of institutional intentions, (usually called a statement of purpose or mission statement), ranged widely from very direct and apparent to almost non-existent. On all campuses in the case study, departments were "told" that their statements of intended educational outcomes should be related to or linked with the statement of purpose for the institution. However, among the case study institutions, approximately one-third made no effort to verify this linkage to or support of the institutional statement of purpose by the statements of intended educational outcomes prepared at the departmental level. On roughly half of the campuses in the case study, some entity (faculty or administrative) reviewed such statements to ensure their linkage to and support of the statement of purpose for the institution. While at less than a quarter of the case study institutions, the mission statement or statement of purpose for an intermediate level organizational unit (division, college, school, etc.) was developed and tied closely to the statement of purpose for the institution. In these instances, the statements of intended educational outcomes for individual academic programs were related to the intermediate organizational unit statement of purpose or mission.

The primary benefit of the intermediate level unit mission approach to linkage with the institutional statement of purpose is that it allegedly provides better "focus" for individual programs and places more "control" in the hands of deans, vice presidents, etc. There are two primary limitations to creating such an intermediate level set of expectations to which program statements of intended educational outcomes are linked. First, the ability to tie back to the statement of purpose of the institution is somewhat blurred by the necessity to translate the relationship through the intermediate level (college, division, etc.) statement. Second, the existence of an intermediary statement of purpose such as that for a college frequently includes the provision for a number of intended educational outcomes which all programs in the college are required to include in their statements; thus, limiting the flexibility of the faculty in each academic program and sometimes leading to accusations of administrative intrusion into a faculty process.

Analysis of the case study institutions' experiences indicated the tendency on the part of the two-year colleges and primarily four-year colleges and universities to relate their statements of intended educational outcomes more directly to the statement of purpose for the institution than at the major research universities. This absence of linkage at the major research universities was in two of the cases attributable to the existence of an essential dysfunctional statement of purpose at the institutional level. One major research university's statement of purpose was described as "much like that from others, in as much as it is so general as to be more or less unrecognizable for any other land grant university."

The approach at Mt. Hood Community College to the linkage of intended educational outcomes to their mission statement was found to be somewhat unique. The college's mission statement was first broken down by various themes, such as student access to technology training. The Strategic Planning Council then identified various activities across the college which supported the themes and intended educational outcomes were defined for these areas. Next, each organizational unit of the college was asked to develop their own statements of intended educational outcomes supporting the mission themes as well as other statements of intended educational outcomes concerning their own organizational unit or department.

Duration of the Process for Faculty Identification of Intended Educational Outcomes—Case study institutions reported taking from two to three weeks to over a year in arriving at statements of intended educational outcomes for academic programs.

Those case study institutions reporting periods of time of less than a month generally fell into two categories. Several institutional implementations (which were not categorized as highly successful by their contributors), pushed faculty in the academic departments and programs to identify statements of intended educational outcomes within several weeks in order to conform to a schedule dictated primarily by the need for the institution to complete its self-study for regional accreditation. In most cases, these "quick and dirty" statements were as quickly forgotten by the departmental faculty even before the self-study was completed. At several other institutions, **initial** statements of intended educational outcomes were framed within a one month or less period and subsequently, **refined** during the next six to nine months to the point of finalization.

While three of the institutions in the case study reported finalization of statements of intended educational outcomes within a one semester period of time, the mode of response time from the case study institutions was nine to twelve months. These institutions reported substantive faculty discussion concerning key issues related to curriculum and educational policy in the course of identifying these intended educational outcomes.

In the author's experience in working on campuses involved in implementation, the identification of intended educational outcomes is the most difficult aspect of the entire implementation process. If done substantively (rather than to meet an externally imposed time schedule or mandate), faculty discussions regarding this issue and narrowing down the long list of proposed statements of intended educational outcomes to three to five statements upon which assessment activities will be initially focused is, in the words of one department chair, "The worst thing I ever had to do as chair of this department." On the other hand, the same chair stated: "After we had completed this process, we knew more about our department, that had absolutely nothing to do with assessment, than we have in a long time."

If the process is hurried for one reason or another, there is strong likelihood that it will be either trivialized by the faculty (resulting in significant problems later in substantiating the use of assessment data to improve programming) or that the faculty will react strongly to being hurried through difficult discussions. Such "feedback" from the faculty concerning the process of implementation can "poison the atmosphere" for constructive change and improvement in academic programming, the intended result of implementation.

Identification of Criteria for Considering the Program Successful —At roughly half of the case study institutions, academic departments initially identified statement of intended educational outcomes or means of assessment which included the criteria or standard which would be utilized for judgment of the program's success. Probably the outstanding example of use of such criteria brought forward by the case study institutions, was that by Coastal Carolina Community College. At that institution, statements of intended educational outcomes have been incorporated into an ongoing planning process documented in their annual publication titled a "Desktop Audit." Each year the accomplishments of the various academic programs are reviewed in a clearly public fashion compared to the criteria which they set for program success and the academic departments are asked (where appropriate) to comment upon their planned actions taken to better achieve their intended educational outcomes. In this case, publication and use of results have led to clear, definitive, and mutually understood criteria for success of each academic program's intended educational outcomes. A brief description of an excerpt from Coastal Carolina Community College's "Desktop Audit" is included as Appendix D.

On the other end of the continuum, were several institutions taking part in the case study whose status was described in the following terms by their contributor:

"Each departmental assessment plan was suppose to be developed using measurable observable outcomes. Criteria for success were suppose to be included as well. However, very few of the departments were able (or willing) to include success criteria in their plans. The process has been in place for nearly three years now and many departments still do not have success criteria in the plans although they have been requested to be specific and include success criteria."

"Departments typically did not identify criteria for considering the extent to which their program was successful. Their statements were general in nature (e.g., develop a working knowledge of the language of chemistry and science to allow effective communication with both scientists and non-scientist). Departmental statements tended to answer the question what should we do, but not the question how much."

"For departments just starting assessment there was a feeling that they did not know, without some baseline data, how to set criteria. There was also some fear that failure to meet explicit criteria would lead to punishment, and therefore it would be better if statements were left vague."

At a number of the institutions in the case study, the extent to which criteria for program success were established can only be described as mixed. At one major research university, the extent to which criteria were established was left entirely to the design of the department faculty. At another institution, "standard setting is encouraged and in some places required." At several of the institutions, the first statements of intended educational outcomes did not include criteria when they were initially drafted. However, as the process has become more mature and sophisticated, such standards are being added often to the description of the means of assessment specified. In addition, the federal Perkins Act requirements calling for occupational/technical programs to set standards in the area of service to special populations (economically or academically disadvantaged, limited english proficiency, etc.), and to report the percent of students achieving standards of academic progress, program completion, job placement, etc., have stimulated standard or criteria setting at some community colleges.

Why is this question regarding criteria for consideration of program success important? The primary purpose in implementing assessment of educational outcomes is the stimulation of the use of results to improve academic programs. In the author's experience, unless criteria or standards for program success are established based upon what the faculty believe students completing their program *ought* typically or on the average should be able to accomplish, then the likelihood of the use of assessment results to bring about change is greatly diminished. Without the establishment of standards or criteria which indicate what the faculty believe to be reasonable levels of student (program) performance, the faculty often tend to view assessment results as confirmation of the existing circumstances rather than as an indicator of the difference between what *ought to be* and *what is*. It is only when we as human beings see such a discrepancy or difference between the current situation and the desired status we have identified in advance that we tend to go about making the changes or improvements in academic programs which are the intended final result of the assessment process.

Whether criteria or standards for program success are articulated as part of the initial statement of intended educational outcomes or are included in the means of assessment associated therewith (as often illustrated in the examples shown in Appendix B) is irrelevant. Either location is appropriate and some departments find such identification of criteria easier at one point in the process than the other. However, to facilitate use of the results to improve academic programming, such standards need to be established *before* assessment activities are conducted.

Approval of Departmental Statements of Intended Educational Outcomes—At a bare majority of the case study institutions, statements of intended educational outcomes originated in academic departments were subjected to "approval" beyond the departmental level.

This approval was reportedly conferred by a number of different institutional sources. On one campus, Jefferson State Community College, statements of intended educational outcomes written for programs in a department were reported as approved by a formal vote of the department faculty. At other institutions, such as Sam Houston State University and Mt. Hood Community College, institutional committees or councils approved statements of intended educational outcomes. At other colleges in the case study, divisional or institutional administrators reviewed proposed statements of intended educational outcomes and approved them prior to finalization.

The purpose of most of these campus reviews of statements of educational outcomes were similar to those at Sam Houston State University where "the criteria for approval does not include...content because it is not the role of the committee to infringe on academic freedom. However, the committee requires that goals and outcomes be measurable..." In most cases reported by institutions in the case study, the purpose of the approval process was not to dictate content, but to review the outcomes oriented nature of the statements themselves and insure their linkage to the institutional statement of purpose.

At some of the other case study institutions, a conscious decision was made not to review the statements submitted by departments. This position tended to be taken most frequently by some of the primarily four-year colleges and universities and particularly the major research universities. At one of the major research universities, there was a concern that the assessment committee should not take on this role and become recognized as the "assessment police" and hence, they declined that responsibility. This committee saw its limits of responsibility as being offering technical assistance and advice, but not passing judgment in terms of approval. On other campuses, the decision not to have a formal approval process was not as dramatically expressed, but nonetheless was as effectively made.

Major Problems in Identification of Intended Educational Outcomes—Over half of the institutions taking part in the case study indicated that among the primary problems in identification of intended educational outcomes was the lack of understanding concerning how to write such statements so that they were in terms of measurable student behaviors which reflected program outcomes. Several case study institutions reported a lack of systematic training for the faculty in how to write such statements as a major hindrance to implementation. How far to go in "dotting the i's and crossing the t's" in preparing statements of intended educational outcomes is a difficult issue. The author has visited campuses upon which the primary institutional focus has been on *how* such statements were written rather than upon the importance of the *substance* contained therein. Such emphasis on the technical merit of such statements can be clearly over done, "turning off" large segments of the faculty to the process. As long as the statements of intended educational objectives are (a) written in terms of what the students will be able to do (as opposed to those at one major research university in the case study which focused upon what the faculty needed to do) and (b) include some rough approximation of a criteria for program success, then the minimum conditions for an "acceptable" statement of intended educational outcomes have probably been met. It should be noted that the establishment of criteria for program success may be accomplished later in identification of the appropriate means of assessment for each intended educational outcomes.

The second most frequently cited problem in identifying statements of intended educational outcomes relates to deciding the substance of these statements. This was also indicated by at least half of the case study institutions and was described as:

- "deciding what to measure."
- "finding the most important key sets of knowledge and skills."
- "lack of agreement on core goals."
- "gaining consensus."
- "lack of agreement upon standards."

Each of the quotes above speak to the difficult value judgments necessary within academic programs in (a) identifying the key concepts or change points upon which the assessment mechanism will need to be focused and (b) setting the criteria for program success.

The third most frequently cited problem in identifying statements of intended educational outcomes was the existence of too many such statements per program. Without the selection of only a portion of the suggested statements of intended educational outcomes upon which to conduct assessment activities, the institutions reported subsequently "choking" on a self-required level of assessment activities totally indigestible on the campus.

In addition to these common issues, case study institutions identified some relatively unique problems. On one campus, spirited discussions took place regarding why all criteria for program success should not be 100% for intended educational outcomes if the institution were indeed conferring a degree. On another campus, initial statements of intended educational outcomes were seen as unchangeable and not subject to refinement or improvement because of their being included in the institution's self-study.

Two very "nuts and bolts" types of problems were cited by other case study institutions. On some campuses, finding the opportunity without any "release time" to prepare these statements within a short period was found to be overly burdensome by the faculty involved. On several other campuses, trying to get faculty initially involved and to maintain the momentum of their involvement without substantive administrative support was found to be difficult at best. This latter circumstance was found most likely to occur at major research universities.

The problems related by the case study institutions reflect accurately the experience of the author in working with many institutions during implementation. The single greatest challenge within the implementation process is the agreement upon (or at least acceptance of) between three and five statements of intended educational outcomes per program that are stated behaviorally and in relatively measurable terms by the faculty. The difficulties in deciding which learning, skills, or attitudes should be measured first, stating those intended educational outcomes in behavioral terms (an act uncommon to many faculty), and then choosing only three to five such statements upon which to initially focus assessment effort, all combine to make an extremely volatile set of circumstances in many departments.

Identification of Intended Educational Outcomes for the General Education Program — It is perhaps reflective of the state of disorganization regarding general education on many campuses that on half of the campuses in the case study, responsibility for intended educational outcomes regarding general education was delegated to the institutional effectiveness/ assessment committee or council. In about half of these cases, the committee or council actually drafted statements of intended educational outcomes for the institution's general education program. In some cases such as Appalachian State University, these statements of intended educational outcomes were based upon participatively arrived at statements of undergraduate goals. In others, they appeared to have sprung exclusively from the imagination of members of the assessment committee. About half of the committees charged with responsibility for identifying intended educational outcomes for the general education program worked directly with individual academic departments to arrive at the necessary statements.

Probably the strongest centralized leadership in general education was evidenced by Stillman College where an existing position of Director of General Education was utilized to coordinate the activity of the individual academic departments in coming forward with their statements of intended educational outcomes for the general education program. Somewhat less directive was the approach taken at Jefferson State Community College at which the academic administrative council (primarily composed of division heads) established the first set of intended educational outcomes for general education which was subsequently modified by a more representative faculty group.

The difficulty in arriving at statements of intended educational outcomes for general education was repeatedly contained in the institutional case study reports. In a number of cases, this difficulty resulted in the institution's treating general education assessment at the individual course level. In time, the result of this action usually became apparent later when assessment activities at the course level were undertaken, found to be excessively burdensome, and abandoned.

Examples of Statements of Intended Educational Outcomes—Contained in Appendix B are example statements of intended educational outcomes by Classification of Instructional Program (CIP) code and degree level (associate, baccalaureate, etc.) from the case study institutions as well as a number of other cooperating institutions. These *are not offered as recommendations or suggestions regarding each discipline*, they are provided solely *as examples* of how such statements have been established by departments in various institutions. *Readers should be careful to note that adoption of any of these statements of intended educational outcomes provided in the examples in Appendix B without careful consideration by the faculty in the institution's departments, represents forfeiture of that department's right to control the curriculum at their institution.*

Summarizing Institutional Experiences in Identification of Intended Educational Outcomes—While the case study institutions reported substantially varying practices regarding identification of intended educational outcomes, the following suggestions regarding this subject are supported by the majority of their experiences:

Summary Suggestions Concerning Identification of Intended Educational Outcomes

- Faculty will become involved when they understand what is expected of them, see potential intrinsic value leading to improved learning, and feel they control the process so that it will not be used against them.
- While the department chair may be expected to provide the needed statement of intended educational outcomes, the chair should be charged with leading and involving the faculty in formulating these statements.
- Guidance of the department through implementation is necessary and should take place at the outset of the implementation process and again before finalization.
  - Initial guidance should include at least minimal instruction concerning preparing statements of intended educational outcomes and examples of such behavioral statements.
  - A "threat-free" peer review process of draft statements of intended educational outcomes may be found useful.
- Linkage of the programmatic statements of intended educational outcomes to the institutional level needs to be monitored either through the peer review process mentioned above or through an "approval" process for such statements by academic administrators.
- Formulation of meaningful statements of intended educational outcomes will take between six months and a year and cannot be substantially shortened without compromising the process in one way or another.
- Statements of intended educational outcomes or the means of assessment later associated therewith should include criteria for program success to encourage subsequent use of assessment results.
- The number of statements of intended educational outcomes upon which assessment activities are to be focused at any given time must be limited to avoid assessment overload.
- Identification of statements of intended educational outcomes for general education will be among the most difficult matters encountered on most campuses.

Concluding Comments Regarding Statements of Intended Educational Outcomes—
The formulation of statements of intended educational outcomes is, in the author's opinion, more important and more difficult than the act of identifying means of assessment. The discussions among faculty members regarding which intended educational outcomes should be included in the "short list" upon which assessment activities will be focused are some of the most heated discussions in which a department may have taken part in a good period of time. If the purpose of implementation is the reform or reconsideration of our curricular practices leading to improve student learning, the identification of intended educational outcomes is the first critical step toward accomplishment of this purpose. It is filled with value judgments regarding the relative importance of the material within disciplines and individual personalities can be expected to play a major role in the discussions concerning this matter. If attempted in a period of institutional financial stress, these discussions can be expected to have a number of hidden agenda related even more strongly than normal to "turf protection" concerns. However, once intended educational outcomes are identified, they clearly point the way to means of assessment which become somewhat mechanical, if unfamiliar, in nature.

Identification of Administrative and Educational Support Objectives

Why is implementation necessary in those areas?—Though clearly not the primary focus of institutional effectiveness or assessment activities across the country, educational support and administrative operations are frequently included in campus implementation for two reasons. First, most regional accrediting policies require implementation of assessment activities in administrative and educational support units at one time or another. This requirement is somewhat more rigorous in SACS than in other accreditation associations; however, nonetheless exists to some extent nationwide. Second, and every bit as powerful, is the argument that if assessment is so good in the academic areas of the institution, why shouldn't the educational support and administrative areas also implement a similar program?

It is the author's impression that implementation of assessment type activities in the educational support and the administrative areas of an institution is generally an easier task requiring roughly half the time of that in academic or instructional areas. This is partially true because the professional staff in these areas, considered as a group, are more predisposed to evaluation or management type activities than the faculty. Frequently department heads and managers in the administrative and educational support units are found to have already implemented some form of Management by Objective or Total Quality Management within their areas of responsibility. Where this is taking place, it is relatively easy to utilize or adapt this existing procedure to fulfill regional accreditation requirements. Second, in administrative areas, the means of assessment most frequently utilized are more direct, as opposed to having to be reflected through the accomplishment of students in the institution's academic programs.

In all but one of the case study institutions, educational support and administrative departments were asked to put forward statements of administrative objectives linked to and supporting the statement of purpose for the institution. It is interesting to note that the case study material from Sam Houston State University clearly stated that "all administrative offices and departments are treated in a fashion identical to academic departments." This is reflective of the feeling on many campuses that "what's good for the goose is good for the gander" regarding assessment.

Determining the Organizational Structure for Statements of Administrative Objectives—Unlike implementation in the academic or instructional aspects of an institution where the structure is relatively clear (academic programs or majors and general education), little guidance is usually provided concerning how to organize or structure statements of administrative objectives within colleges and universities. Resolution of this issue early in the implementation process is important to success in this endeavor.

The simplest, most comfortable, and most frequently utilized structure for organization of administrative objectives in the case study institutions was found in the organization of such statements by administrative departments and divisions. In this arrangement, each administrative officer reporting to the Chief Executive Officer is in charge of a division composed of organizationally distinctive administrative departments with well established functions. Utilization of this model has the advantage of familiarity by the units as well as perhaps budget planning/process statements which may already exist. This model is both feasible and recommended when clearly established department level units exist dealing with relatively well described single functions by each department.

At smaller colleges where frequently those units reporting to an administrative officer who in turns reports to the Chief Executive Officer may not be departmentally organized or single function in nature, establishment of administrative objectives for each of the major functions in a multidimensional department is advised. The classic example, in this regard, is the student affairs division which at smaller colleges is frequently not departmentalized, but may deal with the functions of personal counseling, career counseling, residential life, student activities, intramural athletics, concerts and lectures, admissions, registrar, and financial aid. Clearly under these circumstances, one set of administrative objectives covering this variety of functions would be inappropriate. In this case, the organizational structure for identifying administrative objectives is not the department or division, but the functions conducted within each division.

Quite apart from issues of size or complexity of organizational structures, some institutions choose to organize their statements of administrative objectives around closely related functions. At Jefferson State Community College, "rather than use the organizational structure of the college which is subject to frequent change, the college chose to use a functional structure based on operational units for identification of administrative and educational support objectives. An operational unit is composed of one or more individuals who perform a single function or closely related group of functions (i.e., admissions, budget control, instruction)." This approach is likely to take place at institutions attempting to establish cross functional teams associated with Total Quality Management in the institutions' educational support and administrative operations.

Means of Assessment in Non-Academic Areas—Beyond much question, the most commonly reported means of assessment in non-academic areas were surveys of client satisfaction. Such surveys were frequently of students and faculty, as well as other staff. The primary question asked in most cases related to client (customer) satisfaction with the services provided by the individual administrative/educational support unit or department.

Origination of these surveys varied from campus to campus. On some campuses, measures of client satisfaction with administrative or education services support were conducted institutionally as part of a graduating student survey or other questionnaire. On other campuses, individual educational support and administrative offices asked more detailed questions of clientele either through the mail or at the point of contact at which services were rendered (library books checked out, health services provided, etc.). Where this latter point of service solicitation of clients' satisfaction is practiced, institutions should be careful that clients are not subjected to too many surveys, resulting in low response rates and substantially less creditable feedback. The author has visited campuses that seemed to be awash in client satisfaction measures from educational support and administrative units. Probably the best approach to gauging client satisfaction is to utilize an institution-wide survey, such as a graduating student questionnaire, to identify areas of educational support and administrative services where further study is suggested. Then on a campuswide coordinated basis, a limited number of in-depth point of service surveys should be conducted regarding client satisfaction with specific aspects of the services rendered.

The notion of client or customer satisfaction is directly related to the tenants of total quality management. Among the difficulties in implementation of TQM at campuses is the identification of "who is the client?" It is fairly obvious that the clients of the counseling center are primarily the students enrolled (or formerly enrolled) and that "the client" for the media center are those faculty utilizing audiovisual materials in their classroom presentations. However, the customers or clients of the library obviously include students, but also faculty and potentially users from off the campus.

The second most frequently cited type of assessment in administrative or educational support services by the case study institutions was some type of productivity measure or standardized count of departmental activity. Most of these counts related to the volume of work, the efficiency with which work was accomplished, or in a limited number of instances, error rates. Among these were the amount of time to process travel reimbursements, the number of freshmen applications processed in one week, turnaround time on request for transcripts, etc. Most of these relatively straightforward measures of either the efficiency or quality of services provided were readily identified by the educational support and administrative units taking part.

Two other less frequently identified types of assessment of educational support or administrative units described by case study institutions were external reviews as well as internal reviews of operations. At Sam Houston State University, a series of internal management audits were found to be valuable procedures to assist in administrative objective formulation and measurement. Other institutions reported the use of external regulatory reviews of campus operations (external audit, health inspections, etc.) as valuable means of assessment requiring no additional work on the part of the institution.

In general, the means of assessment identified for educational support and administrative areas were reported to be much simpler, straightforward, and direct than those necessary to demonstrate the effectiveness of the institutions' educational programs.

Staff Involvement in Identifying Statements of Administrative Objectives—The extent of involvement by staff in the establishment of statements of administrative objectives among the case study group appeared to have a direct relationship to the size of the institution. At the larger major research universities, the department head and his/her supervisor (usually a vice president) were often described as being responsible for establishing statements of administrative objectives.

At the primarily four-year colleges and universities, there was clearly a greater expectation that the department head would have established the necessary administrative objectives based upon broadbased consultation with the staff in the office. Ultimately, these administrative objectives required approval by the vice presidential level administrator overseeing each individual department.

At the smaller institutions, all staff down to the clerical level tended to be involved in establishing statements of administrative objectives. It was not infrequent that planning conferences for all employees, retreats, or focus groups were utilized to gather the opinion of all employees involved in establishing administrative objectives.

It was reported by more than one institution participating in the case study that "the process of writing goals of outcomes statements has caused shared vision and a collective purpose as well as provided feedback on performance within numerous administrative and educational support units." Both professional and clerical staff warmed quickly on most campuses to this procedure and were more than willing to take part.

Amount of Time to Prepare Statements of Administrative Objectives—Somewhat surprisingly, administrative and educational support units at the case study institutions were given roughly the same amount of time to prepare their statements of administrative objectives as were the academic programs. One small group of institutions taking part in the case study reported three months or less being given to administrative departments to prepare these statements of administrative objectives. These were generally those institutions in the "heat of" preparing for a self-study visitation. Another group of case study institutions reported providing roughly a semester for administrative units to prepare their statements of administrative objectives, while still a third group allowed up to a year for preparation of these statements.

Based upon experience, it is this author's opinion that this is one area in which on many campuses an institution can accelerate the process somewhat. Identification of both administrative objectives and the manner in which they are to be assessed is distinctly possible within a three- to six-month period without rushing or over burdening the administrative staff involved.

Primary Problems in Implementation Within Educational Support and Administrative Units—The problems in implementation within educational support and administrative units reported by the case study institutions, while similar in many ways to those encountered in academic units, were more campus specific.

A number of campuses in the case study reported difficulties with administrators in framing or drafting statements of administrative objectives. At one institution where some department heads were described as being less than capable of articulating their unit's goals and objectives, "They were encouraged to seek guidance beyond the directions of the planning manual, but some submitted statements that were practically useless." On another campus, considerable confusion resulted from trying to change terminology from a currently functioning system of goals and objectives in administrative areas established during a previous grant to the regional accrediting association's terminology. Among the reasons described as contributing to the inability or difficulty in establishing what should have been relatively straightforward administrative objectives was the focus of initial campus educational experiences or workshops on the preparing of statements of intended educational outcomes. While this early focus on academics is understandable, later and more attention to administrative objectives could easily have avoided the problem on a number of campuses.

Surprisingly, a quarter of the case study institutions indicated a lack of strong administrative leadership in seeing that statements of administrative objectives were established. On one campus, a situation was described in which there was no administrative support for the process, while on another, some administrative unit heads were allowed not to participate in the process. On still other campuses, administrators appeared to be reluctant to commit to certain criteria for the purpose of judgment of their department's success. At one institution, historically departments had been asked to state objectives and measures of success only when seen as "troubled" or scheduled for significant overall reductions.

The expected types of difficulties related to identifying means of assessment were reported by most institutions. Those ranged from difficulty in reaching consensus on objectives through a lack of success criteria, to difficulty in identifying appropriate means of assessment. In the author's experience, most administrative and educational support offices can simplify the process of identifying administrative objectives and ultimately means of assessment by answering in sequence the following three questions:

- What services or functions does our department provide to the college?
- How can we ascertain if these services are being provided efficiently?
- To what extent are our services meeting the needs of our clients?

One of the community college campuses in the case study reported reluctance on the part of the educational support and administrative staff to take into consideration measures of client satisfaction based upon what was perceived as a genuine fear that initial ratings by clients would be less than desirable. This attitude reflected what, in all probability, had been a somewhat less than "service orientation" in the operations of the administrative units in the past on that campus.

Two other substantial problems have emerged in the author's experience working with campuses conducting assessment of administrative objectives. These are the somewhat greater tendency to tie such assessment of accomplishment of administrative objectives to individual administrator's personal evaluation and second, the potential for a "veritable plethora" of client satisfaction surveys discussed earlier in this chapter.

Just as is the case in the academic sector, it is important for administrators to feel that they can take part in this process of identifying administrative objectives and assessing the extent of their accomplishments for formative purposes as opposed to making summary judgments about their individual work performance. On some campuses visited by the author, there is a strong tendency to tie necessary employee evaluations for personnel decision making purposes to such a formative assessment process. This usually results in compromising the integrity of the formative assessment process as individuals take part in "gamesmanship" to make themselves look good rather than assessment to improve support services.

The need to acquire information in terms of client satisfaction can become almost an overwhelming impulse for educational support and administrative department heads. In no time at all, the campus can be awash with client satisfaction measures from the bookstore to the library to the student health center to the bursar's office. The result of this type of uncontrolled proliferation is frequently exceedingly low response rates on the part of the clients or students and real questions regarding the sincerity with which the measures or questionnaires are being completed. Such measures of client satisfaction by individual administrative units should be coordinated at the institutional level.

Summary Comments—In summary, the following comments can be made regarding the case study institutions experience in establishment of administrative objectives and the means for their assessment in educational support and administrative units:

- Ultimately, such a process must be established and the earlier begun the better.
- There will need to be support solicited from the senior administrators to elicit maximum cooperation from their subordinates.
- This process should be separated from the process of evaluating individual administrators or its usefulness will be compromised.
- If an existing process (MBO, TQM, or other variations) is in existence and functioning, do not attempt to change that process, but describe the existing process in terms recognizable by the regional accrediting authority.
- Provide separate implementation guidance for educational support and administrative units from that provided to the institution's instructional components. That guidance should stress the need for client satisfaction measures and maximum involvement of staff in identifying administrative objectives, and the means for assessment of their accomplishment.
- Select no more than three to five administrative objectives per department or function upon which to focus assessment activities at any given time.
- Emphasize the use of results to improve educational support and administrative programming rather than to justify the continuation of such units.

Designing and Conducting the Educational Assessment Process

Most energy and attention on campuses implementing assessment of educational outcomes focuses upon the particular means of assessment utilized. This is probably because of the tangible nature of assessment instruments and procedures; a certain degree of anxiety always associated with a measurement instrument (particularly when it will be utilized in relation to "our" program); and that "assessment" has become the buzzword utilized to describe the entire procedure by the public.

If the institution has proceeded in a systematic fashion from formulation of its statement of purpose through identification of its intended educational outcomes, then the identification of means of assessment to be utilized should flow readily. Unfortunately in many cases, institutions rush to the means of assessment and then try to back into statements of intended educational outcomes and even upon rare occasions into their institutional statement of purpose from these assessment instruments, all in order to meet a deadline related to regional accreditation.

By focusing first on means of assessment rather than intended educational outcomes, many institutional implementations bog down because they consider assessment activities to be a "shotgun" covering the entire field of fire (learning) from which they hope to try to discern something of use among all of the data available. Those more successful institutions tend to view assessment as a "rifle shot" targeted upon the statements of intended educational outcomes identified earlier in the process. Implementation on these campuses is characterized by efficiency of assessment procedures and higher utilization of assessment results.

On the case study campuses, slightly more than half of the assessment effort expended was specifically targeted on intended educational outcomes. Another way of stating this is to say that on these campuses, approximately half of the assessment work conducted was likely to be tied back to intended educational outcomes and yield results which would be utilized to improve academic programming. Conversely, one might say almost one half of the assessment effort created a great flurry of activity, but that its relationship with intended educational outcomes was problematic and that hence, up to half of the assessment effort expended by the case study institutions may have been wasted or ineffective in bringing about use of results to improve programming.

Why did this take place? Failure to focus assessment activities on intended educational outcomes on some of the case study campuses can probably be attributed to three factors: ignorance, haste, and intent. In many academic departments, the act of identifying intended educational outcomes and any form of program assessment was a major accomplishment. In these departments, the need to tie or relate the two together simply was not well communicated in the initial faculty orientation and this relationship can be expected to be tightened in the near future. On those campuses "under the gun" and expecting a regional accreditation visit soon, frequently the need for haste to "make up for lost time" resulted in selection of means of assessment which were not connected to statements of intended educational outcomes, but were readily available. One institution described it this way: "Most departments maintained only a loose connection between their educational goals and their means of assessment. Assessment strategies were proposed and did not link directly with a particular educational goal. Some of these unconnected means of assessment were adopted out of convenience because they were readily available in an existing university report." In only a small number of instances was there an apparent intentional lack of connection between means of assessment and intended educational outcomes reported. In one particular case, the institution was experiencing financial difficulty, reducing programs, and the faculty in the area were extremely reluctant to identify anything which might be used against them.

What then is the result of failing to tie together specific intended educational outcomes with means of assessment? Without making this tie apparent from the beginning, many assessment procedures and instruments will be utilized unnecessarily absorbing precious time, energy, and resources that could have been utilized to focus upon the appropriate means of assessment necessary to ascertain the accomplishment of the statements of intended educational outcomes. Second, the use results of instruments not tied directly to statements of intended educational outcomes is highly problematic. Many faculty frankly won't take time to try to find a use for a mound of data not responsive to their questions (intended educational outcomes). Faculty tend to use data from means of assessment that directly relate to their questions framed in terms of the intended educational outcomes of their programs. Finally, between the wasted effort and the lack of useful results, in many cases what has already been a frustrating process falls apart.

The Use of Standardized Examinations in Assessment—The case study institutions reported the use of both standardized licensure examinations and commercially produced standardized examinations in assessment procedures. Clearly, the most frequently utilized type of standardized examination in use on the campuses in the case study was the licensure exam and the majority of institutions reporting indicated the results of licensure examinations as a viable part of their assessment program.

The use of available standardized test in the major or for general education was reported on barely a majority of the campuses in the case study. Only at the University of Montevallo were commercially available standardized test reported as a primary component of the assessment of educational outcomes. On that campus, "Between 50% and 60% of programs that have nationally standardized content area tests use them." The University of Montevallo also reported use of a standardized instrument for the assessment of general education "for some years." Quite on the contrary, the use of commercially available standardized means of assessment was found to be rather "limited or spotty" on most other campuses taking part in the case study. The use of standardized testing instruments "in all fields available" was reported by only two institutions, both of which were two-year colleges.

Why on campuses relatively mature in their assessment procedures have standardized assessment instruments been utilized so sparingly? Three reasons are reported by the case study institutions. The expected faculty reluctance to utilize standardized means of assessment because of their perceived lack of validity or fit with the institution's educational outcomes was frequently cited by case study institutions and probably is justified in many instances. Second, a concern about the impact of having their program not perform (as demonstrated on the standardized test) at the expected level of attainment and the potential consequences thereof from the administration and/or state governing board was cited. Finally, the cost of the institution paying for these means of assessment was identified by three of the institutions as a reason for either not utilizing standardized means of assessment or discontinuing their use. These latter two justifications, it should be noted, have nothing to do with the appropriateness of the standardized instruments as a means for program evaluation, but are related to institutional politics and perceived financial circumstances.

It is of considerable interest to note that when required by state mandate to utilize standardized subject area tests in the major such as the EXCET subject test required for teacher certification in Texas, the results of such instruments were described as "useful to both departments and the institutional effectiveness committee." It is the author's opinion that in many cases the use of standardized tests is probably warranted, but that until required to do so by an external agency, most institutions will not use them. The danger therein is that the external agency with little institutional input may identify or prepare a test which ultimately shapes the institution's curriculum.

The combined limited use of commercially developed tests and the more widespread (but also limited by availability) use of licensure examinations as means of assessment among case study institutions is probably best exemplified by the primarily four-year university which reported the use of standardized test (commercially available and/or licensure) in *slightly less than half* of the institution's academic departments.

The Use of Locally Developed Means of Cognitive Assessment (Tests)—While virtually all statements of programmatic intended educational outcomes contain one or more statements related to the student's knowledge in the field, the faculty at the case study institutions were, on the whole, even more reluctant to prepare locally developed measures of this knowledge than to adopt standardized commercially available instruments covering these fields. There were, of course, a host of reasons cited by the case study institutions, including the following:

> "Besides the psychometric issues of reliability and validity associated with test development, the lack of normative data on students elsewhere limits the usefulness of test data. While locally developed test are indeed used, departments are strongly encouraged not to rely solely on these measures."

> "There is strong opposition by many faculty to using such exams, although the reason for the opposition has not been clearly identified."

> "This method of assessment only reached the discussion stage. There was general disagreement on what should be measured and how the test should be structured."

> "Problems encountered in the development of locally made exams included the subject matter to be included, the length of the exams, the length of administration, piloting exams, doing item analysis, and the desired level of proficiency. In addition, college personnel were concerned with the reliability of locally developed exams."

However, in the opinion of the author, the essential reason that most case study institutions had not further implemented locally developed comprehensive exams was reported by one primarily four-year college or university which indicated "the primary problem encountered with locally produced tests has been the time required to produce valid instruments." From the author's experience, this is the single greatest impediment to the comprehensive production and use of locally developed examinations. None of the case study institutions reported any release time for faculty to prepare such comprehensive examinations. Such lack of release time is typical of institutions nationwide.

In those few instances in which case study institutions reported use of locally developed examinations, they were most often constructed by assigning faculty teams to the task and to no one's great surprise, these locally developed comprehensive examinations frequently were constructed from test items extracted from course final examinations. Among the more successful implementation of locally developed examinations was that at Coastal Carolina Community College where end of course tests in capstone courses were frequently broadened to make them more comprehensive and then utilized as a means of assessment for the entire program.

Use of Attitudinal Questionnaires for Assessment—If case study institutions reported some reluctance or unevenness in cognitive assessment utilizing standardized or locally developed instruments, they demonstrated absolutely the opposite experience in willingness to ask students, faculty, and alumni about their level of satisfaction with their educational experience at the college or university. Only two of the case study institutions did not report the extensive use of attitudinal questionnaires as a means of assessment on their campus.

On some campuses, such as Clemson University and Collin County Community College, both standardized questionnaires (in this case, the ACT Student Opinion Survey for four- and two-year colleges) were utilized as well as locally developed questionnaires. Some other campus made the conscious policy level decision not to use standardized questionnaires. Their justification for not utilizing standardized questionnaires usually related to the ability of locally developed instruments to fit the specific intended educational outcomes of the program and the apparently lower relative cost per unit of locally developed surveys compared to standardized surveys. However, Sam Houston State University pointed out in its contribution to the case study that "While locally developed surveys may appear to be the least expensive alternative, it may be the institution's goal to produce professional appearing instruments. A significant expenditure in hardware and software is required, but in the end the departments get what they need and want."

Why this apparent rush to embrace the use of attitudinal questionnaires as a means of assessment by the case study institutions? The author believes that there are two reasons for the reported extensive use of attitudinal questionnaires: (1) Attitudinal questionnaires represent a relatively expedient reflection of the perception of program quality or accomplished by its graduates, alumni or employers. These surveys can in many cases be conducted at the institutional level without significant involvement or work by the faculty and represent a "quick fix" to the assessment problem on some campuses. (2) The results of attitudinal questionnaires can be dismissed by faculty as perceptual rather than substantive reflections of accomplishment if the perception does not happen to agree with the intended educational outcomes. It is much easier politically to deal with the students' perception of program quality than to measure that quality or achievement through a cognitive test of one type or another and then perhaps to have to deal with the reality of lesser achievement.

Attitudinal affirmation of program accomplishment or "quality" on various types of questionnaires represents in the author's opinion one of the weakest types of assessment information, but is better than nothing. Regretfully, in order to avoid difficult, technical, and internal political circumstances, many institutions apparently are satisfied with such secondary type of information rather than actually measuring whether the students have the knowledge or skills which our academic programs are intended to convey.

Among the best sets of locally developed surveys identified were those from Coastal Carolina Community College where standardized or commercially available attitudinal questionnaires were rejected because they were too long and the questions were too general, and the belief that they could not be altered sufficiently to meet local needs. Locally developed surveys were then developed for graduates, alumni, and employers. These surveys are automated on scannable forms which greatly increase their ease of use, return rate, and analysis. Among the software packages utilized on the campuses of the case study to produce such locally developed surveys have been those by Bubble Publishing Company and Scantron.

Also noteworthy were those locally developed instruments developed at the University of Kentucky to support their program review based educational outcomes related implementation. Copies of two of those instruments are included in Appendix E as well as a sample of the survey instruments from Coastal Carolina Community College.

The Provision of Centralized Assessment Services—Without exception, all of the case study institutions report some form of assistance provided by the institutions' administration to facilitate implementation of institutional effectiveness or educational outcomes assessment.

At ten of the institutions in the case study, this assistance was provided by a party having in their title the institutional research function. Only three of these ten offices were recently established for the specific purpose of facilitating implementation of institutional effectiveness or assessment of educational outcomes. So in the majority of cases, the existing institutional research offices at the case study institutions were asked to provide additional services supporting institutional effectiveness and assessment of educational outcomes achievement. Regardless of the title of the office, the type of central assessment services provided were remarkably similar from campus to campus in the case study. These services involve leadership or coordination, technical skills, logistical support, and data provision.

At the majority of the institutions in the case study, leadership for overall campus implementation was provided by the individual heading the institutional research/planning component on the campus. This leadership ranged from service as Executive Vice President of the institution, to chair of the institutional effectiveness committee, to overall coordinator of the process. At some institutions, coordination took a relatively direct form of establishing a timeline and assigning responsibilities in implementing assessment activities. On other campuses, it was obvious that campus leadership coordination was more in the collegial style typified by the chairmanship of the institutional effectiveness committee through which campus actions were taken on a consensual basis.

Centralized assessment support services (usually institutional research offices) at all case study institutions provided at least *technical* support in the design and construction of attitudinal surveys of graduating students, alumni, etc. All of these offices also provided *logistical* support to actually conduct attitudinal surveys for their institution. In addition to providing extensive support in the survey design and administration, several of the offices in the case study provided data processing support to extract existing data to support institutional effectiveness operations, while only four of the institutions in the case study reported providing centralized services regarding standardized testing.

Based upon the case study reports, it is clear that the central administration on these campuses was providing the necessary support structure for implementation of a successful program of assessment of educational outcomes. However, the experiences reported by these institutions revealed the marked difference in implementation between the *comprehensive use* of attitudinal surveys accomplished by the central administrative support services and the *relative lack* of implementation of cognitive assessment by the faculty.

Student Motivation—One of the problems faced by all institutions implementing assessment of educational outcomes or institutional effectiveness is the motivation of students to take seriously tests, surveys, and other activities conducted for assessment purposes. It is one matter, and legally very defensible, to require students to take part in such assessment activities. It is impossible to require students to take assessment activities *seriously* and to do their best if they believe that the results of the assessment activity have little or no bearing upon themselves.

In an effort to motivate students to seriously take part in assessment activities, institutions in the case study appealed to the student's commitment to their institution, fit assessment instruments into convenient time packages, incorporated assessment into classwork, offered bribes, and appealed to vest self-interest. Usually the beginning point of the motivational process on a campus is an appeal to the students to take part in assessment activities and to seriously assist the institution in improving its curriculum for future generations of students. This is frequently accompanied by the requirement that in order to graduate or pass through certain periods of their curriculum, students must take an examination or respond to a survey. Usually however, "passing" scores are not required. Such an appeal to the good nature of the student body has, in most instances, fallen on deaf ears and resulted in 10-20% of the students taking a means of assessment seriously once they realize that there "is nothing in it for them."

The University of Montevallo, among the case study institutions, probably has done the most to accentuate this intrinsic motivation for students to take part through building assessment for continuous improvement into the academic culture of the institution. Students are informed during orientation about the institution's assessment program. Freshmen are reportedly required to take the Freshmen Survey during their registration and are told again at that time about the university's overall assessment programs. Seniors are required to take university-wide senior assessments in order to participate in graduation exercises and are notified of this requirement by their senior checksheets as well as by letters informing them of the dates of administration of the surveys. In each case, the use of the assessment results to improve academic and educational support/administrative programming is explained to the students and wherever possible, examples of the use of assessment results in the past are offered.

Convenience of student participation is also normally utilized as a means of student motivation. This convenience may take the form of scheduling "short forms" of some examinations to be taken within a single class period or the shortening of questionnaires or limiting their number so as to ease the burden on the students. Several of the case study institutions reported motivation of students to take part in focus groups by the provision of food and drink. The enclosure of small gifts in questionnaires, and other obviously extrinsic means of motivation for student participation in assessment activities were also reported.

By far, the most common and probably most effective means of student motivation reported by the case study institutions was the integration of assessment activities into existing student academic procedures. This was accomplished by embedding within existing courses means of assessment which were later reviewed for assessment purposes by the faculty overall and the creation or modification of capstone courses within which various means of assessment were administered and after which the results were reviewed by the faculty as a whole for assessment purposes. In both cases, student motivation was assured by using the means of assessment once for individual student grading purposes and then extracting the means of assessment from that environment and reviewing the assessment results a second time as they relate to accomplishment of intended educational outcomes.

There is nothing unethical about utilizing vested student self-interest as a means of motivation for students to seriously take part in assessment activities. One of the case study institutions, Coastal Carolina Community College, reported motivating students within their capstone courses to take a standardized means of assessment seriously so that their scores could be utilized to better help them find employment upon graduation. Likewise, the author is familiar with three other schools which utilize extrinsic forms of motivation or self-interest to get students to take seriously their general education or rising junior examination. At one of these schools (a relatively traditional institution), the order of student registration for classes in the student's junior and senior year is determined by how well they scored on the rising junior or general education exam at the close of the sophomore year. At another residential institution, competition between fraternities and sororities are held concerning whose members can score highest on the rising junior examination. However, the utmost motivation which this author has witnessed takes place at a primarily commuter four-year institution that awards parking passes to the "honors parking lot" located in the center of the campus to those students doing best on the rising junior examination. A number of faculty have asked to take the examination.

Student motivation is particularly important on those campuses implementing assessment of educational outcomes with the purpose of satisfying state accountability requirements. In a number of instances, substantial differences between average scores on assessment instruments from institutions enrolling the same type of students can only be attributed to the manner in which the institutions motivated their students to take part in the assessment program. While this explanation may indeed be correct, it is difficult to persuade legislators that the difference in scores is something other than related to effectiveness of the academic programs.

The Existence and Use of Assessment Plans—The existence of "an assessment plan" was reported at roughly half of the case study institutions. The nature of these plans varied significantly. Some reported rather lengthy documents prepared for state accountability purposes, others reported listings of assessment responsibilities and time tables, while on other campuses they existed primarily at the departmental level. Appendix F provides A Summary of Department Assessment Plans in the Major at SUNY-Albany. There seemed to be a greater tendency on the part of smaller institutions to have prepared an assessment plan integrating activities throughout the institution as opposed to decentralized assessment planning at the larger institutions in the case study.

What are some of the common components of these assessment plans? The assessment plans reviewed, as stated earlier, varied widely in content and purpose. In general, it can be said that they addressed: who, what, when, where, why, and how of assessment to greater or lesser degrees on each campus. None of the plans reviewed were prepared for a regional accreditation agency. It is this author's general opinion that those preparing assessment plans tended to be among those campuses in the case study most likely to have successfully implemented a program of institutional effectiveness or assessment of educational outcomes.

Coordination of Assessment Activities—Case study institutions reported three basic structures for continuing coordination of assessment activities. These were regular administrative operations, separately convened institutional effectiveness or assessment committees, and coordination by a single office.

On several campuses in the case study, the regular administrative structure (presidential cabinet, deans' council, etc.) was utilized to coordinate assessment activities. Where this took place, it was frequently the responsibility of a staff officer to bring to this group's attention the specific matters which needed to be coordinated.

On other campuses, assessment activities were coordinated by a body such as an institutional effectiveness/assessment committee or standing committee specifically charged with this requirement. On several campuses in the case study, committees such as these were charged with beginning the process; however, since have turned the responsibility for its ongoing maintenance over to an individual administrative office.

Offices of institutional research, planning, etc., which frequently were reported as conducting much of the assessment work done on campuses, often also served as the natural location for the coordination of the balance of the work which was accomplished. Offices such as these, in addition to designing and conducting survey research, frequently were found to coordinate other offices conducting such research to prevent duplication of effort and to oversee survey of clientele, schedule of standardized testing, etc., to avoid conflicting assessment activities.

Summary Comments Regarding Designing and Implementing the Educational Assessment Process at Case Study Institutions

The comments below summarize the experiences of individual campuses in the case study regarding the subject:

- Identification of intended educational outcomes led naturally and directly to means of assessment.
- Beginning the process by identification of means of assessment led to institutional efforts which "bogged down" in overwork and underutilization of results.
- While licensure examinations were frequently utilized as a means of assessment, great institutional reluctance to voluntarily use cognitive commercial standardized test was demonstrated.
- The use of locally developed comprehensive examinations was reported in only a limited number of cases.
- All case study institutions reported some use of attitudinal questionnaires (students, graduates, alumni, employers, etc.) as a means of assessment.
- Centralized technical and logistical services to support assessment activities were reported by all institutions and such offices frequently were charged with coordination of the overall process.
- Institutions addressed the issue of student motivation to take part in assessment activities through a number of creative means, but the most widespread and apparently effective was to "embed" means of assessment in a capstone course or other required academic endeavors.
- Existence of institutional plans for assessment were reported by only half the case study institutions, but these institutions tended to be the most successful in implementation.

The experiences of the case study institutions in the assessment process is both reassuring and disappointing. It is reassuring to know that much well-designed and executed assessment has taken place among institutions of higher learning. It is disappointing that among the case study institutions so much wasted effort was reported in accomplishing assessment activities not targeted upon intended educational outcomes and hence, likely to go unutilized. The extent of reliance at the case study institutions on attitudinal affirmation of programs by graduates, alumni, etc., was in the author's opinion somewhat excessive. More substantive ascertainment of student knowledge through locally developed or standardized testing would have provided direct evidence of program accomplishment. The case study institutions represent a reasonable cross section of higher education and in their assessment efforts have occasionally taken the course of least resistance through attitudinal means of assessment which are readily gathered *at the institutional level* rather than, in the author's opinion, the more substantive means of cognitive assessment either through standardized test or locally developed comprehensive examinations *at the program level*. The key element, however, is the use of assessment results to improve programming which is described in the following section.

Use of Assessment Results

All of the assessment activities reported earlier by the case study institutions were for one purpose: to provide assessment results for utilization by the institutions' instructional and educational supportive programs to improve accomplishments. An institution can have failed at any number of the previously discussed activities and redeem itself by the production of information or assessment results which are actually utilized to improve institutional and educational support program performance. This use of assessment results is, to put it in the vernacular, the "bottom line" and has frequently been described as "closing the loop" in the assessment process from intentions to improvements. However, there are a number of critical issues in the use of assessment results on the campus which the case study institutions were asked to address:

- Analysis of Assessment Results
- Establishment of a Clearinghouse for Assessment Information
- Communication of Assessment Results
- Establishment of a Formal Policy Regarding "Use of Assessment Results"
- Documentation of the Use of Assessment Results

Each of these is addressed in turn in the following sections.

Analysis of Assessment Results—The analysis of assessment data is a very sensitive and controversial matter on many campuses. In general, the case study institutions reported that if the assessment activity (attitudinal questionnaires, standardized tests, etc.) was conducted at the institutional level then analysis of the results was provided by that level. However, analysis of data resulting from means of assessment (locally developed examinations, performance assessment, etc.) conducted by various academic and administrative departments was found to be accomplished primarily within each of those individual academic programs and units.

The definition of "analysis" was found to vary from (a) the provision of *statistical data summaries* concerning the results of a means of assessment to (b) the study of the data received through interpretation of the results to *derive their meaning* concerning a program or the institution. Utilizing the definition of analysis that relates primarily to the forwarding of *statistical data summaries* of assessment activities, the clear majority of institutions in the case study reported provision of such analysis concerning institutionally conducted means of assessment by a centralized agency on campus. Typical of the justifications for this action were those cited by Sam Houston State University and Clemson University.

At Sam Houston State University, "Except for a few departments that wish to analyze their own data, analysis is performed in the Office of Institutional Research….The aim of the Office of Institutional Research is to make assessment and the use of assessment results as painless as possible for the departments. We want departments to focus on what needs to be assessed and how the results can be utilized without much emphasis on administration of instruments and data analysis."

At Clemson University, it was found that "perhaps the most significant reason for performing analysis prior to disseminating the information, is the varying degrees of expertise in interpreting data in the various units. Although some units deal with data analysis on a regular basis, others find data analysis to be equivalent to a foreign language. The purpose of analysis performed by the Office of Assessment is to turn the data into information and to point out the implications of the data, if any."

At more technically oriented institutions and quite possibly more generally in the future, such statistical presentation of information regarding assessment data may be accomplished at the department or program level. Appalachian State University already reports an increase in the number of "data sets" forwarded to departments for their own statistical processing.

If the operational definition of "analysis" is that described as leading from the statistical presentation of information to the *derivation of meaning* and potentially implications for academic programs, then such analysis was conducted at all levels by the case study institutions. At some institutions, such as Stillman College and Mt. Hood Community College, analysis of institutionally produced data to the point of derivation of meaning and implications was conducted by an institutionally based group, in the case of Mt. Hood Community College by their institutional research component and in the case of Stillman College by a cross sectional group coordinating the implementation process.

Wherever analysis to the point of derivation of meaning and potential implications is conducted beyond the departmental level, the challenge of bias in the analysis is likely to come forward when the results of the analysis do not meet the ends desired by the operating units. Rather than address educational issues, individuals find it even easier to attack the analysis than to attack the assessment means which were utilized. Any distraction is likely to be offered in order to focus attention on something other than the issues at hand revealed in the assessment results. Most of the case study institutions which had pursued analysis of data to the point of ascertaining or deriving meaning built into their process a procedure for at least recognizing the results of varying data analysis and Mt. Hood Community College, even identified their Program Improvement Council as the place that "any differences in interpretation of results and ratings are reconciled."

At a number of the institutions in the case study, analysis to the point of determination of meaning and implications of the data was accomplished at the department and program level. Such analysis was reported regularly shared within the operating unit and forwarded to the supervisory level (dean or vice president) as use of assessment results are reported.

The Establishment of a Clearinghouse for Assessment Information—The establishment of a common point for collection of assessment information is frequently cited in the literature in the field as a desirable event on campuses implementing programs of assessment of educational outcomes. Such a clearinghouse can coordinate assessment efforts more effectively, cross reference assessment results between programs and departments, and provide a ready depository for review by reaffirmation of accreditation teams or for accountability purposes. The primary issue regarding creation of such a clearinghouse is one of trust on the campus. Does the unit identified as a clearinghouse, enjoy sufficient credibility and trust on the campus to house information which could be potentially damaging to the institution's individual academic programs (as well as the individuals employed therein) with confidence that such information will be utilized for formative program improvement purposes rather than summative decisions concerning programs or personnel?

A bare majority of the institutions taking part in the case study reported the existence of such a clearinghouse function on their campus. These institutions cut across the entire spectrum of institutional types and the reason cited for establishment of this clearinghouse for assessment information included the preparation of state accountability reports and the analysis of all statistical data relating to programs to ascertain meaning and implications.

Two of the other institutions in the case study (not included in the majority referenced above) reported that most campus assessment information was forwarded to a clearinghouse function. Stillman College indicated that although their Office of Institutional Research and Planning "does not currently receive *all* assessment information, campus personnel invariably call on this office to provide assessment results." At Appalachian State University, "The office seeks to monitor and inventory assessment results across the campus rather than actually housing complete copies of all reports."

At two of the case study institutions, a conscious decision not to establish a clearinghouse function was reported. At both of these institutions, the extremely decentralized nature of the implementation design was primarily responsible for this decision. Whether this decentralization was a reflection of a lack of "trust" in the institution's administration to handle the data in a responsible manner is a matter for further conjecture though in the case of one of the institutions, the author is relatively certain that "trust" was not an issue.

Communication of Assessment Results on the Campus—Among the opportunities for creativity in the institutional research community is that of communication of data of all types. Not surprisingly, the case study institutions reported both written and verbal communication of assessment findings on the campuses.

Communication of assessment findings through a written means was reported in tabular, graphic, and narrative form. Such written communications were accomplished in scheduled reports concerning assessment activities such as alumni and graduating student surveys, occasional formal reports of major assessment studies, and ad hoc reports in response to departmental inquiries. A particularly noteworthy means of communication of assessment findings was through the "Institutional Research Newsletter" published by Stillman College as a means for the routine dissemination of assessment information.

The presentation of assessment findings through verbal means was occasioned in three different settings on the case study campuses. First, a series of special presentations to a number of campus groups regarding the implications of the administration of a standardized assessment of general education was conducted at Clemson University. Second, assessment findings were frequently presented verbally at scheduled meetings of the administration and governance structures at case study institutions as issues regarding assessment were discussed. Finally, most institutions in the case study reported individual sessions, on request, with various academic programs to discuss and explain assessment findings which had been forwarded earlier.

Two particular noteworthy and very different means of communication assessment results were reported by the case study institutions. In an attempt to bring various assessment findings together into one very readable publication, a document entitled *Reflections of a*

University: Some Questions Clemson Has Asked was prepared, copies were provided to all deans, directors, department heads, the faculty senate, the Board of Trustees, and other relevant groups at Clemson University. This publication (a portion of which is contained in Appendix G) utilized the results of various surveys (alumni, faculty, student opinion, staff), general education test results, retention findings, etc., to ask and answer questions about many various aspects of the institution. The intention of the publication was to demonstrate how seemingly unrelated pieces of assessment information could be brought together and focused to provide a coherent picture of various university issues. This example is particularly noteworthy because of its relationship of assessment results to issues of concern at the institution level and because of its integration of assessment findings from a number of sources.

Probably the best systematic means for effectively communicating assessment results in a recurring manner and demonstrating their use was found to be the "Desktop Audit" procedure utilized by Coastal Carolina Community College. Other than this author's personal aversion to the title of the document, the procedure utilized and illustrated in Appendix D, is most noteworthy because it combines systematically both written and direct verbal communication of the data while insuring its use on the campus. The process at Coastal Carolina Community College is described in their contribution to the cast study as shown below:

> "Assessment results are communicated to the departments by the printing of a DRAFT Desktop Audit. The draft is sent to each faculty member in November of each year. The Research, Planning, and Institutional Effectiveness Office produces the draft, distributes the copies, and collects the updates from the departments. A great deal of interaction and feedback takes place in December. The final interaction takes place in a formal departmental meeting (December/January) to review the particular "program" Desktop Audit. Present at the meeting are the departmental faculty, the Division Chair, Dean of Curriculum Education, Vice President for Instruction, and the Executive Vice President. Any additional adjustments to the Desktop Audit take place at that time. Over the years, fewer and fewer adjustments have been made because of the increased interaction prior to the final face-to-face departmental meeting. After all of the departmental meetings have taken place, a full book of the desktop audits are printed and distributed to all faculty and staff."

It should be noted that the Desktop Audit and its systematic approach to data communication and utilization have been recognized by the legislature of the State of North Carolina to the extent that a similar type of procedure is now being required of all 58 community colleges within that State.

Establishment of a Formal Policy Regarding "Use of Assessment Results"—All campuses are, to one extent or another, paranoid. The author has visited campuses ranging from rampant paranoia concerning the intrusiveness of the administration into faculty rights and prerogatives (featuring accusations that administration was "going through the garbage" for evidence to use against the faculty), to the most benign situation in which there has been no evidence of inappropriate administrative behavior regarding faculty rights and privileges. But, nonetheless, "they" (the administration) bare careful watching anyway. Given this potential situation and the possible "misuse" of assessment information in an adverse way concerning individuals or programs, some campuses find it important to put together a statement regarding the "use of assessment" results for formative purposes and to publish it broadly on the campus. Two personal illustrations by the author testify to the potential need for such a statement. On one campus, the implementation of outcomes assessment activities was announced at the same faculty meeting at which the institution's first "review" of tenured faculty members was also made. Forever locked in the minds of tenured faculty members at that institution will be the fact that those two issues were coupled together (although completely unintentionally by the institution) and hence, faculty resistance to assessment activities has increased, and in the foreseeable future, will limit implementation on that campus.

On another campus which the author visited, it became abundantly clear shortly into the visit that the entire subject of assessment was receiving an even less enthusiastic response than normal among faculty. Upon inquiry, the author ascertained that the Chief Academic Officer, concerning whom a vote of no confidence had been passed in the previous week, had stated that he would "take care" of his faculty opposition through the "assessment activities" which were about to commence. The reaction of the faculty was a predictable lack of enthusiasm concerning anything connected with assessment. However, the faculty members present were convinced that perhaps the situation could be salvaged by the drafting of a "Statement of Use of Assessment Results" for signature by the Chief Academic and Chief Executive Officers. Initially, the Chief Academic Officer did not wish to sign the statement separating assessment from anything even remotely resembling summative decisions regarding individuals or academic programs. However, the President of the institution (upon whom a vote of confidence was to be taken the next week) convinced the Chief Academic Officer of the wisdom of signing the statement and implementation activities began in earnest on the campus.

Both of the above examples illustrate the fact that if the faculty believes that assessment activities can be used against either themselves or their programs, some will either refuse to take part or "play games" with the process in such a way as to insure that they are placed in the most favorable light. The institution must remove assessment activities from the punitive or reward structure as far as possible in order to facilitate sincere and genuine implementation for program improvement purposes.

The need to put forward a formal written statement regarding the use of assessment results varies from campus to campus. Two of the institutions in the case study found it desirable to state from the outset exactly what assessment data would and would not be used for on the campus. One of these institutions was a major research university and the other a community college. One of the statements emanated from a faculty based assessment committee, while the other was clearly a statement promulgated by the administration. At another institution in the case study, while no written statement existed, the Chief Academic/Chief Executive Officers and other administrative officers were reported to repeatedly emphasize in their verbal comments the separation between the assessment activities and evaluation of individuals.

On three of the campuses in the case study, while no written statement existed, the procedures for both formative assessment of educational outcomes and summative evaluation of faculty were described as being so different as to separate the two processes entirely. It might be pointed out that what is clear to administrative officers, who frequently were the respondents or contributors to the case study, and the perception of individual faculty regarding this matter could be considerably different.

On some of the case study campuses, there was a specific and direct tie between outcomes assessment data and the program review process. Undoubtedly, this raised anxiety among the faculty undergoing program review for both summative and formative purposes and required the institution to exercise close oversight regarding the intended educational outcomes so as to insure that they did not become solely self-serving. Only at Coastal Carolina Community College was the edge taken off the use of assessment results for summative purposes by "guaranteeing" the faculty in programs under review the opportunity for retraining at the college's expense and subsequent continuing employment should their program be terminated.

Perceptions of the faculty regarding the potential use of assessment results is a serious matter. It is not necessary that a statement of use of assessment results be established on every campus as the relative degree of institutional paranoia varies from campus to campus and from time to time. However, if in the judgment of those guiding implementation activities on the campus, there is a significant or potentially well-founded question regarding possible misuse of assessment results for purposes other than originally intended, the situation can be relatively easily resolved by the establishment of such a statement.

Documentation of the Use of Assessment Results—As institutions gain experience and become more mature in their assessment activities, documentation of the use of assessment results becomes more important because of the frequent changes in departmental leadership and the growing expectation on the part of regional accrediting agencies that assessment information has been used for a significant period of time at the institution. Documentation reported by the case study institutions took a number of different forms and was maintained at two relatively distinct levels. All institutions reported the gathering and documenting of the use of assessment results to improve academic programming at the departmental level. The nature of these reports and their frequencies varied significantly. At Clemson University, the assessment plan required reporting each year while at the author's institution a one-page report of assessment activities is required every other year. At Sam Houston State University, an extensive report was required each two years. There is no standardized form for documentation of the use of assessment results, rather the institutional emphasis should be placed on a brief open-ended narrative asking how assessment results were used to improve programming. In most cases, the necessary documentation can be accomplished in one or two pages at the most.

In addition to documentation at the departmental level, institutions frequently felt the need to prepare an annual overall comprehensive report regarding institutional effectiveness or assessment operations on the campus. Among the case study institutions, this is typified by the experience at Clemson University and Appalachian State University where academic departments are required annually to forward a summary of their assessment results and use of the data to the Office of the Director of Assessment and Office of Institutional Research and Planning, respectively, on these two campuses. These offices, in turn, prepare summary reports to satisfy state accountability initiatives.

At Stillman College, a similar annual report was reported as prepared for their Board of Trustees each spring, while at some other campuses in the case study documentation of the use of assessment results was accomplished periodically by program review activities in which assessment data were utilized.

The clear implication, as the assessment movement reaches adolescence, is that those institutions involved should be able to provide a documented trail of the use of assessment results to improve academic programming over an extended period of time. That is the circumstances which regional accreditation teams expect to see after up to ten years of implementation activity in regions of the country.

Examples of Use of Assessment Results—Each of the case study institutions reported ten or more specific examples of use of assessment results to improve academic or other programming. The following constitute the highlights from some of the institutions' reports in this regard:

Stillman College
- The English Department spent two years reviewing, piloting, and revising its basic skills course based on data gathered from student assessments.
- As a result of assessment efforts, a social science department developed and has improved a new basic computer science course for social science majors.
- The English Department developed a capstone course for its majors.
- The Math and Science division developed and implemented a computerized math tutoring component designed to enhance math skills of all students.

Collin County Community College
- In response to a recommendation that the Sociology Department "internationalize the curriculum," the department has standardized its course syllabi making course content more global and has adopted a new introductory course textbook which gives a much more global perspective.

Clemson University
- Senior exit interviews in the medical technology program indicated that the students were generally unprepared for the clinical section on phlebotomy (blood collection for lab analysis). As a result of those interviews, a component of phlebotomy was added to Med Tech 101 which all medical technology majors must take in their first year.
- A senior thesis project was developed in architecture to help assure that students could integrate art, history, technology, and planning.
- Responses to an alumni survey conducted by the Construction Science and Management program identified a curriculum weakness in that graduates felt that an orientation to construction course should be taken during the first year in place of one of the existing courses.
- The Department of Psychology found through the use of an alumni survey that students needed more proactive advising, information regarding career opportunities, and greater awareness of multiculturalism issues. As a result, the department developed a comprehensive handbook for all psychology majors to address the issue of career opportunities and formed peer advising services for freshman and sophomore psychology majors to help make advising more participative.
- The Department of Chemical Engineering identified a deficiency in the area of oral communication through the use of an alumni survey. As a result, the curriculum was revised to replace a required english course with a speech course.

Mt. Hood Community College
- An analysis of student intentions data and other course profile information caused the Computer Science Department to offer weekend courses culminating in a significant increase in enrollment.
- The program improvement process led to numerous modifications including the conversion of a number of associate degree programs to one-year certificate programs, "coring" of first year course across several related programs and other curriculum changes.

Jefferson State Community College
- As a result of various assessment activities, a computer science course was added to selected business programs.

Sam Houston State University
- Analysis of the performance of students on a Geography EXCET Teacher Certification Test identified a weakness in the area of physical geography. Adjustments to the curriculum have been accomplished.
- One former student invited back for an interview as part of assessment of the program presented the Chair with a $10,000 check to establish an endowment. The student has subsequently contributed an additional $13,000 to this fund. Assessment pays big dividends—it causes students and alumni to know that you care.

University of Kentucky – Lexington Campus
A survey of graduating seniors revealed poor perceptions of academic advising. The Chancellor reallocated a substantial amount of funds from a support unit to establish a centralized academic advising center.

Appalachian State University
- Courses have been added, especially senior seminars, to measure students' preparation in their majors.
- Changes have been made in remedial mathematics and english courses to increase success in required general education courses.

Detailed treatment of the use of assessment results on other campuses is contained in Trudy Banta's book *Making a Difference* from Jossey-Bass Publishers, 1994. The early and continued dissemination of how assessment information is being utilized on the campus to improve academic or educational support programming is an excellent stimulus to continued implementation activities throughout the institution.

Concluding Comments Regarding Use of Assessment Results

After careful planning, as well as the expenditure of a considerable amount of time and energy, some institutions "assume" that the assessment results emanating from the process will "automatically" be utilized for the improvement of academic programming on the campus. In general, such use of results will take place; however, the issues reviewed in this section will increase the utilization of such information which is the end result of all previous efforts. In summary, the following points highlight the case study institution's experience regarding the use of results of assessment data:

- Statistically summaries of institutionally conducted means of assessment (question-naires, etc.) were frequently forwarded to the program level.
- Analysis of assessment results to the point of derivation of meaning and implications was accomplished at the departmental and institutional level.
- Most institutions establish a clearinghouse for assessment information to consolidate results from across the campus.
- A systematic process combining both written and verbal communication of assessment information was found to be most effective in dissemination of assessment results.
- Early in the implementation process institutions should identify the purposes for which assessment results will be utilized and those matters which will not be addressed by assessment information.
- Responsibility for and a process to require minimal documentation of the use of assessment results should be established.
- Identification of model examples of the use of assessment results on the campus can stimulate continued implementation across the campus.

Once all of the processes described in this chapter have been initially implemented, the challenge of the institution is their integration into the ongoing life of the campus or the creation of an institutional effectiveness or educational outcomes assessment cycle to continue the process into the future. The experiences of the case study institutions in this regard are described in the following chapter.

Chapter V

ESTABLISHMENT OF THE INSTITUTIONAL EFFECTIVENESS OR ASSESSMENT CYCLE ON CAMPUSES AMONG THE CASE STUDY INSTITUTIONS

The need to regularize or make cyclical institutional effectiveness or assessment of educational outcomes activities on campuses is clearly one of the intended results of the implementation process. Whereas episodic "spasms" of assessment activities associated with regional accreditation reaffirmation visitations are a relatively common experience in higher education today. Each of the case study institutions has, in its own unique way, tried to build assessment activities into the ongoing fabric of the institution so as to create a process for the continuous improvement of institutional operations leading to enhanced student learning. This chapter addresses:

- The nature of the institutional effectiveness/assessment cycles established on campuses and their relationship to other ongoing operational procedures and planning at the institution.
- Problems encountered in integration or meshing of institutional effectiveness and assessment activities with other institutional operations.
- Actions to continue motivation for assessment activities past institutional reaffirmation of accreditation.
- Procedures for evaluation of assessment activities.

The Nature of the Institutional Effectiveness/Assessment Cycles Established

The case study institutions reported three basic patterns of institutional effectiveness or assessment activities on their campuses, (a) those tied with an external reporting requirement, such as, legislature or governing board; (b) those periodic activities scheduled to examine in depth part of the institution every four to six years; and (c) those comprehensive annual planning processes into which assessment and/or effectiveness activities had been integrated.

Assessment and Effectiveness Activities Associated with or Caused by External Reporting Requirements—Tying an institution's effectiveness or assessment cycle to an external requirement can have drastically different consequences depending upon the nature of the external requirement. At Clemson University, the campus assessment/effectiveness cycle was reported as primarily conditioned by an annual requirement for an "institutional effectiveness report" to the South Carolina Commission on Higher Education. The report, consisting of 18 components or measures, is required annually and although not all components are reported upon each year, a cycle has been established so that every three years, narrative explanations of each of the 18 components are to be provided. Also, Clemson is required to provided data under a "report card" type legislative mandate. A separate data file (narrative explanations not allowed) of outcomes assessment data is also forwarded annually to the Commission on Higher Education. Hence, Clemson is forwarding both narrative and summary data as well as raw data files to the State on what amounts to both a one-year and three-year basis.

At Stillman College, a private institution in Alabama, a semi-annual report of the President's office to the Board of Trustees causes twice yearly assessment cycles at the institution-wide and unit levels. *At the institution level*, the cycle includes mission review; review, development, and refinement of intended educational outcomes; adjustment of curriculum and plans for operations and assessment techniques; and preparation of effectiveness reports. These reports are forwarded to the institutional effectiveness unit liaison who forwards them to the Institutional Planning Committee that in turn prepares reports and forwards them to Administrative Council, Vice President for Academic Affairs Advisory Council and the Administrative Cabinet. From these reports, the institutional report on effectiveness activities is prepared for the Board of Trustees and a determination is made of the impact on planning and evaluation processes in each unit. Following that, the information is used as part of an annual planning retreat. *At the unit level*, the cycle consists of a detailed analysis of the unit mission, goals and objectives; the establishment of unit priorities, and intended educational outcomes, strategies, and required resources (fiscal, human, and physical); implementation of goals, objectives, results; data gathering; analysis and refinement; evaluation and report generation; adjustment; and the incorporation of results. The institutional planning cycle is sequenced around the development of the required (February and September) reports each unit must submit to the President's office for preparation of the Board of Trustees reports twice each year.

At Appalachian State University, the assessment activities are being incorporated into the biennial budgetary request in the State of North Carolina. This is partially occasioned by state requirements for assessment information; however, it is primarily connected with strengthening the institution's accountability to the public at the time financial requests for the support of the institution and, indeed, the system are made. Appalachian State University also takes part in a separate phased assessment of its general education program in which components of the program are addressed sequentially.

What are the advantages and disadvantages of tying or relating a campus-based program of assessment of educational outcomes or institutional effectiveness to an external requirement or time table? Clearly the greatest advantage of such action is the use of the external requirement as a lever to initiate, continue or expand assessment activities on the campus. Beyond that one very powerful advantage, few others can be identified. Among the chief disadvantages of relating campus assessment initiatives to external requirements are external control of the sequence of reporting and the nature of the assessment activities. As can be seen from the three examples above (Clemson University, Stillman College and Appalachian State University), the frequency of reporting can vary from twice each year to annually to biennially and even to a three-year cycle without any relationship to institutional need.

Additionally, the nature of the information required for external reporting is usually some-what different from that necessary internally for program improvement within the institution.

However, the greatest single disadvantage of relating institutional processes for effec-tiveness and assessment of educational outcomes to external requirements is that the basic purpose of assessment activities on the campus becomes "creating a favorable impression" on the external agency levying the requirements rather than upon institutional improvement. Wherever data or narrative concerning an institution's performance is produced primarily for the purpose of gaining favor with the external agency, then the great tendency will be to "play the game" rather than to improve institutional operations. Under these circumstances, faculty in particular lose interest in "playing the game" very quickly and are loath to create a second or internal process for program improvement purposes when the institution is obviously focused upon satisfying its external agency. In most cases, data provided to external agencies for accountability purposes is so "politicized" that it is of very limited use on the campus.

Institutionalization of Assessment Activities Through In-depth Periodic Program Review Activities—Many institutions acknowledge that it is a virtual impossibility to con-sider in depth the effectiveness of all units on the campus annually. Rather than the annual cycles described in the following section of this chapter, these institutions have opted for a cycle of four to six years during which they will have covered in detailed or on an in-depth basis each of the major operating units/academic programs at the institution. The nature and administration of these periodic cycles vary significantly from campus to campus.

At the University of Kentucky-Lexington Campus, in-depth consideration of assess-ment activities regarding academic programs has been incorporated into the institution's internal program review schedule which cycles programs through on a four- to six-year basis and is clearly a function of the academic administration of the institution. A description of this periodic review described in the "Review of Educational Units, Regulations, and Instructions" from the University of Kentucky is included as Appendix H. In essence, this procedure sets up an internal program review process complete with self-study, intended educational outcomes, means of assessment and use of results, an internal review team from outside the department, and a summary report.

A more collegial and less administratively directive periodic process or cycle of assessment of student academic achievement was reported by Sam Houston State Univer-sity. "Each summer, the Institutional Effectiveness Committee identifies approximately 15 academic and administrative departments (or 20% of the institution) for participation in the assessment activities with the assistance of the Committee." These departments are notified and ask to appoint a liaison to work with the Committee on behalf of their department. Over the next two years, departments work with the Committee to complete a schedule of assess-ment activities shown in Appendix I. "During the workshops held in the fall, the depart-ments are given an overview of what is expected and an orientation into the methods of assessment they might choose to use." During the first two years of the cycle, shown in Appendix I, the departments received considerable support from the Committee and institu-tional research. "During this period, departments are encouraged to assess those outcomes that are more difficult, require more effort, or that may be more expensive. Not all intended outcomes are addressed simultaneously. Departments continue to assess outcomes over the next three years with minimal assistance from the Committee although they are still given both technical and clerical support by the Office of Institutional Research."

What are the advantages and disadvantages of such an extended or periodic approach to assessment activities in the department or unit? Clearly, this approach recognizes the inability of any institution to focus in depth assessment activities annually without institutional exhaustion or unacceptably high levels of expenditure. By taking this approach, each unit or program is reviewed in greater depth once every four to six years than would be possible on an annual basis.

The primary problem with this approach is that also associated with professional or regional accreditation. What happens between reviews? In both of the examples illustrated above (University of Kentucky-Lexington Campus and Sam Houston State University), activities "between reviews" are described as an effort to sustain a more reduced level of interest between intensive periods of in-depth review. However, in the author's experience, such an extended or stretched version of implementation inevitably leads to "peaks and valleys" in both implementation and, more importantly, use of assessment results for the improvement of programming. Nonetheless, such an extended approach is initially easier to implement, can function without being part of a comprehensive institutional process, and is an attractive alternative.

Comprehensive Programs of Institutional Effectiveness—The four community colleges taking part in the case study (Mt. Hood, Collin County, Jefferson State, and Coastal Carolina) have all implemented relatively comprehensive approaches to assessment of institutional effectiveness or educational outcomes. Each of these colleges, through very different procedures, has incorporated a statement of purpose, statements of intended educational outcomes, assessment, use of results, and budgeting into one relatively cohesive institutional planning and evaluation process. It is of considerable interest to note that such a comprehensive approach to institutional effectiveness or outcomes assessment implementation has been put into place only at the community colleges included in the case study.

The institutional effectiveness cycles established at Collin County Community College and Jefferson State Community College represent excellent adaptations of what otherwise would be described as strategic planning and budgeting processes to the reality of the need for integration of more results or outcomes oriented information into decision making on a systematic basis. Both institutional processes are related to the institutions' budget cycle. Collin County's process, in particular has been developed so as to transcend the requirements of external agencies and to service institutional needs. Both case study institutions begin their process with statements of purpose resulting from strategic planning concerning service to their locality and proceed to relatively institutional level statements of expected results or intended achievement. At Collin County, each degree program has also developed its own strategic plan with statement of purpose and expected results directly related to institution level statements. In both institutions' cases, coverage down to the degree program level is also accomplished through a periodic or cyclical program review process which supports an annual or biennial institutional level budget process. At both institutions, assessment results are formulated for institutional level goals with accomplishment of department and program intended outcomes brought forward on a periodic basis from the program review process to support these institutional level statements of intentions and achievements. At Collin County, however, the degree of accomplishment of intended outcomes for individual programs is also documented in annually updated strategic plans for these programs. The annual or biennial cycle of these institutions' comprehensive approaches to the integration of outcomes assessment to strategic budget planning result in establishment and financing of the institutions' instructional and administrative processes for the forthcoming year. Brief summaries describing the comprehensive planning processes at Jefferson State Community College and Collin County Community College are contained in Appendix I.

The Jefferson State Community College and Collin County Community College models have a comprehensive approach to implementation which primarily emanate from an institutional level of concern that is extended down into the program of the institutions' and their achievements. While, when fully implemented as designed, such programs meet the intent of institutional effectiveness and assessment of educational outcomes, their primary (though not exclusive) focus appears to be at the institutional level. On the other hand, the comprehensive approaches to institutional effectiveness implemented at Mt. Hood Community College and Coastal Carolina Community College are based on and concerned at least as much with the improvement of student learning in their individual educational programs. From that program base has grown a connection to institutional level purposes and budgeting necessary to support such learning and student success.

At Mt. Hood Community College, the initial thrust behind implementation of assessment activities related to improvement of student success. This concern led to the integration of a number of processes into a more or less connected series of activities that was described as their institutional effectiveness cycle. This annual cycle emerged with program review occurring during the year with its completion by spring. Strategic planning commencing in the late spring with completion expected by mid-fall. Upon the completion of strategic planning, budget development began in the mid-fall term with its completion and adoption of the formal budget in the spring. Paralleling this activity in the spring semester, was assessment of the current strategic plan (including student learning/success) and initiation of planning for the following year. It is important to note that while this process was reported as indeed linked to the institution's budgeting process, its focus and emanation was from the standpoint of improvement of student learning or success.

Implementation at Coastal Carolina Community College has grown from the program to the institutional and budget level. The "DeskTop Audit" procedures and publication, described in Appendix D, began as a necessary annual program review endeavor concerned with program continuation, etc. However, in order to meet regional accreditation requirements, this annual review of programs was expanded to include an annual review and publication of programintended educational outcomes as well as data concerning the assessment of these achievements, and a description of how the results were utilized to improve programs. It should be emphasized that what has made this process work at Coastal Carolina Community College is the commitment of the institution to its employees that if their program was discontinued, they would be provided an opportunity for retraining and continued employment at college expense. Hence, the best possible environment for formative assessment was established, one in which a regularly scheduled and highly publicized process requiring faculty to set intended educational outcomes, do assessment, and use the results within a relatively non-threatening environment.

These four comprehensive approaches to institutional effectiveness or assessment of educational outcomes work for their individual institutions and are the result of circumstances unique to each institution at a given time. There is no one comprehensive model that will operate satisfactorily on all campuses; however, in the author's opinion, ultimately institutions will be best served by seeking to establish an ongoing comprehensive program of institutional effectiveness activities tailored to their own needs.

Problems Relating Institutional Effectiveness or Assessment of Educational Outcomes with Existing Institutional Processes

The reports provided by the case study institutions indicate that assessment activities cannot generally survive, not to mention prosper, if they are seen as an "add on" or something extra not connected with other institutional operations. The case study institutions report attempts to integrate institutional effectiveness and assessment of educational outcomes into strategic planning, institutional budgeting, and program review for external and internal purposes, as well as external reporting. The four community colleges in the case study have sought to tie all of the above, including assessment of educational outcomes and institutional effectiveness, into a common process through one means or another.

The common problem related by the case study institutions in establishing a tie or relationship with other institutional processes are "timing" and "focus" in order to have the best opportunity to stimulate faculty use of assessment results. The institutional effectiveness cycle on many campuses provides assessment of the previous year's accomplishments as the faculty commence the academic year at the beginning of the fall semester each year. The need for linkage to budgeting would normally take place at the end of the spring semester of the previous fiscal year. Which process takes priority? Can linkage be established so as to serve both needs? These are the common types of questions with which institutions grapple in trying to tie institutional effectiveness processes to external time tables imposed by agencies other than the institution. Brought into this dilemma is the genuine desire on the part of most institutions not to duplicate activities on the campus.

Some relatively unique approaches to integration of assessment activities were reported by the case study institutions. Unlike other institutions which reported integration of assessment activities with primarily institutional level processes, Sam Houston State University reported trying to integrate such activities with the processes within academic departments and a healthy emphasis upon classroom assessment techniques. Collin County Community College reported easing the coordination burden somewhat by cycling institutional effectiveness operations between planning, budgeting, and program review activities on their campus.

Almost half of the case study institutions reported direct and fully functional linkage between budgeting and institutional effectiveness or assessment cycles on the campus. Those included the four institutions reporting a comprehensive institutional effectiveness or outcomes assessment cycle (the four community colleges taking part in the case study) as well as the University of Kentucky-Lexington Campus. However, the nature of the relationship with budgeting process varied considerably by institution.

The connection or relationship of the budgeting and institutional effectiveness cycle were reported at both the institutional level and within the departments. Some of the institutions reported the primary relationship existed in the assessment of *departmental* accomplishments or achievements which led to both proposals for financial increases as well as judgments regarding departmental program operations. Other institutions reported the primary relationship at the *institutional* level in which strategic planning processes were designed and funds allocated to support certain overall institutional goals and that from these institutional goals, departmental statements of intended educational outcomes and administrative objectives as well as assessment plans were formulated. Two other institutions, Appalachian State University and Stillman College, indicated the desire for direct linkage with planning and budgeting processes, but that the exact relationship remained under development.

On the other end of the continuum were two colleges in which planning and budgeting were not linked materially with the assessment process. The respondent from one of these institutions indicated that he would avoid such linkage at all costs for he feared it represented the "kiss of death" for the assessment activities on his campus.

A close relationship with budgeting is not necessary to be successful in assessment of educational outcomes or institutional effectiveness. The nature of this relationship should be carefully planned on the campus to avoid either the technical problems mentioned or, in the author's opinion, the more substantive problem of dominance by fiscal planning over educational or outcomes oriented planning which takes place on many campuses.

The primary difficulties cited by the case study institutions in meshing assessment activities with other institutional procedures concerned the relationship between the budget cycle and assessment activities. In this relationship, five separate issues were identified:

- *Timing of the Budget Cycle with the Most Likely Assessment Cycle on Campuses*— Provision of assessment data to department/units at the beginning of the fall semester does not fit particularly well with either the request or allocation aspects of most budgetary cycles.
- *Uncertainty of Funding*—The tie to budgeting seems to indicate that unless budget requests are honored, assessment activities will not take place.
- *Openness*—Most institutions felt that in their budget requests and planning processes, they could not achieve the degree of openness with external parties that is internally necessary for the use of assessment data to improve programming.
- *Political Exigencies*—Political decisions are often necessarily reached rather than those based on support of educational learning outcomes.
- *Reluctance/Slowness*—One institution reported a genuine reluctance to incorporate outcomes type information into budgetary justifications, less the legislature actually expect to see the results of assessment of a more comprehensive nature.

Among the problems identified by the case study institutions in meshing assessment with other institutional process were the following:

- *Differences in Terminology*—What may be an "objective" in one institutional process may be called by another title such as "outcome" in another process, leading to confusion on the campuses.
- *Acquisition of the "Baggage of the Other Process"*—When too closely meshed with other processes, assessment tends to "acquire" the on-campus political baggage which other processes have accumulated.
- *Linkages Across Departmental Boundaries*—In working with cross departmental issues in learning outcomes, issues regarding which department must assume responsibility for a particular outcome were encountered.

Most of these issues have been reconciled or resolved by the reporting institutions. However, the most forthright response among the group was Coastal Carolina Community College which stated that they had no problems meshing the processes together "since the president was intent upon so doing."

At a number of institutions in the case study, integration of assessment activities into a comprehensive planning approach progressed in a logical way which made sense internally as well as externally for the institution. The primary danger is that in trying to achieve integration into a single institutional process, the unique formative aspect of institutional effectiveness and assessment of educational outcomes will become subsumed under or overwhelmed by the need to respond to an external agency or campus/system/state politics centered around acquisition or distribution of resources.

Evaluation of the Institutional Effectiveness or Assessment of Educational Outcomes Process

Most of the institutions taking part in the case study had yet to identify a process for evaluating the success of their institutional effectiveness or assessment of educational outcomesactivities. Many had identified a group to conduct such an evaluation and some claimed that evaluation of the process was accomplished annually as part of their comprehensive assessment/institutional effectiveness system.

Sam Houston State University provided the most thoughtful explanation of procedures by which its assessment activities are evaluated through (a) narrative comments listed in departmental reports on their assessment efforts, (b) a survey instrument completed by assessment liaisons, departmental chairs, and administrators at the director or higher level, and (c) a survey question included in the faculty annual survey regarding attitudes toward the administration. Also, Jefferson State Community College indicated its intention to appoint an ad hoc committee after five years of implementation to evaluate the overall effectiveness of the assessment procedures in improving college programs and services.

Clearly the most unusual tribute to an ongoing assessment program reported by the case study institutions was that of Coastal Carolina Community College where the North Carolina Legislature became aware of the "DeskTop Audit" in the Spring of 1993, and were so pleased with its format and usability, that they included it as part of the July 1993 appropriation legislation for the community college system in that state. This bill states that "the State Board of Community Colleges shall study models for measuring institutional effectiveness, such as the desktop audit used by Coastal Carolina Community College, and shall direct community colleges to utilize similar models in providing accountability information to the State Board for the General Assembly." While one might question their motives in this regard, clearly this type of recognition is a positive statement regarding the perceptions of legislative representatives concerning the worthiness of institutional effectiveness or assessment of educational outcomes as practiced at one of the institutions in the case study.

Campus Motivation for Continuation of Institutional Effectiveness or Assessment of Educational Outcomes

Probably more difficult than initial implementation of institutional effectiveness or assessment activities, is their continuation once the immediate or initial threat of campus visitation or state reporting is passed. The case study institutions identified four factors stimulating continuation of assessment implementation:

- Continuation of the institutional effectiveness or assessment cycle itself
- Other external reporting requirements
- Continued visibility and commitment from executive leadership
- Making assessment meaningful.

By far the most frequently cited reason for continuation of assessment activities on the campuses in the case study was the continuation of the cycles or sequence of assessment activities established during initial implementation. If these activities or the sequence of events has been built into the expected operations of the institution, then the momentum of the cycle tends to continue assessment activity into the future. With this type of motivation, it is imperative that institutions reexamine the nature of the cycle and its results, improvement of student learning, and educational support on administrative operations. Otherwise, the institution may only continue "going through the motions" rather than making substantive improvements.

The influence of other external requirements for assessment information encourages continuation of assessment activities on many campuses past the regional accreditation process. State initiatives such as those reported by Clemson University and Appalachian State University provide a powerful mechanism encouraging continuation of assessment efforts. One of the contributors in the case study went as far as stating that "It is my belief that at this school, if not for the...requirements, assessment would not be an issue until the next accreditation visit....Most of the departments are reporting assessment activities only because the necessity to do so continues." In addition to state mandates for assessment information for accountability purposes, the federal requirement for outcomes assessment data to support funding through the Carl Perkins Act stimulates continuation on many two-year college campuses.

Professional accreditation also provides a powerful lever requiring continuation of assessment in the disciplines. Nursing, allied health, teacher education, business, and engineering professional accreditation requirements all contain mandates for assessment of educational outcomes. In those departments seeking or maintaining professional accreditation, the motivation for continuation will be self-sustaining.

The continued visibility and commitment from executive leadership sustains implementation at some institutions. Stillman College reported manifestation of this continuing commitment through the establishment of a senior level position with a responsibility for coordinating continued institutional effectiveness or assessment implementation on the campus.

All of the above mechanisms for fostering continued implementation (continuation of the cycle, external motivation, internal commitment) describe essentially extrinsic levers to foster continuation of assessment activities at an institution. The most desirable basis upon which to foster continuation is, of course, the intrinsic reward experienced by faculty coming from visible observation that the use of assessment results has improved programming. Fortunately, this was reported by several of the case study institutions. Sam Houston State University reported that "the best method of facilitating the continuation of assessment is to make assessment meaningful in the first place." Clemson University reported "There are a few departments which have discovered that assessment can be beneficial and those departments are being reinforced by their own effort. However, they are in the minority."

In the author's opinion, institutional effectiveness and assessment of educational outcomes would not have been implemented on campuses without external stimulus and will not be continued comprehensively within an institution without external stimulus. There are portions of the institution that will grasp the intrinsic value of assessment activities and the use of its results to improve programming. Hopefully, these segments will grow. But for the immediate future, it is important for institutions to bear in mind that external stimulus (regional accreditation, professional accreditation, state reporting, etc.) will be the continuing *occasion* for demonstrating the use of assessment results to improve programming, but not the *reason* for doing assessment, the improvement of programming.

Concluding Comments Regarding the Cyclical Nature of Institutional Effectiveness or Assessment Activities

Among the primary differences brought to campuses by the establishment of an ongoing program of assessment or institutional effectiveness is the establishment of a systematic approach to consideration of educational outcomes between decennial reaffirmation visits by regional accrediting associations. Institutions within the case study have described cycles running from six months to six years in duration; however, all cycles described succeed in the establishment of a systematic approach to consideration of the effectiveness of the institution and its academic programs. The following comments summarize the experiences described in this chapter:

Summary Comments Regarding the Creation of an Institutional
Effectiveness or Assessment Cycle

- While significant initial leverage is gained by closely relating institutionalimplementation to external accountability requirements for assessment data, on balance such requirements are a detriment to complete implementation activities through use of assessment results for program improvement.
- A periodic (once every four to six years) review of academic programs (including intended student academic achievements, assessment, results, and use of assessmentresults) is an attractive institutional implementation cycle, but leads to substantial "peaks and valleys" in departmental level assessment activities.
- Institutions will best be served by establishing comprehensive approaches to institutional effectiveness which are based upon assessment at the program and departmental level and link upward to institutional statements of purpose and budgeting procedures.
- The relationship of assessment activities to other institutional procedures, while highly desirable to avoid duplication of effort and encourage continuation of assessment activities, is fraught with logistical as well as conceptual implications.
- In the immediate future, external stimulus (regional accreditation, professional accreditation, state reporting requirements, etc.) will provide the primary motivation for continuation of assessment activities on most campuses as recognition of the improvements in student learning and campus operation brought about, thereby grows slowly.

Chapter VI

CONCLUDING COMMENTS AND SUMMARY FINDINGS FROM THE CASE STUDY INSTITUTIONS

None of the case study institutions would claim their implementation to be entirely successful, without its trials and tribulations, or completed. However, each has achieved a great deal toward improvement of its institutional and programmatic performances. In this final chapter, the cost of implementation is reviewed as well as the overall factors which have facilitated and impeded implementation on the campuses in the case study.

The Cost of Implementation at Case Study Institutions

One of the most frequently asked questions by institutions beginning the implementation process is "What's it going to cost us?" The institution that believes there are no cost involved in implementation of a program of institutional effectiveness or assessment of educational outcomes is certainly misleading itself. Without much question, the greatest cost on campuses has to do with the time of faculty involvement in the process for which little or no release time is provided and no costing data are available.

Earlier in the assessment movement, a figure of between $10.00 and $12.00 per year per full-time equivalent student for out-of-pocket cost for assessment activities was reported by institutions beginning implementation. Given their heavier reliance on standardized testing at that time, this was a reasonable figure and probably reflected practices four to six years ago. However, the case study institutions reported substantially lower cost for assessment implementation. Among the 11 institutions represented in the case study, ranging from major research universities to community colleges, the overall cost, including both centralized personnel support and out-of-pocket was reported at approximately $10.60 per head count student annually, or $3.70 per head count student in out-of-pocket cost annually. Cost patterns in both cases were examined in relationship to institutional type and full/part-time enrollment patterns. In neither case did there appeared to be a substantial difference in the average cost based upon these factors. As a matter of fact, some of the highest cost per head count student were reported by relatively smaller community colleges in the study enrolling large numbers of part-time students and one of the major research universities enrolling almost exclusively residential students.

While certainly not a random sample of assessment implementation cost nationwide, the above figures are similar to the author's own institutional cost for implementation of assessment activities and do reflect discussions among assessment practitioners nationally. The good news, in this case, is that cost for implementation is apparently less than first indicated, due to many factors including a reduced reliance on standardized testing and surveys, while the bad news is clear verification that additional cost for implementation can be expected.

Factors at Case Study Institutions Facilitating Implementation

As the case study institutions were completing their analysis, they were asked to identify those factors which either assisted or facilitated implementation most on their campuses. The majority of the case study institutions identified the following factors as important in aiding implementation on their campuses:

- Commitment on the part of the chief executive officer
- Appointment of a group responsible for implementation
- Establishment of centralized support services

Those institutions identifying presidential leadership and involvement as a key factor in implementation included community colleges, private institutions, and regional universities. It is significant to note that none of the major research universities indicated this to be of substantial importance on their campus.

The identification of a group responsible for implementation was also cited by the majority of institutions in the case study. At most institutions, this group was faculty dominated; however, at one of the campuses, vice presidential leadership was identified as the overall group responsible for implementation.

It is not surprising that the establishment of centralized support services in the form of an Office of Institutional Research or Assessment was cited by over half of the institutions in the case study as the majority of respondents were employed in or directed such an office or operation. What is important to draw from this response is that without centralized support, leadership, etc., most institutions would find implementation difficult at best.

Slightly less than half of the case study institutions reported the following factors at the departmental and institutional level as key in fostering implementation on their campus:

- Creating a positive atmosphere for implementation at the departmental level
- Supporting departmental implementation activities by the central administration
- Integration of assessment activities with other institutional processes.

Establishing the necessary atmosphere for formative assessment and program improvement was frequently cited by case study institutions as a key factor in facilitating implementation. Even on those campuses in which program review became part of a potentially summative process, assessment information was put in a position of being a positive factor rather than a punitive indicator for support of programs undergoing review. These activities were necessary to foster "faculty buy in" and the belief that assessment activities that were do-able would contribute to student learning and would help the academic programs rather than be used "against us."

Supporting departmental assessment activities was also identified as extremely important by institutions in the case study. This support took the form of training by outside facilitator or consultants, the provision of funds for standardized testing and other departmental expenses, and the provision of tools for assessment, such as institutional questionnaires, etc.

Not surprisingly, integration of assessment activities with other institutional processes, or potentially into an overall planning and evaluation cycle, was frequently cited by case study institutions as a factor facilitating implementation. In some cases, this meant the complete revamping of the strategic planning, budgeting, evaluation cycle at the institution and the integration of assessment activities as an integral part of that series of events. At other institutions, integration of assessment activities with other formerly free standing academic or administrative operations such as program review was viewed as essential in support of implementation.

Several of the case study institutions related (a) the importance of external reporting and (b) the provision of a prescribed or common format for departmental reports as important factors facilitating implementation. The nature of the external reporting required varied among state agencies and regional accreditation bodies; however, in most cases, these requirements were seen as significant levers toward implementation on the campuses. The provision of a prescribed format to the departments for reporting use of results was referenced by more than one institution as a factor significantly facilitating implementation. This was described as a need for people to "see an example" of what they were expected to do and to provide a "format" for them to "fill in."

In addition to those activities commonly identified as factors facilitating implementation, the following four factors were identified by single institutions and yet, in the author's opinion, can be generalized:

- Review of the college mission statement
- Identification of "true believers"
- Adopting principles to guide assessment implementation
- Establishment of an annual report

Detailed consideration of an institution's mission is a key to initiation of assessment activities on some campuses. Activities on the campus should be seen as flowing from the institution's mission to the operating units where the success of those operating units is evaluated and, in turn, fed back for validation of mission accomplishment.

It has been said that "success feeds upon success," and in this case, finding a few success stories or "true believers" on the campus willing to implement assessment procedures and show the use of assessment results to improve programming is an invaluable factor in stimulating implementation throughout the institution. In most cases, these "true believers" will be found in areas requiring assessment activities for professional accreditation purposes; however, they also may be found to exist among faculty, who are particularly committed to the teaching and learning process.

On many campuses, assessment activities are viewed with suspicion by faculty at the onset. The adoption of a set of principles to guide assessment decisions and activities by a primarily faculty-based group will allay many of the concerns felt, if not voiced, by faculty and greatly facilitate implementation.

The best initiated implementation of assessment activities will wither immediately following the reaffirmation committee's visit on many campuses. The establishment of an annual report of departmental assessment activities can be a major factor facilitating implementation if it is followed up as part of an ongoing faculty/administrative review and use of the results each year.

Factors Reported as Impeding Implementation on Case Study Campuses

There was generally much less agreement among case study institutions regarding the factors which hurt or restrained implementation on their campuses than about those factors which aided or facilitated that implementation. The following factors were referenced by several institutions as impeding implementation:

- Lack of Faculty/Staff Commitment or Trust
- Budgetary Constraints
- Difficulties in Integration of Assessment With Other Campus Processes
- Assessment Activities Related to the Core Curriculum or General Education

Slightly more than one third of the case study institutions cited lack of faculty/staff commitment or trust as a major factor impeding implementation. This was reported by the case study institutions in two ways. Several of the institutions reported that the faculty simply lacked faith that carrying out assessment activities would, indeed, lead to improvement of student learning. On the other hand, several of the other institutions portrayed the faculty's basic distrust of any process which might result in change from their existing academic procedures. This distrust is probably reflective of general faculty inertia regarding curriculum reform which is not uncommon throughout higher education.

Budgetary constraints were also frequently cited as an impediment to implementation. The primary problems were related not to out-of-pocket cost (which seem to be readily provided), but to the time and personnel involved. While several comments were reported concerning the lack of time needed to coordinate and support the process, the bulk of the discussion forwarded by the case study institutions focused on the lack of faculty release time to take part in the assessment process. In the author's opinion, the result of this impediment to implementation was also reflected in the relatively few examples of the development of locally constructed cognitive instruments by faculty reported by the case study institutions.

While cited as a key factor in facilitating implementation by some institutions, others cited integration of assessment activities with other ongoing processes as a major impediment at their institution. This was particularly true at institutions where external processes were responsible for driving the internal assessment process which was frequently "jerked around" by seemingly irrational changes in reporting requirements and timelines.

Several of the case study institutions reported significant difficulty in assessment of general education or the core curriculum. In the author's opinion, assessment of this subject is among the most difficult task for colleges or universities because of the diversity of opinion regarding the definition of a liberally or generally educated person. The consequence is fragmentation of this field among many disciplines and a high level of anxiety caused by potential adjustments in this area, resulting in substantial changes in staffing requirements.

Among the other items reported as causing significant grief to the case study institutions in their implementation process were the following:

- Distraction of effort caused by other "crises"
- Conducting the self-study simultaneously with implementation of assessment activities
- Educating faculty and staff about assessment
- Lack of time for reflective thinking about what the college should attempt to accomplish
- Technical problems regarding assessment data.

The response from one of the institutions is probably representative of the general tone of frustration which many of the case study institutions felt regarding implementation of assessment activities. It is related below with only sufficient changes in the report to shield the identity of the institution. The primary factors causing grief in implementation at the institution were:

1. *Battling the Vivid Anecdote*—Lack of an institutional tradition of making decisions based on data, but instead on advice from informal networks and the occasional vivid anecdote.

2. *Mom Says You Have to Do This*—Establishing the process under the auspices of the regional accreditation review and the perception that this was an externally imposed requirement not to be taken seriously.

3. *Who's in Charge?*—Being unclear about who is to provide leadership.

4. *Why Is Anybody in Charge?*—It was unclear what the institution wanted from the assessment process and there were no strong institutional planning goals upon which to build an assessment program.

5. *The Rush to Judgment*—There was a great deal of anxiety about the region a accreditation reaffirmation visit and the need to "have something on paper" for the visit.

6. *Assessment Means Numbers*—Lack of understanding regarding what assessment/institutional effectiveness involved. The perceptions were that assessment was "limited to quantitative tests, bureaucratic intrusiveness, and was not related to what was happening in a classroom. It was seen as an extra task to be accomplished which was loaded with educational jargon and should be more appropriate in high schools than in our type of institution."

The above comments as well as those of many other practitioners are quite easy to illicit and could have filled this book. However, despite the problems, institutions throughout the country are moving ahead with implementation, in most cases, fairly successfully.

The Most Important Single Piece of Advice That Case Study Institutions Would Offer Those Beginning the Process of Implementation

At the close of their input to the case study, institutions were asked to identify the single most important piece of advice which they would pass on to institutions beginning the implementation process. The responses of the majority of institutions are represented in the two items listed below:

- Have the support of senior administrators at the institution
- Fit the institutional implementation process to the way in which the institution currently functions

The visible support of senior administrative officers, including most particularly the Chief Executive Officer, was the single most frequently offered advice by the case study institutions. This support should not be only lip service in nature, but should include a continuing concern for the implementation process and support to the extent of provision of the necessary resources at the institutional and departmental level to see that the process takes place.

Assessment of educational outcomes or implementation of institutional effectiveness activities defies the "cloning process" by which many institutions implement activities successfully accomplished on other campuses. The case study institutions recognize this by their identification of the necessity of fitting the process of implementation at each institution to the manner in which that institution now functions. At one institution in the case study, that meant a very decentralized process focused at the departmental level. On another campus, it meant a very "top down" process, administratively directed, and in both cases, implementation was among the most successful among the case study institutions. While the institutional effectiveness paradigm and generic model for implementation provide a useful framework for adaptation to campus needs, it cannot be adopted without adjustments to campus conditions.

Among those other pieces of advice offered by the case study institutions were:

- Selection of the right implementation team at the institution
- Establishment of a sound institutional research and planning basis before implementation activities
- Focusing upon accomplishment of the institutional mission and linkage of that process down through the institution's units
- Motivation of the faculty to take part in assessment activities through the granting of release time

The Future Implementation of Educational Assessment and Institutional Effectiveness on Campuses

Events during the last several years have clearly indicated the growing breath of implementation of assessment activities across the country. It is now hard to find a college or university that can not point to one type or another assessment activity taking place on the campus. Implementation activities during the next five to ten years will focus upon (a) making, what are now in many cases isolated, assessment activities on campuses more comprehensive across all disciplines and (b) fulfilling the promise of assessment by demonstration of the use of results to improve academic programming. For those progressively fewer faculty in academic departments who have hoped that assessment would "go away" if they ignore it long enough, the day of reckoning is close at hand.

Regretfully as many institutions expand their initial assessment activities to make them more comprehensive and complete, many of the less desirable experiences reported by the case study institutions will be replicated. Some campuses, hopefully those who have benefited from review of the experiences of the case study institutions related in this book, will profit from the shortcomings and successes of previous institutions and craft even more successful strategies for implementation of educational outcomes assessment or institutional effectiveness.

In five to six years, experience with institutional implementation of educational outcomes assessment or institutional effectiveness will have expanded even further and changed substantially in nature these practices become more widespread within institutions. At that time, another series of case studies in implementation will be needed to guide implementation of assessment of educational outcomes and institutional effectiveness into the next century.

APPENDIX A—Revised Outline of Case Study Book Topics

I. "Building the Foundation"

  A. Awareness

    1. What brought subject to institutional attention?

    2. What was the general campus "climate" for implementation?

    3. Were there other assessment related initiatives influencing the institution (accountability requirements, TQM, performance funding, etc.)?

    4. Who was first to become aware of the requirement or need to implement institutional effectiveness or assessment activities?

    5. How was awareness of the need to implement a program of institutional effectiveness or assessment of student academic achievement communicated across the campus and how successful was this effort in motivating staff and faculty?

    6. What was the basis for "selling" the importance of assessment activities to the faculty (program improvement, external account-ability, regional accreditation, professional accreditation, etc.)

    7. To what extent ("lip service" to "driving force") were the Chief Executive Officer and Chief Academic Officer aware and supportive of the need for implementation?

  B. Organization for Implementation

    1. Who was "selected" to lead implementation and what was their background?

    2. Was there an assessment committee appointed and if so, what was its composition and purpose?

  C. Condition of the Institutional Statement of Purpose

    1. Was the originally existing Institutional Statement of Purpose found to be usable for institutional effectiveness purposes? If not, what were its primary problems?

    2. What steps, if any, were taken to modify the originally existing institutional Statement of Purpose?

  D. Inventory of Existing Means of Assessment?

    1. Was an inventory of originally existing campus assessment activities conducted?

    2. If so, how was it utilized?

II. "Detailed Design at the Departmental/Program Level"

  A. Origination of Statements of Intended Student Academic Achievement (Outcomes, Expected Results, etc.) by Academic Programs

    1. How were faculty involved?

    2. What was the role of the departmental chair?

    3. What and by whom was guidance provided to academic departments for this purpose?

    4. How were these statements linked to the Institutional Statement of Purpose?

    5. How long were departments given to develop such Statements of Intended Student Academic Achievement (Outcomes) regarding their majors?

    6. Did the Statements of Intended Student Academic Achievement Outcomes) or the description of the designated Means of Assessment identify the *criteria* (%, x, etc.) for considering the program successful?

    7. Was there a requirement for "approval" of Statements of Intended Academic Achievement (Outcomes, Expected Results, etc.) and if so., by whom was this approval required?

    8. What were the major problems encountered by departments in preparing Statements of Intended Student Academic Achievement?

    9. How was the determination of Intended Student Academic Achievement regarding undergraduate "general education" made?

10. Please provide as many Statements of Intended Student Academic Achievement (Outcomes, Expected Results, etc.) for degree programs or general education as possible.

B. Identification of Administrative and Educational Support Objectives
1. To what extent were such statements identified?
2. What organizational structure was utilized?
3. What were the primary Means of Assessment cited?
4. Who was involved in establishing such statements in most departments?
5. How long were administrative departments given to develop such statements?
6. What problems were encountered?

C. Designing the Assessment Process
1. To what extent were the Means of Assessment identified focused *solely* on the Intended Student Academic Achievement (Outcomes)?
2. In those programs for which standardized cognitive tests were available, what proportion was adopted?
3. What issues/problems were encountered in utilizing locally developed comprehensive tests in the major?
4. Were standardized or commercially available attitudinal questionnaires (graduating student, alumni, employer, etc.) utilized? Why was this alternative chosen?
5. What assessment services were provided by the central administration?
6. How were students motivated to take assessment instruments seriously?
7. Was a formal "assessment plan" written for the institution, colleges/schools, or departments? If so, please explain "why" and forward a copy.
8. Other than by use of a plan, how were various assessment activities coordinated?

D. Assessment Results
1. How much and what type of "analysis" of assessment results was performed prior to their forwarding to those responsible for academic programs?
2. Were all assessment results forwarded to/through a central point creating a "clearinghouse" for assessment results?
3. How were assessment results communicated to the departments?
4. Did the institution establish a formal policy regarding the "use of assessment results" to separate assessment from appraisal of individuals for promotion, etc.?
5. How and by whom was the **use** of assessment results documented?
6. Please cite ten uses of assessment results to improve academic programming on your campus.

III. "Establishment of the Institutional Effectiveness Cycle"

A. Did your institution establish a series of recurring activities which taken as a whole could be identified as an institutional effectiveness or assessment cycle? If so, please describe these recurring activities' substance, duration, and frequency.

B. Assuming that the institution has established some types of institutional effectiveness cycle, how is that set of activities integrated into other operations, procedures, plans, etc., at the institution?

C. What problems did you encounter in meshing institutional effectiveness/assessment planning with other planning related activities at your institution?

D. How is the Institutional Effectiveness Cycle related to budgetary decisions?

E. What arrangements have been made to evaluate the assessment procedures put in place on your campus?

F. What steps have been successful in facilitating continuation of assessment activities after accreditation requirements have been met?

IV. Concluding or Summary Findings
  A. What has been the annual cost for implementation:
    1. Centralized Support & Coordination?_____
    2. Out-of-Pocket?_____
  B. Please list in order of importance the five (5) actions which your institution took that most facilitated implementation?
  C. What factors (3-5) caused your institution the most "grief" in the implementation process?
  D. If you could offer an institution beginning the process of institutional effectiveness or assessment implementation just **ONE** piece of advice, what would it be?

APPENDIX B—Examples of Intended Educational Outcomes and Administrative Objectives, Means of Assessment, and Criteria for Success from a Wide Variety of Disciplines and Administrative Departments

Appendix B is composed of almost sixty examples of statements of intended educational outcomes, means of assessment, and criteria for program success from a wide variety of disciplines. Examples were contributed by the institutions and individuals shown below, in addition to the case study institutions.

Institution	*Contributor(s)*
Cedarville College	Jack Riggs
Central Missouri State University	Jim Sylvester
Central Alabama Community College	Martha Allen, Jane Boos
Chadron State College	David Scott
Clermont College of University of Cincinnati	Grace Murdoch
Eastern New Mexico University	Thurman Elder
Greenville Technical College	Linda Isles Jones
Holmes Community College	Richard Newton
Middle Tennessee State University	Faye Johnson
Ringling School of Art and Design	Mary Ann Stankiewicz
South Seattle Community College	Liz Hildebrant
Southwestern Community College (NC)	Renee Cohen
Troy State University	Angela C. Roling
York Technical College	Sherry J. Glenn

It should be emphasized that the *examples* on the following pages are not offered as *models*, i.e., entirely "correct" statements of intended educational outcomes and means of assessment in each discipline. They are exactly what is stated, *examples* provided by the institutions listed above or the case study institutions. As *examples*, the following pages illustrate typical types of educational outcomes statements and means of assessment for disciplines at two- and four-year colleges. Readers should clearly understand that *adoption of one of these examples by your institution without careful consideration by the faculty in the department constitutes forfeiture of the departmental faculties' prerogatives to control the curriculum and the means of assessment at your institution*. These *examples* should be used as a starting point for discussions within your disciplines, but hardly as ends in themselves.

The following examples from four-year institutions are indeed wide-ranging and demonstrate amply the independence of departmental faculty. However, a number of the associate degree examples tend to bear a strong resemblance to one another. That occurred because one of the two-year colleges submitting these examples (following consultation with the faculty and academic administrators) set general criteria and means of assessment for "employment rate" and "employer satisfaction" across all occupational/technical associate degree programs at the institution. In turn, the institutional level is conducting the required employer, graduate, and alumni surveys to provide the assessment data needed. It should also be pointed out that the definition of "technical proficiency" in each of the associate degree programs at this institution was left entirely to the faculty in each discipline and the entries concerning this subject exhibit the unique character and independence of each of the separate occupational/technical programs.

The examples of intended educational outcomes, means of assessment, and criteria for program success provided in the following pages represent only two of the five components of institutional effectiveness paradigm expected by most regional accrediting associations. The five components are:

- Linkage to Statement of Purpose
- Intended Educational Outcomes/Administrative Objectives
- Means of Assessment and Criteria for Program Success
- Report of Assessment Results
- Use of Results for Improvement of Programming

Illustrated on the following page is a tabular representation of these five components for the "Range Management (BS)" program which is shown in narrative form on the page following the tabular example. Only two components (Intended Educational Outcomes, and Means of Assessment and Criteria for Program Success) are provided in the tabular and narrative presentations of the "Range Management (BS)" example. While there is no single recommended format for displaying the five components of the institutional effectiveness paradigm, it is important that whatever format is utilized, a close relationship between the portion of institutional statement of purpose supported, the intended educational outcome, the means of assessment and criteria for program success, the relevant assessment results, and the use of those results to improve programming be maintained.

UNDERGRADUATE RANGE MANAGEMENT (BS)
CIP 02.0409

Expanded Institutional Statement of Purpose	Intended Educational Outcomes	Means of Assessment and Criteria for Success	Summary Highlights of Assessment Results	Use of Results for Improvement of Programming
	1. Students understand the rangeland resources of soils, plants, and water.	**1a.** At least 70% become certified as Associate Professionals in a technical area as stipulated by the American Registry of Certified Professionals in Agronomy, Crops, and Soils. **1b.** 95% participate in Society for Range Management Plant Identification Contest.		
	2. Students understand range ecosystems and principles applicable to management of range resources.	**2a.** 95% obtain civil service rating of 80% or higher as a Range Conservationist and certified to a U.S. Federal agency for the Office of Personnel Management. **2b.** All students score in top 50% of the Undergraduate Range Management Examination.		
	3. Students familiar with resources to keep abreast of new findings and techniques in the science and art of range management.	**3a.** 95% participate in annual meetings of the Society for Range Management. **3b.** 90% submit a written report showing familiarity with requirements in Civil Service for a Range Conservationist and the Society for Range Management's Accreditation.		
	4. Students have skills to create public appreciation of economic and social benefits obtained from range management.	**4a.** 70% present information concerning technical topics in range management in oral, formal, academic format, informal, functional format, and in written form suited to producers and evaluated by faculty and peers as "effective". **4b.** Students present a technical paper at meeting of the Society for Range Management and 70% judged as satisfactory.		
	5. Students recognize formal training is only the beginning of professional development.	**5a.** 95% are members of the Society for Range Management. **5b.** 90% of graduates report one or more types of continuing education activities completed during the past year on an Alumni Survey.		

UNDERGRADUATE RANGE MANAGEMENT (BS)
CIP 02.0409

Intended Educational Outcomes and Means of Assessment/Criteria for Success

1. Students will have an understanding of the basic rangeland resources of soils, plants, and water.
   a. At least 70% of students will become certified as Associate Professionals in a technical area of their choice through the process established by the American Registry of Certified Professionals in Agronomy, Crops, and Soils (a service of the American Society of Agronomy).
   b. Ninety-five percent of students will participate in the Society for Range Management Plant Identification Contest.

2. Students will have an understanding of range ecosystems and of the principles applicable to the management of range resources
   a. Ninety-five percent of students will obtain a civil service rating of 80% or higher as a Range Conservationist and be certified to a U.S. Federal agency for the Office of Personnel Management.
   b. Students will score within the top 50% of the Undergraduate Range Management Examination administered by the Society for Range Management at the annual winter meeting of the society.

3. Students are familiar with resources available to keep abreast of new findings and techniques in the science and art of range management.
   a. Ninety-five percent of students will participate in annual meetings of the Society for Range Management.
   b. Ninety percent of students will submit a written report exhibiting familiarity with Civil Service requirements for a Range Conservationist and the Society for Range Management's Accreditation requirements.

4. Students possess the skills to create a public appreciation of the economic and social benefits obtained from the range environment.
   a. Seventy percent of students present information concerning technical topics in range management in an oral, formal, academic format, in an oral, informal, functional format, and in a written format suited to producers and evaluated "effective" by faculty and peers in senior seminars.
   b. Students present a technical paper at a meeting of the Society for Range Management. Seventy percent will be judged satisfactory.

5. Students will recognize that formal training received is only the beginning in one's professional development and show evidence of continuing that training.
   a. Ninety-five percent of students will be a current member of the Society for Range Management.
   b. Ninety percent of graduates will report one or more types of continuing education activities taken part in during the past year on an Alumni Survey conducted by the college.

NOT TO BE CONSIDERED AS A MODEL BUT AS AN EXAMPLE

MARKETING/RETAILING (Associate Degree)
CIP 08.0708

Intended Educational Outcomes and Means of Assessment/Criteria for Success

1. Graduates of the Marketing/Retailing program will be employed in the field.
   a. Fifty percent of the responding graduates of the Marketing/Retailing program will report employment in the field or obtaining additional education on the Graduating Student Survey administered within the first five months after graduation
   b. Eighty percent of the responding (previous year) graduates of the Marketing/Retailing program will report employment in the field or in additional education at a four-year institution on the Alumni Survey distributed one year after graduation.

2. Graduates of the Marketing/Retailing program will be technically proficient.
   a. At the close of their final term, 80% of the graduates will be able to identify problems and opportunities and construct good decisions within a given period of time in case studies and computer simulations prepared or "as directed" by the Marketing/Retailing program faculty in the Capstone course Retail Merchandising Management (MKT 249).
   b. Ninety percent of students will successfully complete the Marketing and Retailing internship (MKT 248) with an organization as rated by the employer.

3. Employers of the Marketing/Retailing program graduates will rate the technical and academic skills of the employees as average or above.
   a. The Employer Survey conducted each year will rate the graduates as above average on the three course area performance (competency) survey questions. "Above average" is higher than a 3.0 on a 5.0 scale; however; if any of the three survey questions has an individual rating below 3.0, that individual course area performance will be reviewed further.
   b. Sixty percent of the respondents to an Employer Survey conducted every year will respond that they would employ future graduates of the Marketing/Retailing program.

NOT TO BE CONSIDERED AS A MODEL BUT AS AN EXAMPLE

UNDERGRADUATE RECREATION (BS)
CIP08.0903

Intended Educational Outcomes and Means of Assessment/Criteria for Success

1. Students will have a comprehensive knowledge of components from the National Recreation and Parks Association Exam that are applicable to the University's recreation major.
    a. Eighty percent of recreation graduates will pass the University's exit examination at the 75% level or above.
    b. Eighty percent of recreation graduates responding to the Graduating Student Questionnaire (developed and administered by recreation department faculty) will "agree" or "strongly agree" that they have gained a comprehensive knowledge in the field of recreation equal to or greater than individuals with the same degree with whom they have come in contact.

2. Students will have organization and management skills in recreation.
    a. Eighty percent of the recreation graduates responding to the Graduating Student Questionnaire will "agree" or "strongly agree" they have organization and management skills in recreation.
    b. Eighty percent of the supervisors of internships for recreation students responding to an internship assessment survey will indicate that the students have demonstrated acceptable levels of organization and management skills in the field of recreation.

3. Students will be able to work with diverse populations.
    a. Ninety-five percent of supervisors of the Therapeutic Recreation experience will indicate on the experience evaluation form that the graduate with a major in the field of recreation is able to work with diverse populations.
    b. Eighty percent of the students graduating with a recreation major will "agree" or "strongly agree" on the Graduating Student Questionnaire that they are able to work with diverse populations

4. Students will be prepared for employment in the field of recreation.
    a. Seventy-five percent of graduating recreation majors, who have responded to the placement center's one-year follow-up study will be working in the field of recreation or will be attending graduate school within one year of graduating.
    b. Seventy-five percent of the supervisors of internships for recreation students responding will indicate on an internship assessment survey that the students are prepared for employment in the field of recreation.

NOT TO BE CONSIDERED AS A MODEL BUT AS AN EXAMPLE

UNDERGRADUATE SPEECH COMMUNICATION (BA/BS)
CIP09.0101

Intended Educational Outcomes and Means of Assessment/Criteria for Success

1. Orally communicate with a variety of speaking techniques utilizing audience-centered delivery styles.
   a. All students will complete a public jury performance demonstrating competencies in public address, oral interpretation, and the control of speech apprehension by presentation to the speech department faculty. Ninety-five percent will be judged acceptable by a jury of the faculty.
   b. All students will either compete with the University forensics team or chair a student or civic organization (required of all BA/BS candidates).

2. Students will understand communication events in their historical and social context.
   a. Ninety percent of students will be able to relate rhetorical theory with significant communication events through history (evidence in speech department faculty supervised oral assessments during a capstone course).

3. Students will be able to orally communicate by encompassing ethical and critical thinking skills.
   a. Students will be required to use proper documentation of research sources in a mock debate evaluated by the speech department faculty. Ninety percent will do so on their first evaluation.
   b. Students will explore the different organizational and structural components in preparing an effective speech and apply those components in three speeches presented to the speech department faculty. Eighty-five percent of students will have all three speeches rated acceptable or better by the faculty.

NOT TO BE CONSIDERED AS A MODEL BUT AS AN EXAMPLE

UNDERGRADUATE COMPUTER SCIENCE (BS)
CIP11.0701

Intended Educational Outcomes and Means of Assessment/Criteria for Success

1. Students will be prepared for an entry level job in data processing.
    a. Seventy-five percent of graduates taking the SOCAT competency test in computer science will make a passing score.
    b. Seventy-five percent of graduates will rate "good preparation" or "excellent preparation" in response to the question "How well do you think the institution prepared you for this position?" on the Alumni Survey.

2. Graduates will find employment in a related field or will continue their education.
    a. Sixty-five percent of graduates will indicate that they are currently employed or have accepted a job in their field or are continuing their education in response to the Alumni Survey Questionnaire.

3. Employers of the institution's graduates will be pleased with the education received by their employees.
    a. Eighty percent of employers of the institution's graduates will indicate on a survey a rating of "excellent preparation" or "good preparation" in response to the question "How will prepared was the employee for their position?"

NOT TO BE CONSIDERED AS A MODEL BUT AS AN EXAMPLE

COSMETOLOGY (Associate Degree)
CIP12.0403

Intended Educational Outcomes and Means of Assessment/Criteria for Success

1. Graduates of the Cosmetology program will be technically proficient in hair styling.
    a. At the close of their final term, 90% of the students will be able to perform five different hair cuts or hair styles on live patrons as assigned in a given period of time as evaluated by the Cosmetology program faculty in the Capstone course Advanced Cosmetology Practice (COS 108).
    b. Eighty percent of the Cosmetology graduates will pass the State Board of Cosmetology.

2. Graduates of the Cosmetology program will be technically proficient in hair coloring.
    a. At the close of the final term, 90% of the students will be able to perform three hair coloring assignments on live patrons as assigned by the instructor within a given period of time as evaluated by the Cosmetology program faculty in the Capstone course Advanced Cosmetology Practice (COS 108).

3. Graduates of the Cosmetology program will be technically proficient in permanent waving of the hair.
    a. Prior to graduation, 90% of the students enrolled will be able to give a perm to two live patrons within a given period of time as evaluated by the Cosmetology program faculty in the Capstone course Advanced Cosmetology Practice (COS 108).

4. Graduates of the Cosmetology program will be employed in the field.

   a. Sixty percent of the responding graduates of the Cosmetology program will report employment in the field on the Graduating Student Survey administered within the first three months after graduation.
    b. Eighty percent of the responding (previous year) graduates of the Cosmetology program will report employment in the field on the Alumni Survey distributed one year after graduation.

5. Employers of the Cosmetology graduates will rate the technical and academic skills of the employees as average or above.
    a. The Employer Survey conducted each year will rate the graduates as above average on the three course area performance (competency) survey questions. "Above average" is higher than a 3.0 on a 5.0 scale; however, if any of the three survey questions has an individual rating below 3.0, that individual course area performance will be reviewed further.
    b. Sixty percent of the respondents to an Employer Survey conducted each year will respond that they would employ future graduates of the Cosmetology program.

NOT TO BE CONSIDERED AS A MODEL BUT AS AN EXAMPLE

UNDERGRADUATE HEALTH EDUCATION (BEd)
CIP 13.0101

Intended Educational Outcomes and Means of Assessment/Criteria for Success

1. Students will have knowledge in ten content areas of comprehensive health education curriculum as identified by AAHE and knowledge of the role of health education in society.
    a. Eighty percent of health education graduates will pass at the 75% level or above the University's health education comprehensive exit examination, which tests both content knowledge and role knowledge.
    b. Eighty percent of health education graduates responding on the Graduating Student Questionnaire (locally developed) will "agree" or "strongly agree" that they have a comprehensive knowledge base in health education equal to or greater than individuals with the same degree with whom they have had contact.

2. Students will have the knowledge and skills required for preparing and facilitating lesson plans utilizing a variety of teaching methods in health education.
    a. All students will have available in their professional portfolios a 7-12 year curriculum and a health unit complete with lesson plans prepared for effective instruction.
    b. Student teaching evaluations from classroom teacher, education supervisor, and health education supervisor will be conducted six times during student teaching. Classroom teacher evaluations will indicate recommendations of 95% of students teachers for certification.

3. Students will be prepared to find employment in the field of health education.
    a. Ninety percent of health education graduates registered with the placement service during the year will have received a job offer in education by the fall semester following their graduation (as indicated from the placement service records).
    b. Seventy-five percent of the students holding the health education degree and responding to the placement center's one year follow-up study shall indicate that they are currently employed in the field of education.

NOT TO BE CONSIDERED AS A MODEL BUT AS AN EXAMPLE

UNDERGRADUATE VOCATIONAL EDUCATION (BEd)
CIP 13.0501

Intended Educational Outcomes and Means of Assessment/Criteria for Success

1. Students will be able to articulate the goals, purpose, and philosophy of vocational education in the United States and be capable of interpreting legislation relative to vocational education.
    a. Students are evaluated by a qualitative instrument locally developed by the vocational education staff under the direction of the vocational coordinator. A panel of three vocational education staff members will review the examination papers, evaluating on a four point Likert rating scale. Eighty percent of the students will rate average or above average.

2. Students are capable of identifying/analyzing the common elements of vocational programs and capable of performing in an educational setting as a vocational educator.
    a. Students' performance is measured by a state-wide follow-up survey of program graduates developed by the state vocational coordinators to determine the degree to which this University's program prepares the graduates for the educational work site. Students will receive a score of 75% and above.

NOT TO BE CONSIDERED AS A MODEL BUT AS AN EXAMPLE

UNDERGRADUATE PHYSICAL EDUCATION (BEd)
CIP 13.1314

Intended Educational Outcomes and Means of Assessment/Criteria for Success

1. Students will have a comprehensive knowledge base in physical education as defined by the National Association for Sport and Physical Education.
   a. Eighty percent of physical education graduates will score 75% or above on the state college physical education comprehensive exit examination.
   b. Eighty percent of physical education graduates will "agree" or "strongly agree" on a Graduate Student Questionnaire (locally developed) completed in the HPER methods course that they have a comprehensive knowledge base in physical education as equal to or greater than individuals with the same degree with whom they have come in contact.

2. All physical education students will demonstrate competency in 12 physical education skill areas.
   a. One hundred percent of the candidates to be accepted into the physical education student teaching semester must have passed a standardized skills test at 80% in each of the 12 areas as administered by the physical education staff.
   b. Seventy-five percent of the physical education graduates will "agree" or "strongly agree" on the Graduating Student Questionnaire that they have competency in at least 12 skills areas.

3. Students will demonstrate an acceptable fitness level before entering the professional semester.
   a. All students graduating with a degree in physical education will score 70% or higher in six tests within the University's fitness test prior to entering the professional semester.
   b. Eighty percent of physical education graduates will answer "agree" or "strongly agree" on the Graduating Student Questionnaire to the question, "I feel I have a sufficient level of physical fitness to effectively teach in the area of physical education."

4. Students receiving a degree in physical education will be prepared for their first experience in the field.
   a. Students will compose a portfolio with a personal philosophy of physical education, a teaching unit, and a K-12 physical education curriculum to be evaluated by the physical education department. Ninety percent of this portfolio will be "accepted" by a jury of faculty on first review.
   b. Ninety-five percent of students will successfully complete a ten week teaching experience in a school setting evaluated separately by three supervisors.

5. Students will find employment in the field within one year of graduation (if not in graduate school).
   a. Ninety percent of physical education graduates registered with the placement office will receive a job offer in education during the first year after graduation.
   b. Seventy-five percent of physical education graduates responding to the placement center's one year follow-up survey shall indicate that they are currently employed in the field of education or in graduate school.

NOT TO BE CONSIDERED AS A MODEL BUT AS AN EXAMPLE

UNDERGRADUATE ENGINEERING (BS)
CIP 14.0101

Intended Educational Outcomes and Means of Assessment/Criteria for Success

1. Students completing the Baccalaureate program in Engineering will be able to perform at an acceptable level of technical competence denoted by national professional requirements.
    a. Graduating seniors will pass the national FE examination (Fundamentals of Engineering) at a rate which will exceed the average rate of passing in the state of Ohio for first-time test takers.

2. Engineering students will be able to prepare and present technical briefings and reports.
    a. Seventy-five percent of graduating seniors will be deemed competent in the area of communications as assessed by external consultants in their review of the senior Capstone project.

3. Engineering graduates will be able to find employment in the professional market place.
    a. Ninety percent of those graduates seeking employment will be employed within one year following graduation.

4. Students completing the Baccalaureate program in Engineering will demonstrate adequate preparation for graduate school.
    a. Ninety percent of those seeking advanced degrees will be enrolled in a graduate program within two years following graduation.

5. Engineering students will demonstrate an awareness of the need for technology in missions.
    a. Engineering students as a group will participate in short-term mission projects at a rate which exceeds the overall percentage of students who attend the University.

NOT TO BE CONSIDERED AS A MODEL BUT AS AN EXAMPLE

UNDERGRADUATE ARCHITECTURAL TECHNOLOGY (Associate Degree)
CIP 15.0101

Intended Educational Outcomes and Means of Assessment/Criteria for Success

1. Graduates will be technically proficient in manual and computer-aided drafting techniques, construction terms and techniques, as well as presentation techniques.
   a. At the close of their final term 90% of the students will be able to prepare a portfolio and meet the quality control and evaluation of the Architectural Technology program faculty in the Capstone course (ARC 220) portfolio.

2. Graduates will be employed in the field.
   a. Forty percent of the responding graduates of the Architectural Technology program will report employment in the field on the Graduating Student Survey administered within the first three months after graduation.
   b. Sixty percent of the responding (previous year) graduates of the Architectural Technology program will report employment in the field on the Alumni survey distributed one year after graduation.

3. Employers of the Architectural Technology program will rate the technical and academic skills of the employees as average or above.
   a. The Employer Survey conducted each year will rate the graduates as above average on the three course area performance (competency) survey questions. "Above average" is higher than a 3.0 on a 5.0 scale; however, if any of the three survey questions has an individual rating below 3.0, that individual course area performance will be reviewed further.
   b. Sixty percent of the respondents to an employer survey will respond that they would employ future graduates of the Architectural Technology program if a position were available.

NOT TO BE CONSIDERED AS A MODEL BUT AS AN EXAMPLE

ELECTRONICS AND COMPUTER ENGINEERING (Associate Degree)
CIP 15.0301

Intended Educational Outcomes and Means of Assessment/Criteria for Success

1. Graduates will have a strong basic understanding of the fundamental principles of electricity and electronics and specific technical expertise in their area of specialization.
   a. Seventy-five percent of graduating students responding to a survey will indicate that they "strongly agree" or "agree" that they have a basic understanding of the fundamental principles of electricity, electronics, and specific technical expertise in their area of specialization.
   b. Seventy percent of those employers responding to the Employer Survey will "strongly agree" or "agree" that the students educated by the institution at hand have a basic understanding of the fundamental principles of electricity, electronics, and specific technical expertise in their area of specialization.

2. Graduates will be able to obtain gainful employment by applying the above skills to business and industry.
   a. Sixty percent of graduates responding will be employed in the field or enrolled in a four year institution when surveyed one year after graduation.

3. Employers of the new graduates will indicate a willingness to hire more graduates of the program.
   a. Seventy-five percent of employers of recent Electronics and Computer Engineering graduates will indicate in a telephone survey that they are satisfied with the level of training the employee has for the workplace.

NOT TO BE CONSIDERED AS A MODEL BUT AS AN EXAMPLE

ELECTRONIC ENGINEERING TECHNOLOGY (Associate Degree)
CIP 15.0303

Intended Educational Outcomes and Means of Assessment/Criteria for Success

1. Graduates of the Electronic Engineering program will be employed in the field or continue their education.
   a. Forty percent of the responding graduates of the Electronic Engineering program will report employment in the field on the Graduating Student Survey administered within 90 days of the time of program completion.
   b. Seventy-five percent of the responding (previous year) graduates of the Electronic Engineering program will report employment in the field on the Alumni Survey distributed one year after graduation.

2. Graduates of the Electronic Engineering program will be technically proficient.
   a. At the close of their final term, 100% of the students will be able to complete within a given period of time a student project "prepared" or "as directed" by the Electronic Engineering faculty in the Capstone course Electronics Design Project (ELN 246).

3. Employers of the Electronic Engineering program graduates will rate the technical and academic skills of the employees as average or above.
   a. The Employer Survey conducted each year will rate the graduates as above average on the three course area performance (competency) survey questions. "Above average" is higher than a 3.0 on a 5.0 scale; however, if any of the three survey questions has an individual rating below 3.0, that individual course area performance will be reviewed further.
   b. Ninety percent of the respondents to an Employer Survey conducted every year will respond that they would employ future graduates of the Electronic Engineering program.

NOT TO BE CONSIDERED AS A MODEL BUT AS AN EXAMPLE

UNDERGRADUATE INDUSTRIAL TECHNOLOGY (Associate Degree)
CIP 15.0699

Intended Educational Outcomes and Means of Assessment/Criteria for Success

1. Students completing the Baccalaureate program in Industrial Technology will be prepared in a specialized professional area.
    a. Ninety percent of the students will successfully complete an internship or teaching experience with a satisfactory performance evaluation by the on-site and campus supervisor.
    b. In a follow-up attitudinal measure examining employer and employee satisfaction, 80% of those surveyed will state satisfaction.

2. Students completing the Baccalaureate program in Industrial Technology will be able to internalize the philosophical base of industrial technology. These are: to identify how technology is organized into a meaningful whole within the humanities, sciences, and education of future citizens; order and structure the discipline of technology; analyze technology's component parts; understand how technical means have increased the potential for survival; and, explore possibilities of new technologies and question their impact on the environment, society, and the world.
    a. Students will score at least 75% on comprehensive tests administered during the senior year.
    b. Students complete a locally developed Likert scale survey given to assess attitudes toward the philosophical elements. Eighty percent of students will "agree" or "strongly agree" with statements relative to philosophical elements.

3. Students completing the Baccalaureate program in Industrial Technology will be able to demonstrate processes essential to professional technologists. Processes include: communication, critical thinking, analytical thinking, reasoning, creative thinking, and problem-solving.
    a. Ninety percent of students will successfully develop a professional portfolio or complete the appropriate licensure examination which directly addresses competence in an area of specialization.
    b. Seventy-five percent of students will successfully complete a comprehensive test administered during the senior year and developed by the department to address the above skills.

NOT TO BE CONSIDERED AS A MODEL BUT AS AN EXAMPLE

SURVEYING TECHNOLOGY (Associate Degree)
CIP 15.1102

Intended Educational Outcomes and Means of Assessment/Criteria for Success

1. Graduates of the Surveying Technology program will be technically proficient.
   a. At the close of their final term, 90% of the graduates will be able to design a 20-30 lot subdivision plot as directed by the Surveying Technology program faculty in the Capstone course Mapping & Subdivision Planning (SRV).
   b. Ninety percent of the graduates will be able to design a grading and drainage plan for a 20-30 lot subdivision as directed by the Surveying Technology program faculty in the Capstone course Mapping & Subdivision Planning (SRV 214).
   c. Ninety percent of the graduates will be able to draw, plan, and profile sheets for streets in a 20-30 lot subdivision as directed by the Surveying Technology program faculty in the Capstone course Mapping & Subdivision Planning (SRV 214).

2. Graduates of the Surveying Technology program will be employed in the field.
   a. Eighty percent of the responding graduates of the Surveying Technology program will report employment in the field on the Graduating Student Survey administered within the first five months after graduation.
   b. Ninety percent of the responding (previous year) graduates of the Surveying Technology program will report employment in the field on the Alumni Survey.

3. Employers of the Surveying Technology program graduates will rate the technical and academic skills of the employees as above average.
   a. The Employer Survey conducted each year will rate the graduates as above average on the three course area performance (competency) survey questions. "Above average" is higher than a 3.0 on a 5.0 scale; however, if any of the three survey questions has an individual rating below 3.0, that individual course area performance will be reviewed further.
   b. Eighty percent of the respondents to an Employer Survey conducted every year will respond that they would employ future graduates of the Surveying Technology program.

NOT TO BE CONSIDERED AS A MODEL BUT AS AN EXAMPLE

FOREIGN LANGUAGE (BA)
CIP 16.0101

Intended Educational Outcomes and Means of Assessment/Criteria for Success

1. Students will be able to speak the language so as to be understood by a native of the target culture, using correct pronunciation, stress, rhythm, and intonation.

   a. Ninety-five percent of the students taking the ACTFL examination at the time of graduation will achieve the "passing score" established by faculty in the department for each specific language.

2. Students will be able to write so as to be understood by an educated native of the target culture, using correct spelling, punctuation, vocabulary, and grammar.

   a. Students completing the program will be required to write a 20-page autobiographical sketch in the language of their major. Ninety percent of these sketches will be judged to use correct spelling, punctuation, vocabulary, and grammar by a jury of departmental faculty including at least one native speaker of the target country.

NOT TO BE CONSIDERED AS A MODEL BUT AS AN EXAMPLE

HOME ECONOMICS (BS)
CIP 19.0101

Intended Educational Outcomes and Means of Assessment/Criteria for Success

1. Students will gain the knowledge and ability to maintain a safe and healthy learning environment for children ages birth to six years.
   a. Students will participate in a practicum, applying didactic child development skills. Eighty percent of the practicum supervisors will rate student knowledge and ability as "adequate" or better.
   b. In Home Economics 432, a Capstone course, 95% of the students will be able to correct a simulated home environment (designed by the department faculty) so that it meets minimal safety and health standards.

2. Students will gain the experience necessary for a career in managing, buying, promoting, producing, and selling in the clothing and textiles industry.
   a. Students will be assessed by advisors and peer appraisals on the extent to which the student is able to synthesize knowledge, skill, and attitudes in a practical on-the-job training experience. The supervisors of such experiences will rate at least 70% of the students as possessing the knowledge and skills for a career entry position.
   b. Fifty percent of those graduates responding to the Alumni Survey will indicate employment in the field five years after graduation.

3. Students will gain the scientific and technical knowledge of foods and nutrition, skills, and the educational methods needed to apply the knowledge to meet society, regional, and professional needs in the profession.
   a. Seventy percent of graduates will pass the National Registration Examination within one year of graduation.
   b. Employers responding to the annual survey will indicate no less than an average 3.5 (on a scale of 5.0) rating of graduates knowledge in each of the areas identified.

NOT TO BE CONSIDERED AS A MODEL BUT AS AN EXAMPLE

PARALEGAL TECHNOLOGY (Associate Degree)
CIP 22.0103

Intended Educational Outcomes and Means of Assessment/Criteria for Success

1. Graduates of the Paralegal Technology program will be employed in the field.
   a. Fifty percent of the responding graduates of the Paralegal Technology program will report employment in the field on the Graduating Student Survey administered at the time of program completion.
   b. Seventy-five percent of the responding (previous years) graduates of the Paralegal Technology program will report employment in the field or seeking additional education on the Alumni Survey distributed one year after graduation.

2. Graduates of the Paralegal Technology program will be technically proficient in assisting attorneys in most facets of the law.
   a. Ninety-five percent of internship supervisors (practicing attorneys and public legal services personnel) in the Capstone course (LEX 245) will rate students supervised as technically proficient to perform the tasks required.

3. Employers of the Paralegal Technology program graduates will rate the technical and academic skills of the employees as average or above.
   a. The Employer Survey conducted each year will rate the graduates as above average on the three course area performance (competency) survey questions. "Above average" is higher than a 3.0 on a 5.0 scale; however, if any of the three survey questions has an individual rating below 3.0, that individual course area performance will be reviewed further.
   b. Eighty percent of the respondents to an Employer Survey conducted every year will respond that they are satisfied with the employees and they would employ future graduates of the Paralegal Technology program.

NOT TO BE CONSIDERED AS A MODEL BUT AS AN EXAMPLE

UNDERGRADUATE GENERAL STUDIES (BA)
CIP 24.0102

Intended Educational Outcomes and Means of Assessment/Criteria for Success

1. Program will assist students in the development of the abilities to reason critically, analyze and solve problems objectively, and think creatively.
    a. The critical thinking section of the Collegiate Assessment of Academic Proficiency (CAAP) test is administered as a pre-test to randomly selected general studies courses in as many of the 13 core areas as possible. The students' tests are administered as a post-test to the same courses annually. Post test scores will be higher in 70% of the course sections.
    b. The College Outcome Measures Program (COMP) test is administered to 80% of first-year general studies students in their first semester and to graduating general studies students in their final semester. The solving problems section of the test will be targeted specifically for the assessment of this objective, and the students' overall percentile will be 60% or above.

2. The program will assist the students in the development of proficiency in written and oral communication and in the language and symbols of mathematics.
    a. The Pre-professional Skills Test (PPST) is administered to all students seeking teacher certification. Each student will achieve a score of at least 170 on the reading portion, 171 on the mathematics portion, and 172 on the writing portion.
    b. The COMP test is administered to 80% of first-year students in the fall semester and 80% of graduating seniors in the spring semester. The average score of students taking the examination as a senior will be score at the 50th percentile or above in the communicating section of the COMP test.

3. The program will enhance the ability of the students to understand personal values, the values of others, and the ethical and moral implications of that knowledge.
    a. The Defining Issues Test (DIT) is administered to all students in required ethics courses as pre- and post-tests to ascertain the development of values in students. Average scores on post tests will increase in 90% of the courses.
    b. The COMP test is administered to 80% of first-year students in their first semester and to graduating seniors in their final semester. The clarifying values section of the test will be targeted specifically for the assessment of this objective and the students' overall scores fall at the 55th percentile or above.

NOT TO BE CONSIDERED AS A MODEL BUT AS AN EXAMPLE

UNDERGRADUATE LIBRARY MEDIA (BA/BSEd)
CIP 25.0101

Intended Educational Outcomes and Means of Assessment/Criteria for Success

1. Library Media graduates will exhibit knowledge of the five major curriculum content areas including the philosophy of library services, information services and question negotiation, organization of materials, selection of resources, and administration of media services.
    a. Ninety-five percent of students will receive a satisfactory score on the comprehensive oral examination administered by the departmental faculty during the semester in which the students are enrolled in LM 439 (practice and procedure).
    b. Ninety-five percent of students will receive satisfactory evaluations by department faculty and the cooperating practicum librarians from area schools and public libraries during the semester in which the students are enrolled in LM 439 (practice and procedures).

2. Students will exhibit a knowledge of and a sensitivity to cooperation, partnerships, and networking among all types of libraries.
    a. Students maintain a journal during their practicum experiences in which they will detail their observations of and reactions to the similarities and differences in libraries, services, and management styles. Ninety percent will be judged acceptable by a jury of faculty.
    b. Eighty-five percent of students exhibit satisfactory understanding and use of the Internet, list servers, and e-mail in order to network effectively with other media specialists and librarians on a departmentally developed performance examination administered during a Capstone course in the student's senior year.

3. Students will be able to indicate to the department faculty and to potential employers their preparation for positions in school media centers or other library work.
    a. Students exhibit in their portfolio examples of their work in each major area of library study, an abstract of their journal of practicum experience, evaluations from practicum supervisors, a resume, and a copy of the faculty evaluation of one's comprehensive examination process. A jury of potential employers will judge the portfolios of 90% or more of the graduates each year as "demonstrating proficiency."

NOT TO BE CONSIDERED AS A MODEL BUT AS AN EXAMPLE

UNDERGRADUATE GENERAL BIOLOGY (BA/BS)
CIP 26.0101

Intended Educational Outcomes and Means of Assessment/Criteria for Success

1. Students will understand and explain biological concepts and principles.
    a. Fifty percent of general biology students will score at or above the 50th percentile on the "Biology" section of the MFAT.
    b. Seventy percent of students will pass an oral exit interview (approximately one to two hours in duration) presented by the biology department faculty one semester prior to graduation.

2. Students will understand and employ the scientific method in an investigation of living organisms including the interpretation of data, communication of these results to others, and the use of these data to predict the outcome of similar research with other organisms.
    a. Students will develop and complete a research project with the results communicated in writing and orally to the biology department faculty and students during the final semester of their senior year. Seventy percent of the projects will be judged to meet the criterion outlined above by a faculty jury.

3. Students will develop the skills needed for biological research in the lab and in the field.
    a. The research project described above will be reviewed by the same faculty jury to ascertain the proper use of biological research laboratory and field research techniques. Ninety percent of the projects reviewed will be found to have demonstrated laboratory and/or field research techniques in accordance with commonly held principles of good practice.

NOT TO BE CONSIDERED AS A MODEL BUT AS AN EXAMPLE

UNDERGRADUATE BIOLOGY (BA/BS)
CIP 26.0101

Intended Educational Outcomes and Means of Assessment/Criteria for Success

1. Students completing the baccalaureate degree program in biology will compare favorably in their knowledge of biology with those students completing a similar program nationally.
    a. ETS Field Test in biology or GRE with specialization in biology scores will be at or above the national mean.

2. Graduates will be prepared to pursue discipline-related activities which would utilize skills from the program.
    a. As determined by the Alumni and Senior Survey data, 75% of students applying to graduate or professional schools will be accepted.
    b. As determined by the Alumni and Senior Survey data, 75% of students seeking employment will be employed in discipline-related areas.

3. Students completing the program will be able to locate and use biological literature to support research utilizing the scientific method.
    a. Students will be required to complete an original research project. These projects will be reviewed by the departmental faculty and 90% will be judged to have appropriately demonstrated the use of the scientific method and support by the biological literature available in the particular field of inquiry.

4. Graduates will be prepared to pursue discipline-related activities which would utilize skills from the program.
    a. As determined by Alumni Survey data, 80% of students who apply will become employed in discipline-related areas.
    b. As determined by Alumni Survey data, 90% of students will express satisfaction with the degree program.

NOT TO BE CONSIDERED AS A MODEL BUT AS AN EXAMPLE

UNDERGRADUATE MATHEMATICS (BA/BS)
CIP 27.0101

Intended Educational Outcomes and Means of Assessment/Criteria for Success

1. Students' interests are broadened and they develop inquiring minds, while learning to communicate effectively.
    a. At least 50% of the institution's mathematics graduates achieve at the 50th percentile or above on "communicating" and "solving problems" subscores on the ACT COMP.
    b. Eighty percent of all graduates denote on the Graduating Student Survey that the institution has added to their ability to use mathematics in everyday life.

2. Students think logically, creatively, and imaginatively while provided with resources to encourage research and public service.
    a. Twenty-five percent of graduating mathematics majors will have participated in undergraduate research.
    b. One hundred mathematics students annually will participate in Pi Mu Epsilon, the Mathematics Organization, or Statistics, and Actuarial Organization activities.

3. Students acquire a basic understanding of a discipline or a group of related disciplines.
    a. Ninety percent of mathematics majors in education will pass the state department of education's requirement in the specialty area of the NTE.
    b. Fifty percent of graduating mathematics majors achieve at least the 50th percentile on the ETS Major Field Achievement Test.
    c. Students' pass rate on the first two Society of Actuaries Professional Examination will exceed the national pass rate.

4. Students will actively participate in communities by seeking and sharing knowledge, expertise, and creative undertakings.
    a. One hundred practicing teachers will participate in continuing educational activities offered through the Mathematics department.
    b. Ninety percent of participants in continuing education activities indicate on the department's locally developed program evaluation questionnaire activity contributes to professional growth.

NOT TO BE CONSIDERED AS A MODEL BUT AS AN EXAMPLE

UNDERGRADUATE GENERAL CHEMISTRY (BA/BS)
CIP 40.0501

Intended Educational Outcomes and Means of Assessment/Criteria for Success

1. Students attain the knowledge of chemical concepts and their application.
    a. Students score near the 50th percentile on the Standardized General Chemistry Test from the American Chemical Society (ACS).
    b. Seventy-five percent of students will agree, "the major in chemistry prepared me to take the ACS General Chemistry Test" on the Graduating Student questionnaire.

2. Students learn the process in chemistry for investigating chemical phenomena, interpreting the findings, communicating the results, and predicting chemical properties.
    a. Students compose a research paper and/or seminar literature review. As part of a Capstone course in chemistry, graduating students will be presented with a problem which they are likely to encounter in laboratory work. Ninety percent of the students will investigate the problem, interpret findings, communicate the results of findings, and predict the resulting chemical properties in such a manner as to be considered appropriate by a panel of chemistry department faculty.

NOT TO BE CONSIDERED AS A MODEL BUT AS AN EXAMPLE

UNDERGRADUATE GENERAL PHYSICS (BS)
CIP 40.0801

Intended Educational Outcomes and Means of Assessment/Criteria for Success

1. Students have a working knowledge of basic concepts and principles in at least three areas of physics.
   a. Fifty percent of students who take the physics section of the GRE will score at the 50th percentile or better.
   b. Eight percent of students will successfully complete an exit interview/oral examination conducted by the physics department faculty (based on a rubric).

2. Students possess sufficient science process skills which include critical thinking, creative problem-solving, hypothesizing, interpretation of data, prediction, interference, and communication of results.
   a. Eighty percent of students will satisfactorily complete (based on a process skills rubric) an exit interview/oral examination conducted by physics faculty.
   b. Eighty percent of students will demonstrate these abilities by exhibition to the physics faculty through a professional portfolio consisting of samples of the students undergraduate work.

3. Students will be admitted to graduate school or obtain employment in fields related to physics.
   a. Eighty percent of students will be admitted to graduate school or employed in physics-related jobs within one year of graduation as determined by follow-up questionnaires through the alumni office.

NOT TO BE CONSIDERED AS A MODEL BUT AS AN EXAMPLE

UNDERGRADUATE PSYCHOLOGY (BA)
CIP 42.0101

Intended Educational Outcomes and Means of Assessment/Criteria for Success

1. The student will be able to demonstrate his mastery of the knowledge base in the discipline of Psychology.
   a. As a group, students completing the BA in psychology in any graduation year will score at the 50th percentile on a Standardized Psychology Achievement Test. This test will cover Abnormal, Experimental, Design, Statistics, History and Systems, Personality, Theory, Clinical and Counseling, and Social Psychology.

2. The student will be prepared for advanced work in Psychology in graduate school.
   a. The Department will track (going back 5 years) the number of Psychology majors applying to graduate school each year. A 70% acceptance rate at various graduate schools will be achieved.

3. The student will demonstrate entry level skills in Psychology. Preparation for entrance into a Psychology-related vocation will be demonstrated in that 70% of our interns will be rated in the good or superior categories on a rating scale by their internship supervisors.

NOT TO BE CONSIDERED AS A MODEL BUT AS AN EXAMPLE

CRIMINAL JUSTICE TECHNOLOGY (Associate Degree)
CIP 43.0104

Intended Educational Outcomes and Means of Assessment/Criteria for Success

1. Graduates of the Criminal Justice Technology program will be employed in the field.
   a. Fifty percent of the responding graduates of the Criminal Justice Technology program will report employment in the field on the Graduating Student Survey administered at the time of program completion.
   b. Eighty percent of the responding (previous year) graduates of the Criminal Justice Technology program will report employment in the field on the Alumni Survey distributed one year after graduation.

2. Graduates of the Criminal Justice Technology program will be technically proficient.
   a. Students will prepare a case file for prosecution of a mock investigation of a crime in the Capstone course Fundamentals of Investigation II, (CJC 211) and 90% of those evaluated by the Criminal Justice program faculty upon completion of the course will be judged acceptable.

3. Employers of the Criminal Justice Technology program graduates will rate the technical and academic skills of the employees as above average.
   a. The Employer Survey conducted each year will rate the graduates as above average on the three course area performance (competency) survey questions. "Above average" is higher than a 3.0 on a 5.0 scale; however, if any of the three survey questions has an individual rating below 3.0, that individual course area performance will be reviewed further.
   b. Eighty percent of the Criminal Justice Technology respondents to an Employer Survey conducted every year will respond that they would employ future graduates of the Criminal Justice Technology program.

NOT TO BE CONSIDERED AS A MODEL BUT AS AN EXAMPLE

CRIMINAL JUSTICE (Associate Degree)
CIP 43.0104

Intended Educational Outcomes and Means of Assessment/Criteria for Success

1. Students will gain the skills necessary to continue education in the field of Criminal Justice without the loss of credit and without the increased time input at the institution.
   a. Ninety percent of all graduates will continue their education by transferring to four year institutions in an attempt to attain baccalaureate degrees.
   b. Ninety percent of all Criminal Justice graduates attempting to obtain baccalaureate degrees will report no increase in expended time input at the institution to which they transfer and will receive comparable credit hours for classes taken at the institution to which they transfer.

2. Students not desiring a baccalaureate degree will be able to enter into and be successfully employed within the criminal justice field.
   a. Thirty percent of all graduates not desiring a higher degree will report employment in one of the four basic subsystems of the criminal justice field (i.e., courts, corrections, law enforcement, or probation/parole) on the Alumni Survey conducted annually.
   b. Twenty percent of all graduates not desiring a higher educational degree will report employment in a related private security position that will directly utilize the knowledge base obtained from their associate degree educational experience as reported by respondents to the Alumni Survey conducted annually.

3. Students will be proficient in and possess an in-depth understanding of the criminal justice system and they will be capable of applying this knowledge in the field upon graduation.
   a. Eighty percent of all graduates will be prepared during their seventh quarter of study to complete and successfully pass a locally developed and standardized Criminal Justice Proficiency Examination.
   b. Seventy percent of all Criminal Justice employers responding to the Employer Survey will indicate that 90% of their agency's employees, who graduated in Criminal Justice from the institution at hand, have the necessary skills and knowledge base to successfully be rated as highly competent employees.

4. Criminal Justice agencies will be more receptive to hiring college graduates possessing associate degrees in Criminal Justice.
   a. Criminal Justice agencies and practitioners will indicate a 90% approval rating of hiring Criminal Justice graduates from the institution on the Employer Survey.

5. Graduating students desiring to enter the law enforcement profession will be certified in the Basic Law Enforcement Training Program.
   a. One hundred percent of all Criminal Justice graduates desiring to enter into the law enforcement profession as an active law enforcement officer will be certified in the Basic Law Enforcement Training Program during the eighth quarter of studies at the institution.
   b. One hundred percent of all Criminal Justice graduates participating in the Basic Law Enforcement Training Program will indicate on the Alumni Survey that the institution adequately prepared them for the academic work related to the program.
   c. Eighty percent of all Criminal Justice graduates will score 80% or higher on the Criminal Justice Standards Examination.

NOT TO BE CONSIDERED AS A MODEL BUT AS AN EXAMPLE

UNDERGRADUATE CRIMINAL JUSTICE (BA)
CIP 43.0104

Intended Educational Outcomes and Means of Assessment/Criteria for Success

1. Students completing the baccalaureate program in Criminal Justice will compare favorably in their knowledge of the criminal justice system, the causes of deviant behavior, evaluation of and design correctional responses, and basic law enforcement principles with those students completing a similar program nationally.
    a. The average scores of the criminal justice (BA) graduates on the Area Concentration Achievement Tests (ACAT) in criminal justice will compare favorably with those students from other institutions taking the same test.
    b. Ninety percent of these graduates will "agree" or "strongly agree" with the statement, "I feel I am well prepared and adequately educated into the field of criminal justice."
    c. The average scores of these graduates on the ACAT will be significantly improved over the average scores of entering criminal justice students on the ACAT.

2. Students completing the Baccalaureate program in criminal justice will compare favorably in reading and writing skills with those students completing a similar program nationally. Each criminal justice Baccalaureate candidate will submit a legal memorandum and a brief to the criminal justice department. The Criminal Justice Department faculty will determine the extent to which the writings evidence having been adequately researched, edited, proofread, and presented. Seventy-five percent will be found to meet or exceed department standards reflective of national expectations.

NOT TO BE CONSIDERED AS A MODEL BUT AS AN EXAMPLE

BASIC LAW ENFORCEMENT (Associate Degree)
CIP 43.0107

Intended Educational Outcomes and Means of Assessment/Criteria for Success

1. Graduates of the Basic Law Enforcement program will be technically proficient.
   a. Prior to graduation, 90% of the students will be able to pass the North Carolina Education and Training Standard Commission test for certification.

2. Graduates of the Basic Law Enforcement program will be employed in the field.
   a. Seventy percent of the responding graduates of the BLET program will report employment in the field on the Graduating Student Survey administered within the first three months after graduation.
   b. Eighty percent of the responding (previous year) graduates of the BLET program will report employment in the field on the Alumni Survey distributed one year after graduation.

3. Employers of the Basic Law Enforcement program graduates will rate the technical and academic skills of the employee as above average.
   a. The Employer Survey conducted each year will rate the graduates as above average on the three area performance (competency) survey questions. "Above average" is higher than a 3.0 on a 5.0 scale; however, if any of the three survey questions has an individual rating of 3.0 or below, that individual course area performance will be reviewed further.
   b. Eighty percent of the respondents to an Employer Survey conducted each year will respond that they would employ future graduates of the BLET program.

NOT TO BE CONSIDERED AS A MODEL BUT AS AN EXAMPLE

FIRE PROTECTION (Associate Degree)
CIP 43.0201

Intended Educational Outcomes and Means of Assessment/Criteria for Success

1. Graduates of the Fire Protection Technology program will be technically proficient in the inspection and maintenance of building fire protection systems.
   a. At the close of their final term, 90% of the students will be able to inspect and evaluate fire protection systems as assigned by the instructor and make practical recommendations on their effectiveness, safety, and quality within a given period of time as evaluated by the Fire Protection program faculty in the Capstone course Inspection Principles and Practices (FIP 235).

2. Graduates of the Fire Protection Technology program will be employed in the field.
   a. Sixty percent of the responding graduates of the Fire Protection Technology program will report employment in the field on the Graduating Student Survey administered within the five months after graduation.
   b. Eighty percent of the responding (previous year) graduates of the Fire Protection Technology program will report employment in the field on the Alumni Survey distributed one year after graduation.

3. Employers of the Fire Protection Technology program graduates will rate the technical and academic skills of employees as average or above.
   a. The Employer Survey conducted each year will rate the graduates as above average on the three-course area performance (competency) survey questions. "Above average" is higher than a 3.0 rating on a 5.0 scale; however, if any of the three survey questions has an individual rating below 3.0, that individual course area performance will be reviewed further.

b. Sixty percent of the respondents to an Employer Survey conducted every year will respond that they would employ future graduates of the Fire Protection Technology program.

NOT TO BE CONSIDERED AS A MODEL BUT AS AN EXAMPLE

UNDERGRADUATE SOCIAL WORK (BA)
CIP 44.0701

Intended Educational Outcomes and Means of Assessment/Criteria for Success

1. Students completing the BA in social work will compare favorably in their knowledge of social work with other students completing a similar program nationally.
   a. The average score on the Project of Area Concentration Achievement Testing (PACAT) Social Work Achievement Pattern C test (which is taken one semester prior to graduation) will be in the upper two-thirds of the national scores.

2. Students will demonstrate competency in a wide range of social work practice skills.
   a. All students will successfully complete at least 12 hours of volunteer work in human service agencies during their junior year. Success is measured by a review of a student-maintained journal by the field practicum coordinator and by receipt of reports of completed assignments signed by the field practicum supervisors. Eighty-five percent will be judged successful.
   b. Students will successfully complete 425 hours of field practicum experience during their senior year. Success will be measured by their achievement of a "satisfactory" or above rating on their field practicum evaluation. Ninety-six percent will be so measured.

3. Alumni will report that they have found the social work knowledge, skills, and values learned at the University useful on their jobs.
   a. Eighty percent of those graduates who respond to a college administered survey one year after graduation, will "agree" or "strongly agree" that they have been adequately educated at the University in social work knowledge, skills, and values.

NOT TO BE CONSIDERED AS A MODEL BUT AS AN EXAMPLE

SOCIAL WORK (BA)
CIP 44.0701

Intended Educational Outcomes and Means of Assessment/Criteria for Success

1. Students will develop knowledge, values, and skills in the area of social work.
   a. At least 75% of the social work graduates, who take the Social Work Licensing Examination., will pass the examination.
   b. Ninety-five percent of all students will pass a locally developed exit examination, which is comprehensive in knowledge, values, and skills areas.

2. Students will gain the skills necessary to gain employment in the field.
   a. At least 75% of social work graduates will work in a social work setting in their initial employment.
   b. At least 75% of the initial employers in social work settings will be satisfied with the graduate's academic preparation for beginning practice.
   c. At least 80% of social work graduates will be generally satisfied with their academic preparation for initial professional employment, as reported on the Graduating Student Questionnaire.

NOT TO BE CONSIDERED AS A MODEL BUT AS AN EXAMPLE

UNDERGRADUATE GENERAL SOCIAL SCIENCE (BS IN EDUCATION)
CIP 45.0101

Intended Educational Outcomes and Means of Assessment/Criteria for Success

1. Students completing the BS in Education in social science will compare favorably in subject knowledge and reading and writing skills with those students completing a similar program at other institutions nationally.

    a. Students will average in at least the second quartile of an accepted national examination for students with a social science endorsement (e.g., Educational Testing Service Major Field Achievement Test in the area of social science). The test is to be taken one semester prior to graduation.

2. Graduates will be satisfied with the program and show evidence of success.

    a. All graduates will be polled concerning their opinions of the quality of their training during their undergraduate program. This poll will be conducted three times (shortly prior to graduation, after three years, and after six years). At least 80% will "agree" or "strongly agree" with the statement "I am well satisfied with my academic program." The student poll will also collect information regarding post-graduation honors received and the quality of performance in any further higher education endeavors.

    b. Employers will be polled concerning their perception of the competency of the University's social science majors. This will be done within one year of graduation. Eighty percent of employers will indicate their willingness to employ additional program graduates.

NOT TO BE CONSIDERED AS A MODEL BUT AS AN EXAMPLE

UNDERGRADUATE ECONOMICS (BA/BS)
CIP 45.0601

Intended Educational Outcomes and Means of Assessment/Criteria for Success

1. Students will gain knowledge and understanding of the current theory and practice of economics, including an understanding of current micro and macroeconomic theory and how it applies to and affects business behavior, and an understanding of the importance of the free enterprise system and when government intervention is necessary.
   a. At least 50% of students will score at or above the national average on the ETS Business Core Examination for business.
   b. At least 50% of students taking the MFAT will score in the 50th percentile.
   c. At least 60% of students will be able to correctly identify major areas requiring additional managerial attention and study, based on a case-study analysis by department faculty.
   d. At least 60% of students will be able to demonstrate detailed knowledge regarding a functional strategy (i.e., economics), supporting the business strategy, and developing illustrative policies to support that functional strategy, based on a case-study analysis by department faculty.

2. Students will have the preparation to gain entry level employment in business or a business related field or admittance into graduate studies.
   a. At least 75% of the graduating seniors in economics will rank the quality of education received as adequate to pursue their career objectives, based on data collected from the Exit Assessment Instrument.
   b. At least 50% of respondents to the Alumni Survey will report they have achieved employment positions that are connected with their degree program one year after graduation.
   c. Of respondents to the Alumni Survey, at least 80% of the alumni eligible for salary increases or promotions in rank have achieved these advances within five years of graduation.

NOT TO BE CONSIDERED AS A MODEL BUT AS AN EXAMPLE

UNDERGRADUATE POLITICAL SCIENCE (BA/BS)
CIP 45.1001

Intended Educational Outcomes and Means of Assessment/Criteria for Success

1. Students completing the program in political science will compare favorably in subject knowledge with those students completing a similar program at other institutions nationally.
    a. Students will average at least in the second quartile of an accepted national examination of political science majors (e.g., Educational Testing Service Major Field Test in Political Science) taken just prior to graduation.

2. Graduating seniors will demonstrate an understanding of current political and governmental affairs both nationally and worldwide.
    a. Students in their final semester will submit a five-page analysis of a randomly assigned present-day political/governmental situation. Students will use perspectives of political science when composing this analysis and 80% of these analyses will be judged acceptable by a departmental jury.
    b. Students in their final semester will take a college developed examination to measure their awareness of current conditions and events of interest to political scientists. Their average scores will be 80% or higher.

3. Graduates will be satisfied with the program and will show evidence of success.
    a. Upon graduation 90% of graduating political science seniors will "agree" or "strongly agree" that they have been adequately educated in political science.
    b. The number of political science graduates who pursue further education and their graduation rate will be analyzed and 75% of these applying for graduate school in political science will be accepted.

NOT TO BE CONSIDERED AS A MODEL BUT AS AN EXAMPLE

UNDERGRADUATE POLITICAL SCIENCE (BA)
CIP 45.1001

Intended Educational Outcomes and Means of Assessment/Criteria for Success

1. Students will exhibit knowledge of government and politics.
   a. Graduates will score on the GRE at or above the national average.
   b. Graduates will score at or above others at correlating institutions within the region.

2. Students will be satisfied with the education they received in their majors.
   a. A majority of the graduates agree that their education compares favorably with those in similar positions as determined by Alumni Survey data.

3. Students will be employed in a public service-related field.
   a. Fifty percent of majors are employed in a public service/government-related field, as determined by Alumni Survey data.

NOT TO BE CONSIDERED AS A MODEL BUT AS AN EXAMPLE

UNDERGRADUATE SOCIOLOGY (BA/BS)
CIP 45.1101

Intended Educational Outcomes and Means of Assessment/Criteria for Success

1. Sociology majors completing the BA/BS program in sociology will compare favorably in knowledge of social structure and process, social thought, and sociological methods with those students completing a similar program nationally.
    a. Students will average at the 51st percentile or above on the Major Field Test in Sociology. This test is to be administered at the completion of the senior seminar in sociology (a required course for all BA/BS students)

2. Sociology majors will recognize the value of the sociology curriculum to themselves and to society.
    a. Ninety percent of the students will state their recognition of the value of the sociology curriculum in an assigned paper in the senior seminar in sociology.
    b. Graduates of the BA/BS program in sociology will be interviewed and/or surveyed five years after graduation and asked whether the knowledge and understanding they gained through their study of sociology has benefited them. They will also be asked if they have benefited society through their sociologically informed actions. These questions will be asked on the Five Year Alumni Questionnaire sent by the Career Development Center. Ninety percent of those who respond will state that their education in sociology has been of benefit to themselves and to society.

3. Majors in sociology will understand the process of research and be able to write analytically and theoretically.
    a. Students taking research methodology must complete a quantitative research project, including theoretical rationale and data analysis.
    b. Students must write a paper on the field of sociology, its scope, methods, and direction in the senior seminar on sociology (a required course for all BA/BS students).
    c. A sociology department faculty member who has not supervised the student in writing the research/senior paper will be asked to read the research/senior paper and evaluate this paper using criterion of readability, coherence, and scope. Eighty percent will be judged acceptable.

NOT TO BE CONSIDERED AS A MODEL BUT AS AN EXAMPLE

AUTOMOTIVE TECHNOLOGY (Associate Degree)
CIP 47.0604

Intended Educational Outcomes and Means of Assessment/Criteria for Success

1. Graduates of the Automotive Technology program will be technically proficient in trouble shooting and repairing automotive and mechanical problems.
   a. At the close of their final term, 90% of the students will be able to trouble-shoot and repair automotive mechanical problems on live test cars in an assigned given period of time as evaluated by the Automotive Technology program faculty in the Capstone course Automotive Service Operations (AUT 225).
   b. Eighty percent of the Automotive Technology graduates who attempt the voluntary National Automotive exams (ASE) will pass the ASE examination.

2. Graduates of the Automotive Technology program will be technically proficient in diagnosing and estimating automotive mechanical repairs.
   a. At the close of their final term, 90% of the students will be able to diagnose and estimate the cost of repairs needed on an automobile as assigned within a given period of time as evaluated by the Automotive Technology program faculty in the Capstone course Automotive Service Operations (AUT 225).

3. Graduates of the Automotive Technology program will be employed in the field.
   a. Sixty percent of the responding graduates of the Automotive Technology program will report employment in the field on the Graduating Student Survey administered within the first five months after graduation.
   b. Eighty percent of the responding (previous year) graduates of the Automotive Technology program will report employment in the field on the Alumni Survey.

4. Employers of the Automotive technology program graduates will rate the technical and academic skills of the employees as above average.
   a. The Employer Survey conducted each year will rate the graduates as above average on the three course area performance (competency) survey questions. "Above average" is higher than a 3.0 on a 5.0 scale; however, if any of the three survey questions has an individual rating below 3.0, that individual course area performance will be reviewed further.
   b. Eighty percent of the respondents to the Employer Survey conducted each year will respond that they would employ future graduates of the Automotive Technology program.

NOT TO BE CONSIDERED AS A MODEL BUT AS AN EXAMPLE

UNDERGRADUATE INTERIOR DESIGN (BA)
CIP 50.0408

Intended Educational Outcomes and Means of Assessment/Criteria for Success

1. Students will utilize elements and principles of design in both two-and three-dimensional applications.

    a. Ninety percent of the portfolios reviewed will be found to meet the above criteria.

2. Students will understand the physical and psychological effects the build environment has on the individual.

    a. Interior design majors will complete a research paper on the effects of design on the environment and individuals to be evaluated by department faculty. Seventy percent of these papers will be accepted.

    b. In a Capstone course during their last semester, students will be asked to describe the psychological impact of five interior designs selected by the departmental faculty. Ninety percent of their descriptions will match that agreed upon by the departmental faculty.

    NOT TO BE CONSIDERED AS A MODEL BUT AS AN EXAMPLE

UNDERGRADUATE THEATER (BA/BS)
CIP 50.0501

Intended Educational Outcomes and Means of Assessment/Criteria for Success

1. Students completing the BA/BS in theater will have the skills to act, direct, and work in any of the technical areas of theater.
    a. All theater majors will complete a public jury in the second semester of their senior year, which will allow students to demonstrate specific competencies in acting, directing, and technical theater and be adjudicated by the theater department faculty. Seventy percent will be judged "outstanding" and no more than 10% "unacceptable."
    b. Students will direct a cutting from a play to be presented to members of the theater department faculty. The students will through this project prepare for and execute production as if directing the full work. Sixty percent will be judged "acceptable" for public exhibition by the jury.

2. BA/BS candidates in theater will demonstrate an understanding of the significance of the history of theater from its origins to present day.
    a. All students will be able to relate the 'poetics' of Aristotle with significant works of drama from Aeschylus to Shakespeare, to Brecht, to O'Neill, to Mamet as determined by an oral evaluation conducted by the theater department faculty.

3. Senior candidates for the BA/BS in theater will demonstrate an accessibility to and knowledge of a broad and inclusive body of theater literature.
    a. All students will read a minimum of 35 play scripts which will be accounted for in their personal portfolio through critiques, reviews, synopses, and analyses over the course of their studies. Eighty-five percent of the portfolios reviewed will meet departmental standards.

NOT TO BE CONSIDERED AS A MODEL BUT AS AN EXAMPLE

UNDERGRADUATE ART (BA/BS)
CIP 50.0701

Intended Educational Outcomes and Means of Assessment/Criteria for Success

1. Students will compare favorably with students completing a similar program nationally in the creation of visual art.
    a. Ninety percent of students will complete a comprehensive exhibition competitive with students nationally judged by the art department faculty.
    b. Five years after graduation, seventy-five percent of those surveyed will "agree" they were adequately educated in the visual arts compared to others nationally.

2. Students will be able to execute, publicize, and document a public exhibition of their creative ventures.
    a. All seniors graduating from the art program will assemble and promote an exhibition of their artistic works, while following guidelines established by the art department faculty.
    b. Students will provide a documentation portfolio of their work for assessment and retention by the art faculty. Eighty-five percent will be judged adequate or better on their first presentation.

3. Graduating seniors from the art department will possess the skills to create art, critique art, and instruct in the visual arts.
    a. The senior exhibit and portfolio will be reviewed by the art department faculty to determine the extent to which a student shows evidence of the ability to create and critically analyze one's own work. Ninety percent of students work will be judged adequate or better.
    b. Seventy-five percent of graduating seniors will "agree" that they have been adequately prepared to create, critique, and instruct in a variety of areas.

NOT TO BE CONSIDERED AS A MODEL BUT AS AN EXAMPLE

UNDERGRADUATE FINE ARTS (BFA)
CIP 50.0799

Intended Educational Outcomes and Means of Assessment/Criteria for Success

1. Students will develop an individual body of work culminating in a senior exhibition with skills in presentation, composition, design, and artistic ability.

    a. Students will compile a portfolio of all work completed while in the Fine Arts program to be critiqued by the department faculty. Ninety percent of the portfolios will be judged to represent "acceptable" work on first review.

    b. Department faculty will rate the performance of materials at the senior exhibition as superior, satisfactory, average, or in need of remedial work. At least 40% will be judged "superior" and no more than 10% "in need of remedial work."

2. Students will develop competence in the techniques of art and design as well as the abilities to understand and communicate through the language of art and design.

    a. All graduating students will participate in at least four evening critique sessions with the department faculty, prepare and present a draft thesis, participate in a formal thesis course, complete a bound and illustrated thesis book, and participate in an oral review of the thesis work before the department faculty panel. No more than one student per year will be found inadequate in the oral defense of their thesis.

NOT TO BE CONSIDERED AS A MODEL BUT AS AN EXAMPLE

UNDERGRADUATE GENERAL MUSIC (BA)
CIP 50.0903

Intended Educational Outcomes and Means of Assessment/Criteria for Success

1. Students will demonstrate a level of technical skill and musicianship in their major performance area comparable to music majors in similar programs across the nation.
   a. All music majors will perform at least once per semester in a student recital on their major instrument and will pass a "jury examination" each semester.
   b. All students will pass a majority vote of the music faculty on a Sophomore Qualifying Examination in their major performance field. This is done at the end of the sophomore year or after one semester on campus for students who transfer with a two-year degree.

2. All students will demonstrate a knowledge of the theoretical and historical foundations of music.
   a. Students will be asked questions about the style and technical terms of their compositions at each jury examination and will be expected to answer 75% of the questions correctly.
   b. Seniors will take the MFAT in music before qualifying for graduation and score no lower than the 40th percentile.

3. Students in B.S. (K-12 endorsement) will demonstrate skill in the techniques of the major instrumental families and in classroom instruments and sightsinging.
   a. Students will be tested on instrumental fingerings, transpositions, and similar items before being approved for student teaching and they must score at least 75% correct on these tests.
   b. Students will pass (with at least a 75% accuracy rate) a sightsinging test devised and administered by the music department faculty.

4. Students will demonstrate an acceptable level of conducting skills and knowledge of rehearsal techniques.
   a. Ninety-five percent of students will conduct all common beat patterns fluently, display proficiency in cuing, and demonstrate the ability to read vocal and instrumental scores as evaluated by the faculty.
   b. Ninety-five percent of students will also demonstrate mastery of Kodaly hand signals and other techniques appropriate for younger students to a faculty jury.

NOT TO BE CONSIDERED AS A MODEL BUT AS AN EXAMPLE

DENTAL HYGIENE (Associate Degree)
CIP 51.0602

Intended Educational Outcomes and Means of Assessment/Criteria for Success

1. Graduates of the Dental Hygiene program will be able to demonstrate a sound grasp of basic skills and knowledge in the basic sciences, dental sciences, general education, and dental hygiene science.
   a. Eighty-five percent of the Dental Hygiene program graduates taking the Dental Hygiene National Board will pass the examination.

2. Graduates of the Dental Hygiene program will be technically proficient.
   a. At the close of their final term, 100% of the graduates will be able to demonstrate dental hygiene skills with a 77% proficiency rate as evaluated by the Dental Hygiene program faculty in the Capstone course Clinical Dental Hygiene V (DEN 217).
   b. Eighty-five percent of the Dental Hygiene program graduates taking a State Licensure Examination will pass the examination.

3. Graduates of the Dental Hygiene program will be employed in the field.
   a. Fifty percent of the responding graduates of the Dental Hygiene program will report employment in the field on the Graduating Student Survey administered in the first five months after graduation.
   b. Seventy-five percent of the responding (previous year) graduates of the Dental Hygiene program will report employment in the field on the Alumni Survey distributed one year after graduation.

4. Employers of the Dental Hygiene program graduates will rate the technical and academic skills of the employees as average or above.
   a. The Employer Survey conducted each year will rate the graduates as above average on the three course area performance (competency) survey questions. "Above average" is higher than a 3.0 on a 5.0 scale; however, if any of the three survey questions has an individual rating below 3.0, that individual course area performance will be reviewed further.
   b. Seventy-five percent of the respondents to an Employer Survey conducted each year will respond that they would employ future graduates of the Dental Hygiene program.

NOT TO BE CONSIDERED AS A MODEL BUT AS AN EXAMPLE

EMERGENCY MEDICAL SCIENCE (Associate Degree)
CIP 51.0904

Intended Educational Outcomes and Means of Assessment/Criteria for Success

1. Graduates of the Emergency Medical Science program will demonstrate competency in paramedic skills and procedures.

    a. At the close of the final term, 90% of the students will be able to demonstrate with 77% accuracy the ability to perform appropriate paramedic skills and procedures and to utilize the paramedic skills to deliver safe patient care as evaluated by the EMS program faculty in the Capstone course Field Internship III (EMS 241).

    b. Ninety percent of the EMS program graduates will pass the State Office of EMS Paramedic Certifying Examination.

2. Graduates of the EMS program will be employed in the field.

    a. Seventy percent of the responding graduates will report employment in the field on the Graduating Student Survey administered five months after graduation.

    b. Ninety percent of the responding (previous year) graduates will report employment in the field on the Alumni Survey administered one year after graduation.

3. Employers of the EMS program graduates will rate the technical and academic skills as average or above.

    a. The Employer Survey conducted each year will rate the graduates as above average on the three course area performance (competency) survey questions. "Above average" is higher than a 3.0 on a 5.0 scale; however, if any of the three survey questions has an individual rating below 3.0, that individual course area performance will be reviewed further.

    b. Eighty percent of the respondents to the Employer Survey conducted each year will respond that they would employ future graduates of the EMS program.

NOT TO BE CONSIDERED AS A MODEL BUT AS AN EXAMPLE

MEDICAL LABORATORY TECHNOLOGY (Associate Degree)
CIP 51.1004

Intended Educational Outcomes and Means of Assessment/Criteria for Success

1. Graduates of the Medical Laboratory Technology program will be technically proficient in clinical laboratory determinations.
    a. At the close of their final term, 90% of the students will be at the career entry level in the collection, processing, and performance of analytical tests on body fluids, cells, and products, within predetermined limits as evaluated by the laboratory's clinical supervisors and MLT program faculty in the Capstone course Clinical Practice (MLA 222).
    b. Eighty percent of the Medical Laboratory Technology program graduates will pass the American Society of Clinical Pathologists Board of Registry MLT Certification Examination.

2. Graduates of the Medical Laboratory Technology program will be employed in the field.
    a. Sixty percent of the responding graduates of the Medical Laboratory Technology program seeking employment will report employment in the field on the Alumni Survey distributed one year after graduation.
    b. Eighty percent of the responding (previous year) graduates will rate the technical and academic skills of the employees as above average.

3. Employers of the Medical Laboratory Technology program graduates will rate the technical and academic skills of the employees as above average.
    a. The Employer Survey conducted each year will rate the graduates as above average on the three course area performance (competency) survey questions. "Above average" is higher than a 3.0 on a 5.0 scale; however; if any of the three survey questions has an individual rating below 3.0, that individual course area performance will be reviewed further.
    b. Sixty percent of the respondents to an Employer Survey conducted each year will respond that they would employ future graduates of the Medical Laboratory Technology program.

NOT TO BE CONSIDERED AS A MODEL BUT AS AN EXAMPLE

NURSING (Associate Degree)
CIP 51.1601

Intended Educational Outcomes and Means of Assessment/Criteria for Success

1. Graduates will be successfully employed in health care.
   a. Upon program completion, 75% of the institution's graduates will have a commitment for employment as denoted by respondents to the Graduating Student Survey.
   b. Of those who respond to the one year Alumni Follow-up Survey, 95% of those who desired employment in health care will be employed.

2. Graduates will be academically prepared for the NCLEX-RN examination.
   a. Results from the Mosby RN Assess Test will evidence preparedness for the success on the licensure examination with at least 90% of the institution's graduates scoring at or above the national average.

3. Graduates will be at least minimally competent to practice nursing within the state.
   a. Ninety percent of the graduates will initially be successful in their efforts to pass the NCLEX-RN.
   b. Ninety-five percent of the graduates will be successful in passing the NCLEX-RN examination in two attempts.

4. Graduates will be readily assimilated into their chosen health care fields.
   a. Ninety percent of the employers contacted by the annual Employer Survey will respond in a positive way about the institution's graduates that they employ.

NOT TO BE CONSIDERED AS A MODEL BUT AS AN EXAMPLE

NURSING (Associate Degree)
CIP 51.1601

Intended Educational Outcomes and Means of Assessment/Criteria for Success

1. Graduates of the Associate Degree in Nursing will demonstrate proficiency in nursing skills and procedures and will use the nursing process in the delivery of safe patient care.
   a. At the close of the final term, 90% of the students will be able to demonstrate with 77% or higher accuracy, the ability to perform appropriate nursing skills, procedures, and care as evaluated by the ADN program faculty in the Capstone course in Nursing of Adults in Health and Illness III (NUR 208).
   b. Ninety percent of the Associate Degree Nursing program graduates (first-time writers) will pass the NCLEX-RN examination.

2. Graduates of the Associate Degree Nursing program will demonstrate professional behaviors appropriate to the practice of nursing.
   a. At the close of their final term, 90% of the students will demonstrate with 77% or higher accuracy, behaviors appropriate to the practice of nursing as evaluated by the ADN program faculty in the Capstone course Nursing of Adults in Health and Illness III (NUR 208).

3. Graduates of the ADN program will be employed in the field.
   a. Fifty percent of the responding graduates will report employment in the field on the Graduate Student Survey administered five months after graduation.
   b. Ninety percent of the responding (previous year) graduates will report employment in the field on the Alumni Survey administered one year after graduation.

4. Employers of the ADN program graduates will rate the technical and academic skills of the employees as above average.
   a. The Employer Survey conducted each year will rate the graduates as above average on the three course area performance (competency) survey questions. "Above average" is higher than a 3.0 on a 5.0 scale; however, if any of the three survey questions has an individual rating below 3.0, that individual course area performance will be reviewed further.
   b. Eighty percent of the respondents to the Employer Survey conducted each year will respond that they would employ future graduates of the ADN program.

NOT TO BE CONSIDERED AS A MODEL BUT AS AN EXAMPLE

UNDERGRADUATE BUSINESS AND ECONOMICS (BBA)

CIP 52.0101
Intended Educational Outcomes and Means of Assessment/Criteria for Success

1. Students understand the basic principles of business and economics.
    a. Students average at least in the second quartile of the Major Field Achievement Test in business produced by the Educational Testing Service. This test is taken in the students' final semester.

2. Students will be employed in a business related field.
    a. Eighty-five percent of graduating seniors, actively seeking employment, will be employed in an entry level position within six months of graduation as indicated by the data gathered through the Career Development and Placement Center.
    b. Eighty percent of the graduating seniors completing the attitudinal survey administered by the Career Development and Placement Center will indicate "agree" or "strongly agree" with the statement: "In the field of business, I feel as well prepared as the majority of individuals nationwide who have completed a similar degree during the past year."

3. Students graduating with a degree in business will be able to demonstrate acceptable communicative skills.
    a. Students' average score will be 70% or greater on a departmentally developed communications examination to be administered as a culminating exercise in the BE 331 class (i.e., Business Communications).

NOT TO BE CONSIDERED AS A MODEL BUT AS AN EXAMPLE

OFFICE TECHNOLOGIES (Associate Degree)

CIP 52.0101
Intended Educational Outcomes and Means of Assessment/Criteria for Success

1. Graduates of the Office Technologies program will be employed in the field.
   a. Fifty percent of the responding graduates of the Office Technologies program will report employment in the field on the Graduating Student Survey administered at the time of program completion.
   b. Seventy percent of the responding (previous year) graduates of the Office Technologies program will report employment in the field on the Alumni Survey distributed one year after graduation.

2. Graduates of the Office Technologies program will be technically proficient.
   a. At the close of their final term, 90% of the graduates will be able to pass with 70% accuracy the Office Proficiency Assessment and Certification (OPAC) examination within a given period of time on IBM microcomputers using WordPerfect 5.1, dBase IV, and Lotus software as directed by the Office Technologies faculty in the Capstone course Office Simulation (OSC 214).

3. Employers of the Office Technology program graduates will rate the technical and academic skills of the employees as average or above.
   a. The Employer Survey conducted each year will rate the graduates as average or above on the stated Modules of the Office Proficiency Assessment examination. "Average" equals a 3.0 rating on a 5.0 scale; however, if any of the Proficiency Assessment questions has an individual rating below 3.0, that individual course area performance will be reviewed further.
   b. Eighty percent of the respondents to an Employer Survey conducted each year will respond that they would employ future graduates of the Office Technology Program.

NOT TO BE CONSIDERED AS A MODEL BUT AS AN EXAMPLE

UNDERGRADUATE GENERAL BUSINESS (BBABA)
CIP 52.0101

Intended Educational Outcomes and Means of Assessment/Criteria for Success

1. Employers will be satisfied with the institution's preparation of business students.
    a. Seventy-five percent of employers of the institution's alumni will report in a telephone survey satisfaction with their knowledge and skill level.
    b. Seventy-five percent of employers will express satisfaction with the institution's Business Alumni's professional attitude and responsibility as indicated through a telephone survey.

2. Students will express an appreciation and understanding of the importance of lifelong learning.
    a. Seventy-five percent of the institution's Business alumni will respond positively to lifelong learning question on an annual follow-up Alumni Survey.

3. Former students will be able to meet entry level requirements for employment.
    a. Sixty-five percent of new graduates will gain employment or continue their education within six months of leaving the institution.
    b. At least 60% of the employed former students will become employed in a *field related to their program of study* according to data collected from a six-month follow-up survey.

4. Students will be able to apply classroom learning in order to problem solve effectively in the work setting.
    a. Eighty percent of the business students will demonstrate ability to apply knowledge to different settings through classroom projects according to data collected from case studies/group projects in one or more capstone courses where students are asked to identify key factors, prioritize and problem-solve as evaluated by departmental faculty.
    b. Eighty percent of business students will be able to solve a typical computer simulation problem according to data collected from a module of practical application of problem-solving in computer environment developed for a capstone course.

NOT TO BE CONSIDERED AS A MODEL BUT AS AN EXAMPLE

BUSINESS ADMINISTRATION (Associate Degree)
CIP 52.0201

Intended Educational Outcomes and Means of Assessment/Criteria for Success

1. Graduates of the Business Administration program will be technically proficient in management and related skills.
   a. At the close of their final term, 85% of the students will be able to evaluate an organization's major managerial, production, financial, and marketing problems as demonstrated in the Capstone Report based upon a comprehensive case problem assigned by the program faculty in a Capstone course Management and Policy (BUS 235).
   b. At the end of their final term, 85% of the students will be able to recommend courses of action to address the major managerial, production, financial, and marketing problems of an organization as demonstrated in the Capstone Report based upon a comprehensive case problem assigned by the program faculty in the Capstone course Management and Policy (BUS 235).
   c. At the end of their final term, 85% of the students will successfully defend orally the Capstone Report based upon a comprehensive case problem assigned by the program faculty in the Capstone course Management and Policy (BUS 235).

2. Graduates of the Business Administration program will be primarily employed in management and functionally related areas.
   a. Fifty percent of the responding graduates will report employment in management or in the related fields of finance, production, or marketing on the Graduate Student Survey administered within the first five months after graduation.
   b. Seventy-five percent of the responding (previous year) graduates will report employment management or in the related fields of finance, production, or marketing on the Alumni Survey distributed one year after graduation.

3. Employers of graduates of the Business Administration program will rate the academic and technical skills of the employees as "above average."
   a. The respondents to an Employer Satisfaction Survey concerning the Business Administration program graduates will rate the graduates above average, higher than 3.0 on a 5.0 scale in each of the following five performance (competency) areas: Effectiveness of communication; demonstration of math skills; problem analysis and logical decision-making; and, demonstration of good work habits. If any area should receive a score below 3.0, the individual course area and related courses of study will be reviewed further.
   b. Sixty percent of the respondents to an Employer Survey conducted each year will respond that they would employ future Business Administration program graduates.

NOT TO BE CONSIDERED AS A MODEL BUT AS AN EXAMPLE

UNDERGRADUATE ACCOUNTING (Associate Degree)
CIP 52.0301

Intended Educational Outcomes and Means of Assessment/Criteria for Success

1. Graduates of the Accounting program will demonstrate proficiency in the major subject area.
   a. One-hundred percent of the accounting internship students in the Cooperative Education course (COE 211) will be evaluated as above average by their supervising employer.
   b. Eighty percent of the students will score 70% or higher on a departmental proficiency examination administered near the end of the sophomore year in a Capstone course (Advanced Accounting). The examination will be written and evaluated by the Accounting program faculty.

2. Graduates of the Accounting program will be employed in the field.
   a. Fifty percent of the responding graduates of the Accounting program will report employment in the field on the Alumni Survey administered within the first five months after graduation.
   b. Seventy percent of the responding (previous year) graduates of the Accounting program will report employment in the field on the Alumni survey distributed one year after graduation.

3. Employers of the Accounting program graduates will rate the technical and academic skills of the employees as above average.
   a. The Employer Survey conducted each year will rate the graduates as above average on the three- course area performance (competency) survey questions. "Above average" is higher than a 3.0 on a 5.0 scale; however, if any of the three survey questions has an individual rating below 3.0, that individual course area performance will be reviewed further.
   b. Ninety percent of the respondents to an Employer Survey will respond that they would employ future graduates of the Accounting program if a position were available.

NOT TO BE CONSIDERED AS A MODEL BUT AS AN EXAMPLE

UNDERGRADUATE ACCOUNTING (B ACCY)
CIP 52.0301

Intended Educational Outcomes and Means of Assessment/Criteria for Success

1. Students will gain knowledge and understanding of the current theory and practice of accounting, including a conceptual framework upon which to build accounting principles and codes of ethics.
    a. At least 50% of students will score above the 50th percentile on the ETS Business Core Examination for business.
    b. Graduates who take the CPA examination will have a pass rate that equals or exceeds the state average results on the examination.
    c. On the Graduating Senior Questionnaire, 75% of the graduating seniors from the accounting program will rank the quality of education received at least adequate to pursue career objectives.

2. Students will have the skills to gain entry-level employment in an accounting or accounting-related field, or gain acceptance into graduate studies.
    a. At least 50% of respondents to the Alumni Survey will report they have achieved employment in positions associated with their degree program or been accepted into graduate school within one year of graduation.
    b. Of respondents to the Alumni Survey, 80% eligible for salary increases or promotions in rank have achieved these advances within five years of graduation.

NOT TO BE CONSIDERED AS A MODEL BUT AS AN EXAMPLE

BUSINESS COMPUTER PROGRAMMING (Associate Degree)
CIP 52.1202

Intended Educational Outcomes and Means of Assessment/Criteria for Success

1. Graduates of the Business Computer Programming program will be employed in programming and related fields.
    a. Fifty percent of the responding graduates of the Business Computer Programming program will report employment in programming and related fields within five months of graduation.
    b. Eighty percent of the responding (previous year) graduates of the Business Computer Programming program will report employment in the field on the Alumni Survey distributed one year after graduation.

2. Graduates of the Business Computer Programming program will be technically proficient.
    a. At the close of their final term, 80% of the graduates will be able to design, code, and test RPG programs using RPGII, RPG III, and RPG400 programming techniques within a given period of time as evaluated by the Business Computer Programming faculty in the Capstone course Advanced Report Program Generator (CSC 225).

3. Employers of graduates of the Business Computer Programming program will rate the academic and technical skills of the employees as "above average".
    a. The Employer Survey conducted each year will rate the graduates as above average on the three course area performance (competency) survey questions. "Above average" is higher than a 3.0 on a 5.0 rating scale; however, if any of the three survey questions has an individual rating below 3.0, that individual course area performance will be reviewed further.
    b. Sixty percent of the respondents to an Employer Survey conducted each year will respond that they would employ future Business Computer Programming Graduates.

NOT TO BE CONSIDERED AS A MODEL BUT AS AN EXAMPLE

MANUFACTURING AND BUSINESS SYSTEMS (BBA/BA)
CIP 52.9999

Intended Educational Outcomes and Means of Assessment/Criteria for Success

1. Graduates of division programs will be readily employed in positions both generally and within their specific fields of training.
    a. Eighty-five percent of graduates will be employed or in specialized training programs within six months of graduation according to the Alumni Survey of new graduates conducted annually six months after each graduation period.

2. Students will possess the critical thinking and problem-solving skills necessary to be versatile and productive workers and to adapt to changes in the labor market.
    a. Seventy percent of graduates will report on a six-month follow-up survey of graduates that they felt their training improved their critical thinking and problem-solving skills.
    b. Seventy percent of employers will be satisfied with the level of critical thinking and problem-solving demonstrated by employed graduates according to data collected on the follow-up survey to employers of former students and an Industry Contact Log, which questions in detail the competency of graduates.

3. Students will be satisfied with the quality of the education process provided within the division.
    a. Eighty percent of graduates will rate their courses positively according to data collected from the six-month follow-up survey of graduates.
    b. Seventy percent of graduates indicate they would recommend the division to relatives interested in technical training according to data collected from the six-month follow-up survey of graduates.

4. Graduates of divisional programs will understand the value of continuing education in maintaining and upgrading technical skills.
    a. Fifty percent of graduates report they will enroll in on-going education after they are employed according to data collected from the six-month follow-up survey of graduates.

NOT TO BE CONSIDERED AS A MODEL BUT AS AN EXAMPLE

GRADUATE MANAGEMENT (MS)CIP 52.9999

Intended Educational Outcomes and Means of Assessment/Criteria for Success

1. Students will gain the knowledge and intellectual maturity to perform at the graduate level with the application of the following skills: analysis, explanation, recommendation, and synthesizing of old and new skills.

    a. All students will complete with at least 75% a comprehensive final examination, which will require each student to analyze, explain, question, consider, and synthesize old and new knowledge and skill gained from the entire curriculum.

    b. All students must submit a comprehensive portfolio of all work completed while a student in the program. This includes all acceptance letters and correspondence with faculty and administrators. The portfolios will be subject to review by the department faculty and determined to be acceptable or not acceptable according to consensus of the student's quality and quantity of work. Ninety-five percent will be judged acceptable.

    c. Of those respondents on the Student Exit Assessment Survey, at least 75% of the students will rank the quality of education received at least adequate to enhance their career objectives.

2. Students will develop the skills necessary to gain employment in the field.

    a. Of those respondents on the Alumni Survey, 50% will have achieved employment positions or raises/promotions that are connected with their degree program one year beyond graduation.

    b. Of those respondents on the Alumni Survey, 80% who were eligible for salary increases or promotions have achieved these advances within five years of graduation.

NOT TO BE CONSIDERED AS A MODEL BUT AS AN EXAMPLE

ADMINISTRATIVE DEPARTMENT
Bookstore and Cashiering Department

Administrative Objectives and Means of Assessment/Criteria for Success

1. The bookstore will provide students and faculty with the required textbooks and supplies on a timely basis.
   a. Seventy percent of the students responding to the Graduating Student Survey will "agree" or "strongly agree" with the statement "I am well satisfied with the service provided by the bookstore."
   b. Eighty percent of the faculty responding to an annual survey will respond either "agree" or "strongly agree" with the statement "The bookstore's performance in ordering textbooks and supplies meets my expectations."

2. Bookstore employees provide accurate information and training regarding policies and procedures for the campus community.
   a. Eighty percent of the faculty responding to an annual survey will indicate satisfaction with the information and training provided by the bookstore concerning the ordering of textbooks and supplies.
   b. Ninety percent of textbook orders will be received by the bookstore on or before the due date.

3. The bookstore will provide a friendly and helpful environment for the campus community.
   a. Results from a four joint faculty-student focus groups and selected by the Counseling Center and interviewed quarterly, will describe the service provided by bookstore employees as friendly and helpful.
   b. The number of complaints received by the manager of the bookstore regarding service from bookstore employees will not exceed two per year.

NOT TO BE CONSIDERED AS A MODEL BUT AS AN EXAMPLE

ADMINISTRATIVE DEPARTMENT
Campus Security and Safety

Administrative Objectives and Means of Assessment/Criteria for Success

1. The campus will be a safe and secure environment for employees and students.
    a. No more than five violent crimes will be reported annually.
    b. Ninety percent of the graduates will "agree" or "strongly agree" with the statement on the Graduating Student Survey, "I feel comfortable and safe while attending classes and living on the campus."

2. The campus community (students, faculty, administrators, and staff) understand and use crime prevention strategies.
    a. Sixty percent of a randomly drawn sample of campus employees will be able to identify two crime prevention strategies applicable to their area.
    b. The number of thefts which are described in crime reports as "easily preventable by appropriate crime prevention strategies" will not exceed 15 on the campus each fiscal year.

3. The physical environment on the campus will be consistently improved from the standpoint of safety.
    a. The quarterly physical safety inspections will reveal no increase in the number of deficiencies noted.
    b. The number of OSHA safety violations will not exceed three in any one fiscal year.

NOT TO BE CONSIDERED AS A MODEL BUT AS AN EXAMPLE

ADMINISTRATIVE DEPARTMENT
Admissions Office

Administrative Objectives and Means of Assessment/Criteria for Success

1. The proportion of the entering freshman class with SAT averages between 1325 and 1350 will be increased by focusing merit scholarship offers in this range.
    a. Review of the entering freshman class profile provided by the Office of Institutional Research each fall semester will indicate an increase in the proportion of entering students with SAT scores in the 1325-1350 range each year.
    b. Analysis of the merit scholarship offers made by the university each year to entering freshmen will indicate at least twice the proportion of offers to students in 1325-1350 SAT range as in other 25-point SAT ranges.

2. Applicants for admission with an SAT score less than 1100 will not be eligible for financial aid from university funds.
    a. Analysis of the Financial Aid Office annual report will not indicate offers of university-funded financial aid to entering students with an SAT score of less than 1100.

3. The proportion of each entering freshman class composed of National Merit finalists will increase each year.
    a. Review of the entering freshman class profile each year will indicate a continued increase in the number of National Merit finalists each year as well as the proportion that they comprise of Our University's entering freshman class.

NOT TO BE CONSIDERED AS A MODEL BUT AS AN EXAMPLE

ADMINISTRATIVE DEPARTMENT
Sponsored Research

Administrative Objectives and Means of Assessment/Criteria for Success

1. The majority of the research proposals for external funding forwarded through the Office of the Associate Vice Chancellor for Research and Dean of the Graduate School will be directly linked to local or regional (within the state) industries.

   a. Each proposal for externally funded research will be accompanied by a one-page transmittal sheet explaining if and how the proposal relates to a local or regional industry. At the end of the fiscal year, the transmittal sheets will be reviewed, and 50% or more will be judged as directly linked to local or regional industries by the Our University Research Board.

2. The proportion of those proposals for external funding that are directly linked to local or regional industries and are funded will substantially exceed all other such proposals submitted.

   a. Following annual identification of those research grant proposals directly linked with local or regional industries, analysis of actual funding will reveal that twice the proportion of such proposals, compared to all proposals submitted, receive funding.

3. Local industries will be aware of Our University's efforts to seek funding in research areas related to their fields.

   a. Of those proposals for external funding identified as being directly linked with local or regional industries, half or more will include a letter of support, endorsement, or cooperation from the appropriate local or regional industry.

   b. Half of those CEOs of major local industries responding to a letter from Our University's CEO (25% sample each year) will be able to identify research performed by Our University that has been directly related to their products.

NOT TO BE CONSIDERED AS A MODEL BUT AS AN EXAMPLE

ADMINISTRATIVE DEPARTMENT
Physical Plant

Administrative Objectives and Means of Assessment/Criteria for Success

1. The majority of existing classroom facilities will be renovated during the next 5 years.
   a. Review of the university's inventory of general purpose classrooms compared to its list of renovation projects completed each year will indicate that at least 10% of the classrooms have been renovated each year.
   b. Each year the proportion of respondents to the Graduating Student Questionnaire indicating that they "agree" or "strongly agree" with the statement "classroom facilities were conducive to learning" will increase.

2. Improved energy management activities will result in savings for the university.
   a. Each year more square feet of space at the university will be controlled by automated energy management systems.
   b. Utility expenditures per square foot in existing structures (excluding the impact of rate increases and structural changes) will decline each year.

3. The level of safety from food poisoning for all faculty, staff, and students eating at Our University will substantially exceed state standards.
   a. The number of cases of food poisoning (possibly resulting from the student dining halls) reported to the Student Health Center will not exceed two per year.
   b. State Health Department inspections of campus food-service facilities will indicate an average score at least 10 points (on a scale of 100) above the average for commercial establishments in the city.

NOT TO BE CONSIDERED AS A MODEL BUT AS AN EXAMPLE

ADMINISTRATIVE DEPARTMENT
Computer Center

Administrative Objectives and Means of Assessment/Criteria for Success

1. Make mainframe and microcomputer support readily accessible on the campus.
   a. Either a terminal to the mainframe or a microcomputer will be found in each classroom building and dormitory on the campus.
   b. All faculty requesting computer access will have been provided either a terminal to the mainframe or a microcomputer.
   c. The campus microcomputer laboratory will be open between 8:00 A.M. and 12:00 P.M., 7 days per week during the fall and spring semesters.

2. Support integration of computer-assisted instructions (CAI) into classes.
   a. Current CAI software will be available in the computer center.
   b. Five percent of the faculty will have attended a CAI workshop presented by the Our University Computer Center each year.

3. Provide a wide variety of elementary programming languages and user-friendly software packages.
   a. Access through either the mainframe or microcomputer laboratory to Pascal, Basic, APL, and/or PLI will be provided to students in each introductory programming class.
   b. Current word-processing and spread-sheet packages will be readily available to students and faculty through the mainframe, microcomputer laboratory, or computer terminals/facilities in each dormitory and faculty office.

NOT TO BE CONSIDERED AS A MODEL BUT AS AN EXAMPLE

ACCOUNTING DEPARTMENT
Magnolia State University

Administrative Objectives and Means of Assessment/Criteria for Success

1. Maintain financial systems in accordance with commonly accepted accounting practices.
   a. The University will receive an unqualified financial audit report each year.
   b. Each year a portion of the institution's accounting function will be reviewed for conformance with NACUBO procedures by a representative of the University's Accounting Department and 90% of the recommendations contained in the report of each review will be implemented within one year thereafter.

2. Provide timely, complete, and understood reports by object of expenditure concerning expenditures and remaining balances to departments.
   a. Monthly reports of expenditures and remaining balances by object of expenditure will be found to have been produced within the first three working days of the past twelve months.
   b. Ninety percent of those completing a two-hour workshop for department heads/chairs each year will "agree" or "strongly agree" with the statement "I understand and feel comfortable with the monthly financial statement" contained on a survey of participants conducted at the end of the workshop.

. Process vendor statements for services promptly.
   a. Vendor statements for services will be "date stamped" upon their arrival and again as they are paid. A random sample of ten such statements monthly will reveal no more than average of five working days between receipt and payment.
   b. Each year a random sample of vendors will be drawn to receive a brief questionnaire regarding their business relationship with the University. Seventy-five percent of the respondents to that questionnaire will "agree" or "strongly agree" with the statement that "Magnolia State University processes its statements for payment as fast or faster than others with whom I do business."

NOT TO BE CONSIDERED AS A MODEL BUT AS AN EXAMPLE

ADMINISTRATIVE DEPARTMENT
Library Periodicals

Administrative Objectives and Means of Assessment/Criteria for Success

1. Conduct a careful analysis of existing periodical subscriptions linking each to the institution's: General Education, Liberal Arts and Sciences, or Graduate Programs.

    a. Within the first six months, a listing of each of the Library's then current periodical subscriptions and the specific departments/programs which they support will have been published.

2. Poll the university's academic departments to ascertain the adequacy of current periodical subscriptions and to obtain a rank ordering of periodicals in each field in accordance with their importance to the academic programs of Our University. Where appropriate, departments should relate specific periodicals to the accomplishment of expected educational results.

    a. Within the first nine months, a poll of the university's academic departments will have resulted in a rank ordering of available periodicals (both currently subscribed to and other) in accordance with their importance to the academic programs at Our University.

    b. Where possible, individual periodical subscriptions will be found to have been linked to specific statements of expected educational results.

3. 3.Revise the Library's periodical subscription policies and expenditures in accordance with the priorities identified by the academic departments as reviewed by the Chief Academic Officer.

a. At the close of the first year, a revised list of periodical subscriptions, resulting from the department's rankings, recommended by the Director of the Library, and approved by the Chief Academic Officer will have been found to be established.

NOT TO BE CONSIDERED AS A MODEL BUT AS AN EXAMPLE

APPENDIX C—Examples of Institutional Statements of Purpose or Mission from Mt. Hood Community College / University of Montevallo / University of Mississippi

MISSION STATEMENT — It is the mission of Mt. Hood Community College to fulfill the following commitments: MHCC shall provide access to technological education and training, a wide variety of transfer programs, developmental education and comprehensive community services. MHCC shall strive to help students discover their own potential, respect the uniqueness of others, and develop ethical values. MHCC shall provide enthusiastic and dedicated instruction to students of diverse cultural and economic backgrounds. MHCC shall collaborate with agencies, organizations and businesses to best serve students and the community and to be responsive to the realities and demands of a changing world. As part of the global community, MHCC shall cultivate international understanding through education and partnerships. MHCC shall be a community of caring individuals who strive for excellence in all facets of college life.

* * * * * * * * * * * *

THE MISSION — The mission of the University of Montevallo, unique in higher education in Alabama, is to provide to students from throughout the State an affordable, geographically accessible, "small college" public higher educational experience of high quality with a strong emphasis on undergraduate liberal studies and with professional programs supported by a broad base of arts and sciences, designed for their intellectual and personal growth in the pursuit of meaningful employment and responsible, informed citizenship.

- The University shall continue to maintain its reputation as a public university of high quality.
- Quality teaching is and shall continue to be the preeminent activity of the University.
- The University shall remain predominantly an undergraduate university.
- The University shall continue to offer and to support graduate programs in selected areas.
- The University shall develop and utilize and on-going strategic planning process.
- The University shall maintain student enrollment consistent with its quality programs, its traditionally close student-faculty relationships, and effective use of resources.
- The University shall maintain a student body, faculty and staff reflecting the racial, cultural and ethnic diversity of contemporary society.
- The University shall endeavor to keep tuition affordable and slightly above the state average tuition of public universities.
- The University shall endeavor to prepare its students for their chosen occupations.
- The University shall support programs that facilitate the total development of each student and his or her total being: physical, emotional, social, and spiritual as well as intellectual.
- Research shall be an important function of the University.
- The University shall maintain a creative and continuously evolving faculty and staff development program.

- The various cultural and scholarly activities of the University, especially the visual and performing arts, shall be promoted and utilized by members of the University community in order to make the campus as intellectually and culturally exciting as possible.
- The University shall maintain its commitment to a competitive program in selected intercollegiate athletics for both men and women, consistent with the other educational goals of the University.
- The University shall emphasize the international dimensions of its curricula and encourage understanding of global concerns through such resources as its international students, its study-abroad programs and its foreign language programs.
- The University shall provide opportunities for the continuing education of persons beyond the traditional college-age group.
- University governance shall involve the University community in institutional decision-making through appropriate mechanisms and thereby maintain the vitality of collegiality at UM.
- The University shall engage in public service programs with business, industry and labor, public and private schools, governmental agencies and the general public.
- The University shall seek increased funding and other institutional support by communicating the role of the University to the general public; to local, state and federal government agencies; to alumni and friends of the University; and to those private individuals, agencies, corporations, foundations and institutions willing to provide assistance.
- The University shall explore, and where appropriate, implement cooperative efforts with neighboring educational institutions.
- The University shall develop mutually beneficial relationships with junior and community colleges.
- The University shall provide leadership in higher education in Alabama.

* * * * * * * * * * * *

STATEMENT OF ACADEMIC FOCUS FOR THE 1990s
The University of Mississippi Oxford Campus

The University of Mississippi is the oldest public institution of higher learning in the state. Its fundamental purpose is the creation and dissemination of knowledge. Throughout its long history the University has enhanced the educational, economic, and cultural foundations of the state, region, and nation. As a comprehensive, doctoral-degree granting institution, the University offers a board range of undergraduate and graduate programs as well as opportunities for continuing study.

While recognizing that its primary role is to serve the state of Mississippi, the University educates students to assume leadership roles in both the state and nation through its nationally recognized programs of undergraduate, graduate, and professional study. Its teaching, research, and service missions are characterized by equal access and equal opportunity to all who qualify. Within this framework, the University will focus its resources on

Science and Humanities. The University will continue its traditional leadership in the Liberal Arts by emphasizing existing programs of strength in the sciences and humanities and programs that sustain nationally important centers of research and service.

Health. The University will continue to provide the professional education of those who deliver and administer human health services and those who perform research aimed at improving the efficiency, effectiveness, quality, and availability of health care.

Legal Education. The University will continue to provide the initial and continuing professional education of those who formulate, interpret, and practice law.

Business Development and Economic Growth. The University recognizes that economic growth and business development are essential to the future of Mississippi in the increasingly integrated world economy. The University will enhance the development of entrepreneurial, financial, managerial, and information-processing activities through existing pre-professional, professional, and public service programs.

Communication and Related Technologies. The University recognizes that communication technology will be one of the most important growth areas of the next century. The University will continue developing programs that sustain the communication and telecommunication industries. This area of focus crosses disciplinary boundaries and incorporates expertise from specialties such as foreign languages, journalism, engineering, computing, and distance learning.

UNIVERSITY OF MISSISSIPPI OXFORD CAMPUS
Goals for the 1990s

- The University will improve undergraduate education, especially in lower-division courses.
- The University will concentrate graduate education and research in areas of strength consistent with the Focus Areas.
- The University will increase employee compensation to the Southern University Group (SUG) average in order to attract and retain a highly qualified faculty and staff.
- The University will improve educational support services (library, computer networking, database availability, instructional support, etc.) to increase access to information and communication on the campus.
- The University will disseminate its expertise and knowledge to non-academic communities throughout the state of Mississippi and the Midsouth region.
- The University will continue to develop leadership and to instill in its students a sense of justice, moral courage, and tolerance for the views of others.
- The University will maintain efficient and effective administrative services to support the University's instructional, research, and public service programs.
- The University will increase faculty and staff involvement in University planning.
- The University will increase its efforts to secure support from federal, state, and private sources.

APPENDIX D—Extract from *1992-93 Desktop Audit: Program and Support Services Review*, Coastal Carolina Community College[1]

The Desktop Audit is an **annual assessment** of all instructional programs which promotes continued quality at Coastal Carolina Community College. The Desktop Audit annually facilitates institutional planning, program maintenance, program improvement, and program accountability. The Desktop Audit is designed to provide the date necessary for decision making while causing minimum interruption of current operations. The process is planned to achieve the following goals:

1. Provide *continual (broad-based) feedback* to and from instructors on the quantitative and qualitative assessment measurements using "benchmarks" to enhance their program planning and decision-making effort.

2. *Meet the requirements* for program review established by the Department of Community Colleges (22 of the 36 Critical Success Factors), program accountability of the North Carolina State Legislature, and program assessment requirements established by SACS.

3. Organize internally collected data to allow *trend analyses* (five-year) in quantitative and qualitative measurements for use in strategic planning.

4. Provide a data base for *linking budget* development with the planning process.

5. Identify instruction programs *(early warning)* in need of expansion or modification before a trend becomes critical.

6. Identify instructional programs where some *action* is necessary for a program to meet its goals. The action could be *expansion, modification, consolidation, reduction,* or *discontinuation.* When program discontinuation appears to be the option, faculty are retrained at college expense and transferred into a growing curriculum.

Data on costs, enrollment, job [placement, staffing, and the labor market are gathered and analyzed for the vocational/technical programs. In the College Transfer Division, the assessment examines unit costs, enrollment, completions, number of transfers, and the grade point averages of those who transfer to senior institutions.

For the programs in which the Desktop Audit indicates a need for additional review, a more detailed study is performed before deciding to take action concerning a program. The program advisory committees provide an excellent resource for the additional program review. The Vice President for Instruction, deans and instructors, with input from the Advisory Committees, can use the Desktop Audit to provide the data needed for additional review and recommendations for expansion, modification, consolidation, reduction, or discontinuation. The effectiveness and decision-making process of the College is improved through the broad-based involvement and information in the Desktop Audit.

---

[1] Including attachments from *1992-93 Program Outcomes Booklet*

COASTAL CAROLINA COMMUNITY COLLEGE
PROGRAM AND SERVICES ASSESSMENT TIMETABLE

May -July
Planning Office
sends out previous year's 1) Institutional Goals
and 2) Program Outcomes to VP's and faculty/staff for
update and review. Vice Presidents and Deans confer
with faculty/staff. The revised Institutional Goals
and Program Outcomes are returned to the Planning Office

July
Planning Office
begins data collection from Instruction,
Student Services, Business Services for
yearly Desktop Audit on all programs
and services

August
Executive Vice President analyzes data, updates the Desktop
Audit and writes <u>alerts</u> based on benchmarks.
Faculty and staff provide input on measures and benchmarks.

September - October
1) Preliminary Desktop Audit written, 2) Revised Institutional
Goals, and 3) Revised Program Outcomes mailed to DCC
by September. Copy and present to the President,
Vice Presidents, Deans, faculty/staff. Revisions made.
Strategic Planning session to gain consensus on short- and long-term
goals, set priorities, and establish a resource plan.

October - December
Programs/services planning and decisions to improve instruction
or service are made by faculty/staff. Planning Office surveys
and updates Desktop Audit on graduate placement and employer
satisfaction (**October-November**). Periodic updates are provided
to faculty/staff for their review, modification and input. Tentative,
final Desktop Audit is presented to each faculty department
or support service staff (**November-December**). Final Desktop Audit
printed and distributed to all faculty and appropriate staff (**January**)

March
President and Vice
Presidents make
management decisions on
DTA program
Alert responses, resource
allocation, and direction

(Closes the Loop)

Programs and services needing further review	*Programs and services **not** needing further review*
September - February Vice Presidents, Deans, faculty present DTA to program Advisory Committee or appropriate group. Alerts from DTA must be addressed and a response written (any time **between September and February**).	**September - February** Vice Presidents, Deans, faculty present DTA to Program Advisory Committee or appropriate group. Program or services refinement and modifications only as needed (any time **between September and March**). No report needed, but the Advisory Committee minutes need to address the Desktop Audit and Program Outcomes.

(Closes the Loop)   **(Closes the Loop)**

OCCUPATIONAL EDUCATION DESKTOP AUDIT

CODE: T176	PROGRAM: AUTOMOTIVE TECHNOLOGY
	REVIEW: 1992-93 December 1993

I.   Description/Purpose

Automotive Mechanics was one of the first five programs begun by the Onslow County Industrial Education Center on the Highway 17 campus in 1965.

The Automotive Mechanics (2yr.) curriculum was upgraded to an Automotive Service Technology (T156) associate degree program (1989-90) and changed again to Automotive Technology (T176) in 1990-91 which provides a training program for developing the basic knowledge and skills needed to inspect, diagnose, repair and adjust automotive vehicles.

II.   Staffing (Full & Part-time) (SACS 4.4.2)

This program is staffed by two full-time faculty and 0.04 part-time (units) faculty who meet SACS criteria.

III.   Analysis Of Desktop Audit Data (Data Attached)
Quantitative Measurements (SACS 4.1)

A.   **Operating (Dept.) Cost:** The unit cost has remained in the third quartile (upper 50%) for the last four years due to a program change from a vocational to a technical program which reduced the number of shop hours taught and increased unit cost.

B.   **Equipment (Dept.) Expenditures:** $1,019 was spent on equipment.

C.   **Enrollment (1 year old Data):** The 1992-93 day enrollment increased 50% over the 1991-92 enrollment. Instructional department 3-quarter FTE decreased slightly due to the hospitalization of an instructor and night classes had to be canceled because of the illness.
Plus the current Fall/winter FTE and Headcount provided at the Departmental final review meeting.

D.   **Demographics (1 year old Data) (DCC-IV-a, c):** The annual enrollment (1992-93) consisted of 25 males and no females, the majority being white male students in their twenties. Of the overall enrollment, 3 were 1991-92 high school graduates. Two of the high school students were from Jacksonville and 1 was from Swansboro.

E.   **Carl Perkins-Federal Vocational Funds Eligibility** (2 year old Demographic Data): Automotive Technology does not qualify to receive Carl Perkins Federal Vocational funds in 1993-94. The Special Population qualifications are listed on page 8.

(bracket label at left: Future Planning)

Qualitative Measurements (SACS 4.1)

F.   **Graduation Rate (DCC-I-f); State Law S 27 (1993)):** The graduation rate is (Degree-80%, 8 students); (Certificate-17%, 2 students). Total combined graduation rate is 45% compared to the state average of 11%. Internally evaluated (benchmarked) the Coastal degree graduation rate is excellent.

G.   **Job Placement (SACS 3.1; DCC-V-d):** The related employment rate (benchmark) is excellent (86%). The One-Year Follow-up (Alumni Survey) of 91-92 graduates showed that 83% found related employment which is (internal benchmark) excellent.

H.   **Employer Survey Results (SACS 3.1; DCC-V-c; State Law S 27 (1993)):** The graduates working within the field of Automotive Technology were rated average to above average by their employers. 100% of the employers responded that they would hire future graduates.

I.   **Certification/Licensure (DCC-I-e):** The percent passing rate has been excellent (100%) for five years.

J.   **Advisory Committee (SACS 6.1.3):** The Advisory Committee met in 1992-93 (benchmark) and minutes were kept.

K.   **Literacy (GED/AHS) Students Entering Curriculum Programs (DCC-I-b)** In 1992-93, one student entered.

L.   **Program/Student Outcomes at Program Completion (SACS 3.1, 4.1.4):** The student outcome measures were revised in the 1992/93 academic year.   The outcome measures are used to inform students prior to entering college and during the program via handouts. *See "1992-93 Program Outcomes" booklet.*

Extract from *1992-93 Program Outcomes booklet*

Automotive Technology

1992-93

Program/Student Outcomes/Objectives at Program Completion (SACS 3.1,4.1.1):

1. Graduates of the Automotive Technology program will be technically proficient in trouble

92-93 DTA shooting and repairing automotive mechanical problems

Postponed until Spring 1994
    1a. At the close of their final term, 90% of the students will be able to troubleshoot and repair automotive mechanical problems on live test cars in an assigned given period of time as directed by and to the quality control and evaluation of the Automotive Technology program faculty in the Capstone course - Automotive Service Operations (AUT 225)

100% 1b. 80% of the Automotive Technology graduates who attempt the voluntary National Automotive exams (ASE), will pass the ASE exam.
    Note: The ASE exam is an eight part exam. Each part is indepenent of the other. A test taker usually takes one or two exams a year.

2. Graduates of the Automotive Technology Program will be technically proficient in diagnosing and estimating automotive mechanical repairs

Postponed until 1994
    2a. At the close of their final term, 90% of the students will be able to diagnose and estimate the cost of repairs needed on an automobile as assigned within a given period of time as directed by and to the quality control and evaluation of the Automotive Technology program faculty in the Capstone course - Automotive Service Operations (AUT 225)

3. Graduates of the Automotive Technology program will be employed in the field.

100% 3a. 60% of the responding graduates of the Automotive Technology program will report employment in the field on the Graduating Student Survey administered within the first five months after graduation.

83% 3b. 80% of the responding (previous year) graduates of the Automotive Technology program will report employment in the field on the Alumni Survey.

4. Employers of the Automotive Technology program graduates will rate the technical and academic skills of the employees as above average.

(1) 4.33
(2) 4.33
(3) 3.33
    4a. The Employer Survey conducted each year will rate the graduates as above average on the three course area performance (competency) survey questions. "Above average" is higher than a 3.0 rating on a 5 point scale; however, if any of the three survey questions has an individual rating below 3.0, that individual course area performance will be reviewed further.

100% 4b. 60% of the respondents to an Employer Survey conducted each year will respond that they would employ future graduates of the Automotive Technology program.

Note: If graduates do not give permission to contact their employer, the Research Office cannot survey the employer.

M. Early Leavers *(Official, Registrar's Office)* **(State Law S 27 (1993)):** In 1992-93, 4 students withdrew and 3 (75%) responded to the survey. One student was referred to Coastal's Re-entry and Assistance program. The others could not be provided assistance because of their reason for leaving, i.e., moving from the area.

N. Goal Accomplishment (SACS 6.2.1): The program is fulfilling its purpose because:
1. The majority of graduates responding (100%) stated that their goal was to obtain a degree or skills.
2. Of the graduates responding (85.7%) said that they had fully accomplished their goal while the early leavers equally responded that they fully, partially, or did not accomplish their goal.

Grads Primary Goal	Goal Accomplishment	Grads (7 of 9)	Early Leavers (3 of 4)
(7 of 9 (78%) students)	Fully	6	1
Degree 3 (28.6%)	Partially	1	1
Job Skills 4 (71.4%)	Not	0	1

O. Student Opinion Survey (5-point scale) (SACS 3.1, 4.1.4) (State Law S 27 (1993)): The opinion survey reveals that Current Students rated Instruction, Equipment, Teaching Facilities, Faculty Advising and Job Placement above average. The Early Leavers rated Faculty Advising, Facilities and Equipment as average; Instruction and Job Placement below average. The Graduates rated Instruction, Faculty Advising, Equipment, Teaching Facilities and Job Placement Services above average.

P. Placement Tests (SACS 4.1.1): Most (above 50%) of the 1992-93 students completed the ASSET placement test which is an increase over 1991-92.

Q. Curriculum Currency (SACS 4.1.3, 4.1.4): The curriculum was modified in the last 3 years (benchmark) in order to maintain currency and relevance.

R. Tech Prep/Vocational Scholarships & Enrollment (DCC IV- c): Six scholarships were awarded. The day enrollment increased 50%.

S. Instructor/Division Chair Responded To Last Years Desktop Audit Alert (SACS 3.1):
No alerts, therefore, no response necessary.

IV. Program Status & Plans - Next 1 to 2 Years *(Faculty/Dept. Head/Division Chair/Dean Section)*
Status
A. Facilities & Equipment (SACS 4.0; DCC II-d):
Labs - space adequate; *Classrooms* - space adequate; *Equipment* **(DCC-II-d)** - the exhaust system for the automotive shop needs to be upgraded to a powered exhaust system similar to that in the diesel shop.

B. Employment Demand - In the local job market, all graduates have found employment. The demand for graduates is strong.

C. Trends - Working directly with the high school vocational instructors and Tech Prep is expected to increase enrollment and academic strength of students.

D. Strengths - The close cooperation with the auto servicing businesses; the up-to-date equipment; there are more jobs available than there are graduates. Vocational scholarships have provided support to the program.

E. Weaknesses - The general population does not yet realize the great job opportunities available. Some equipment is out-of-date.

Program Objectives/Action for the Next Year (SACS 4.1):
Objectives (3 to 5):
1. To completely update the curriculum through the competency (Outcomes-measures) based project now underway.
2. To develop a multi-year equipment plan.
3. To strengthen equipment and curriculum ties with the high school Automotive programs through Tech Prep.

V. Summary Data - Automotive Technology

A. Operating (Dept.) Cost: Unit Cost = Total annual salaries and supplies/Annual FTE (6/30/93 financial report)

1992-93	$756.86	per annual FTE	1989-90	$580.63	per annual FTE
1991-92	551.78	per annual FTE	1988-89	366.29	per annual FTE
1990-91	648.56	per annual FTE			

B. Equipment (Dept.) Expenditures: (6/30/93 financial report)

1992-93	$1,019.00	1989-90	11,170.00
1991-92	$21,935.64	1988-89	12,819.90
1990-91	0.00		

Graduation Rate/Job Placement Scale (Internal Benchmark)

Needs Improvement	Good	Excellent
0-39%..............................40-69%.................................70-100%		

C. Enrollment (Dept.): *(Generated from Registrar's Office)*

Degree	# Grad	*Percent Completers	Headcount (Fa. Qtr.) FRS	State Percent Completers	T176 Student Fall FTE	Dept. 3-Quarter Avg. FTE	Dept. Units
1992-93	8	80	15	11	41.50	33.00	1.51
1991-92	4	44	10	11	NA	36.75	1.69
1990-91	1	11	09	12	34.50	27.17	1.29
1989-90	**	--	11	--	NA	25.33	1.21
1988-89	***10	--	09	--	NA	42.13	2.01

Headcount is form a selected course.
*Percent Completers is calculated by dividing the latest year graduates by the previous year freshman (FRS) headcount.
**Changed to a 2-year degree program - no graduates in 1990
*** Vocational Diploma Program

Certificate			Night
1992-93	2	17	12
1991-92	7	41	17
1990-91	1	08	12
1989-90	2	11	19

D. Job Placement Follow-Up Results:

Degree /Cert.	Responses	Related Employ.	Related Employ. Wages	Un-related Employ.	Un-employ.	Unknown	1 - Year Follow-up Related Emp.
1992-93	09	09 (100%)	$10.29	0	0	1	
1991-92	06	04 (67%)	9.00	1	1	5	5 (83%)
1990-91	02	02 (100%)	9.50	--	--	--	NA
1989-90	***	--	--	--	--	--	
1988-89	****10	10 (100%)	$6-9	_	--		

***Changed to a 2-year degree program - no graduates in 1990
**** Vocational Diploma Program
Note: Employment status percents are calculated using the number of responses.
Note: One Year Follow-up Surveys (Alumni Survey) were sent to students who were in unrelated fields or unemployed upon graduation only. The related employment responses to the Alumni Survey were added to related employment upon graduation.

E. Certification/Licensure Results: Automotive Services Exam (ASE) (Voluntary)

	No. Tested	No. Passing	No. Failed	% Passing
1992-93	09	09	0	100
1991-92	15	15	0	100
1990-91	10	10	0	100
1989-90	09	09	0	100
1988-89	05	05	0	100

Note: Test takers must have 2 years experience in the field. The Automotive Service Excellence (ASE) exam is an eight part exam. Each part is independent of the other. A test taker may test only in the area he wants to specialize in or test for a general field. The test taker may take the different parts of the exam over different periods of time.

	Excellent	Above Avg.	Average	Below Avg.	Poor

F.   Student Opinion Survey Results: 5 ....|............. 4 ....|............. 3 ....|............. 2.............|............. 1

	Graduates	Early Leavers	Current Students
Overall Instruction	4.43	2.00	4.39
Faculty Advising	4.14	2.50	4.08
Teaching Facilities	4.14	2.50	4.27
Equipment	4.29	2.50	4.18
Job Placement Services	4.14	2.00	3.96

G.   Employer Survey Results: **Evaluation of Students In Related Field Only**

Employer Response to Survey Questions

1.	Performance of vocational or technical skills	4.33
2.	Effective communication in speaking, writing, reading and listening	4.33
3.	Demonstrates the needed math skills	3.33
4.	Uses information to analyze problems and make logical decisions	4.33
5.	Demonstrates good work habits	4.67
6.	If the need arises, would you hire a CCCC graduate in the future?	100% Yes

H.   Vocational Scholarships:

	# Granted	Withdrew	% Change in Day Enrollment	% Change in 3-Quarter Avg. FTE
1992-93	6	0	50%	[10%]
1991-92	5	2	11%	35%

OCCUPATIONAL EDUCATION DESKTOP AUDIT

CODE: T018　　　　　**PROGRAM: BUSINESS ADMINISTRATION**
　　　　　　　　　　　REVIEW: 1992-93　December 1993

I.　Description/Purpose
The Business Administration Program began in 1968 on the Georgetown campus.

The Business Administration curriculum is designed to develop competencies in the application of management principles, critical thinking and decision-making skills applicable to profit and nonprofit organizations. Through the development of these competencies, the graduate will be able to function as a contributing member of a management team.

II.　Staffing (Full & Part-time) (SACS 4.4.2)
The Business Administration program is staffed by 3 full-time faculty and 0.45 part-time (units) faculty who meet SACS criteria.

III.　Analysis Of Desktop Audit Data
Quantitative Measurements (SACS 4.1)

A.　**Operating (Dept) Cost:** Instructional unit cost remained in the first quartile (lower 25%)in 1992-93.

B.　**Equipment (Dept) Expenditures:** No equipment was purchased, however, shared computers were purchased through the BCP program.

C.　**Enrollment (1 year old Data):** Business Administration fills two roles: 1) Major Program of Study and 2) Support courses for College Transfer. The instructional department 3-quarter FTE measures the combination of both roles and it increased 13.6% over the prior year figure. As a major program of study, erosion has been experienced from year-to-year in the measures of program unduplicated Fall headcount, 53% (137 to 65) decline in total headcount and 40% (52 to 31) decline in Freshman headcount in the last 5 years. In response to the 1991/92 DTA Alert, program revisions were made to the management focus and flexibility of the program. this broadened the program's appeal, particularly to the large number of enrolled technical special-studies students not declaring a major. The result in Fall 1992/93 was that the Freshman headcount increased by 41% (22 to 31). This was the first increase in five years.
*Plus the current Fall/winter FTE and Headcount provided at the **Departmental final review meeting.***

ALERT, Year 3: Progress is being made with increasing enrollment (Freshmen); therefore, this alert is only to assist in monitoring further progress. A response to the alert needs to be made by March 1, 1994.

D.　**Demographics (1 year old Data) (DCC-IV-a, c):** The annual enrollment (1992-93) consisted of 27 males and 83 females, the majority being white female students in their thirties. Of the overall enrollment, 7 were 1991-92 high school graduates. Two of the high school students were from Jacksonville, 1 from White Oak, 2 from Swansboro, 1 from Dixon High and 1 from Richlands High.

E.　**Carl Perkins-Federal Vocational Funds Eligibility** (2 year old Demographic Data): Business Administration does qualify to receive Carl Perkins Federal Vocational funds in 1993-94. Through the BCP program, shared computers ($57960.80) were purchased. The Special Population qualifications are listed on page 8.

(left margin, rotated: Future Planning)

Qualitative Measurements (SACS 4.1)

F.　**Graduation Rate (DCC-I-f; state law S 27 (1993)):** The graduation rate is (Degree-45%, 10 students). Graduation rate is 45% compared to the state average of 10%. The Coastal number of graduates and percent completers has been stable for three years. Internally evaluated (benchmarked) the Coastal graduation rate is good.

G.　**Job Placement(SACS 3.1; DCC-V-d):** The 92-93 related employment rate (benchmarked) is excellent (88%). The One-Year Follow-up (Alumni Survey) of 91-92 graduates showed that 100% found related employment which (internal benchmark) is excellent.

H.　**Employer Survey Results (SACS 3.1; DCC-V-c; state law S 27 (1993)):** The graduates working within the field of Business Administration were rated above average to excellent by their employers. 100% responded that they would hire future CCCC graduates.

I.　**Advisory Committee (SACS 6.1.3):** The Advisory Committee met in 1992-93 (benchmark) and minutes were kept.

J.　**Literacy (GED/AHS) Students Entering Curriculum Programs (DCC-I-b):** In 1992-93, one student entered.

K. Program/Student Outcomes at Program Completion (SACS 3.1, 4.1.4): The student/outcome measures were revised in the 1992/93 academic year. The outcome measures are used to inform students prior to entering college and during the program via handouts. *See "1992-93 Program Outcomes" booklet.*

L. Early Leavers *(Official, Registrar's Office)* **(state law S 27 (1993):** In 1992-93, of the 13 students withdrawing, 12 (92%) responded to the survey. Because of their reasons for leaving, i.e., moving from the area, Coastal could not provide assistance.

M. Goal Accomplishment (SACS 6.2.1): The program is fulfilling its purpose because:
1. The majority of graduates responding (100%) stated that their goal was to obtain a degree or skills.
2. Of the graduates responding (87.5%) said that they had fully accomplished their goal while the majority of early leavers responding said they partially accomplished their goals.

Grads Primary Goal	Goal Accomplishment	Grads (8 of 10)	Early Leavers (8 of 12)
(8 of 10 (80%) students)	Fully	7	0
Degree 7 (87.5%)	Partially	1	6
Job Skills 1 (12.5%)	Not	0	2

N. Student Opinion Survey (5-point scale) (SACS 3.1, 4.1.4; state law S 27 (1993)): The opinion survey reveals that Current Students rated Instruction, Equipment, Teaching Facilities, Faculty Advising and Job Placement above average. The Early Leavers rated Instruction, Faculty Advising, Facilities and Equipment above average; Job Placement as average. The Graduates rated Instruction, Teaching Facilities and Equipment above average; Faculty Advising and Job Placement Services average.

O. Placement Tests (SACS 4.1.1): Most (above 50%) of the 1992-93 students have completed the ASSET placement test which is an increase over 1990-91.

P. Curriculum Currency (SACS 4.1.3, 4.1.4): The curriculum was modified in the last three years (benchmark) in order to maintain currency and relevance.

Q. Instructor/Division Chair Responded To Last Years Desktop Audit Alerts (SACS 3.1): Yes, *See "1991-92 Desktop Audit Responses" booklet.*

IV. Program Status & Plans - Next 1 to 2 Years *(Faculty/Dept. Head/Division Chair/Dean Section)*

Status

A. Facilities/Equipment (SACS 4.0; DCC II-d)
Classrooms - Space is more than adequate due to the Business Technology Building;
Equipment (DCC-II-d) - Equipment is up-to-date and state-of-the-art due to new equipment purchases for the new Business Technology Building.

B. Employment Demand - Business firms, government agencies and public agencies in NC have above average need for personnel trained in the management field.

C. Trends: With the full implementation of the substantial revisions to the Business Administration program and adequate promotion, freshman enrollment has attained an upward movement.

D. Strengths: The close cooperation with the business community.

E. Weaknesses: Under marketed to prospective new and technical-special students

Program Objectives/Action for the Next Year (SACS 4.1):

Objectives (3 to 5)
The Business Administration program continues to be revised to include the following features:
1. A clear management focus providing program differentiation
2. Higher mastery levels in Mathematics, English/Communications, and Computer Applications
3. Opportunities for in-depth study of selected advanced technical topics
4. Opportunities for additional study in the liberal arts as well as other technical areas

Extract from *1992-93 Program Outcomes* booklet

Business Administration
1992-93

Program/Student Outcomes/Objectives at Program Completion (SACS 3.1,4.1.1):

1.   Graduates of the Business Administration program will be technically proficient in
92-93 DTA management and related skills.

88%   1a.   At the close of their final term 85% of the students will be able to evaluate an
organization's major managerial, production, financial, and marketing problems as
demonstrated in the Capstone Report based upon a comprehensive case problem
assigned by the program faculty in Capstone Course - Management and Policy
(BUS 235).

88%   1b.   At the end of their final term 85% of the students will be able to recommend courses
of action to address the major managerial, production, financial, and marketing
problems of an organization as demonstrated in the Capstone Report based upon a
comprehensive case problem assigned by the program faculty in Capstone Course -
Management and Policy (BUS 235).

88%   1c.   At the end of their final term 85% of the students will defend orally the Capstone Report
based upon a comprehensive case problem assigned by the program faculty in
Capstone Course - Management and Policy (BUS 235).

2.   Graduates of the Business Administration program will be primarily employed in
management and functionally related areas.

88%   2a.   50% of the responding graduates will report employment in management or in the
related fields of finance, production, or marketing on the Graduate Student Survey
administered within the first five months after graduation.

100%   2b.   75% of the responding (previous year) graduates will report employment in management
or in the related fields of finance, production, or marketing on the Alumni Survey
distributed one year after graduation.

3.   Employers of graduates of the Business Administration program will rate the academic and
technical skills of the employees as "above average".

3a.   The respondents to an Employer Satisfaction Survey concerning the Business Administration program graduates will rate the graduates above average, higher than 3.0 on
a 5 point scale in each of the following five performance (competency) areas:
Performance of technical skills;

(1) 4.33   Effectiveness of communication;
(2) 4.67   Demonstration of math skills;
(3) 4.00   Problem analysis and logical decision making;
(4) 4.67   Demonstration of good work habits.

If any area should receive a score below 3.0, the individual course area and related
courses of study will be reviewed further.

100%   3b.   60% of the respondents to an Employer Survey conducted each year will respond that
they would employ future Business Administration program graduates.

V. Summary Data - Business Administration

A. **Operating (Dept) Cost:** Unit Cost = Total annual salaries and supplies/Annual FTE (6/30/93 financial report)

1992-93	$325.93	per annual FTE	1989-90	$*301.27	per annual FTE
1991-92	324.08	per annual FTE	1988-89	318.03	per annual FTE
1990-91	358.52	per annual FTE			

*This is the first year that financial costs and FTE have been separated between the Business Admin. & Accounting Programs.

B. **Equipment (Dept) Expenditures:** (6/30/93 financial report)

1992-93	0.00		1989-90	0.00
1991-92	0.00		1988-89	0.00
1990-91	502.95			

Graduation Rate/Job Placement Scale (Internal Benchmark)

Needs Improvement	Good	Excellent
0-39%.....................	............40-69%..............	...............70-100%

C. **Enrollment (Dept):** *(Generated from Registrar's Office)*

Degree	# Grad	*Percent Completers	Headcount (Fa. Qtr.) FRS.	Total	Percent Completers	State Student Fall FTE	T018 3-Quarter Avg. FTE	Dept Units
1992-93	10	45	31	65	10	52.94	134.14	6.15
1991-92	18	44	22	80	10	NA	118.05	5.41
1990-91	19	44	41	113	10	84.38	119.23	5.68
1989-90	27	52	43	121	--	NA	**147.33	7.02
1988-89	27	42	52	137	--	NA	237.07	11.09

Headcount is from "Annual Statistics Report" generated by the CCCC Registrar
*Percent Completers is calculated by dividing the latest year graduates by the previous year freshman (FRS) headcount
**This is the first year that financial costs and FTE have been separated between the Business Admin. & Accounting Programs.

D. **Job Placement Follow-Up Results:**

Degree	Responses	Related Employ.	Related Employ. Wages	Unrelated Employ.	Un-employ.	Un-known	1 - Year Follow-up Related Emp.
1992-93	08	07 (88%)	$7.87	0	1	01	
1991-92	14	12 (86%)	$8.46	--	2	04	14 (100%)
1990-91	12	05 (42%)	$7.27	2	5	07	09 (75%)
1989-90	00	--	--	--	--	27	
1988-89	00	--	--	--	--	27	

Note: Employment status percents are calculated using number of responses.
Note: One Year Follow-up Surveys (Alumni Survey) were sent to students who were in unrelated fields or unemployed upon graduation only. The related employment responses to the Alumni Survey were added to related employment upon graduation.

E. **Student Opinion Survey Results:**

Excellent | Above Avg. | Average | Below Avg. | Poor
5................|...............4.................|...............3................|...............2.............|................1

	Graduates	Early Leavers	Current Students
Overall Instruction	4.13	4.14	4.39
Faculty Advising	3.13	3.86	4.08
Teaching Facilities	3.75	4.14	4.27
Equipment	3.63	4.00	4.18
Job Placement Services	3.00	3.40	3.96

F. **Employer Survey Results:**   **Evaluation of Students in Related Field Only**

Employer Response to Survey Questions

1.	Performance of vocational or technical skills	4.33
2.	Effective communication in speaking, writing, reading and listening	4.33
3.	Demonstrates the needed math skills	4.67
4.	Uses information to analyze problems and make logical decisions	4.00
5.	Demonstrates good work habits	4.67
6.	If the need arises, would you hire a CCCC graduate in the future?	100% Yes

OCCUPATIONAL EDUCATION DESKTOP AUDIT

CODE: T041	PROGRAM: ARCHITECTURAL TECH.
	REVIEW: 1992-93 December 1993

I. Description/Purpose

The Architectural Technology program was instituted at Coastal Carolina Community College in 1988 replacing the Architectural Drafting program. It has traditionally emphasized residential and light commercial applications in architectural technology.

The Architectural Technology curriculum provides individuals with the knowledge and skills that will lead to employment and advancement in the field of architectural technology.

II. Staffing (Full & Part-time) (SACS 4.4.2)

The program is staffed by two full-time faculty who meet SACS criteria. Both hold an Associate degree and both instructors have considerable experience in modern computer aided drafting techniques. Part-time faculty are hired on a quarter by quarter basis, as the need arises. All part-time faculty meet SACS requirements.

III. Analysis Of Desktop Audit Summary Data

Quantitative Measurements (SACS 4.1)

A. **Operating (Dept.) Cost:** The unit cost remained in the second quartile (lower 50%) in 1992-93.

B. **Equipment (Dept.) Expenditures:** $13,523 was spent on equipment.

C. **Enrollment (1 year old Data):** The enrollment has been excellent and at or close to maximum for the last four years.
²Plus the current Fall/winter FTE and Headcount provided at the Departmental final review meeting.

D. **Demographics (1 year old Data) (DCC-IV-a, c):** The annual enrollment (1992-93) consisted of 25 males and 19 females, the majority being white males in their twenties. Of the overall enrollment, 9 were 1991-92 high school graduates. Five of the high school students were from Jacksonville, 1 from East Duplin High, 1 was from Wallace-Rose Hill High, 1 from Richlands and 1 from West Carteret High.

E. **Carl Perkins-Federal Vocational Funds Eligibility (2 year old Demographic Data):** Architectural Technology does not qualify to receive Carl Perkins Federal Vocational funds in 1993-94. The Special Population qualifications are listed on page 8.

(Left margin, rotated: Future Planning)

Qualitative Measurements (SACS 4.1)

F. **Graduation Rate (DCC-1f; state law S 27 (1993)):** The graduation rate is (Degree-33%, 6 students); (Certificate-none). Total graduation rate is 33% compared to the state average of 13%. Internally evaluated (benchmarked) the Coastal degree graduation rate needs improvement.
ALERT: A response to the alert is needed by March 1, 1994

G. **Job Placement (SACS 3.1; DCC-V-d):** The related employment rate (benchmark) is excellent (83%). The one-year follow-up (Alumni Survey) of 91-92 graduates shows that 60% found related employment which is (benchmarked) good.

H. **Employer Survey Results (SACS 3.1; DCC-V-c; state law S 27 (1993)):** The graduates working within the field of Architectural Technology were rated average to above average by their employers. 100% responded that they would hire future CCCC graduates.

I. **Advisory Committee (SACS 6.1.3):** The Advisory Committee met in 1992-93 (benchmark) and minutes were kept.

J. **Literacy (GED/AHS) Students Entering Curriculum Programs (DCC-I-b):** In 1992-93, no students entered.

K. **Program/Student Outcomes at Program Completion (SACS 3.1, 4.1.4):** The student outcome measures were revised in the 1992/93 academic year. The outcome measures are used to inform students prior to entering college and during the program via handouts. *See "1992-93 Program Outcomes" booklet.*

L. **Early Leaver Students *(Official, Registrar's Office)* (state law S 27 (1993)):** In 1992-93, of the 6 students withdrawing, 2 (33%) responded to the survey. Coastal could not provide assistance because of their reason for leaving, i.e., moving from the area.

Extract from *1992-93 Program Outcomes* **booklet**

Architectural Technology
1992-93

Program/Student Outcomes/Objectives at Program Completion (SACS 3.1,4.1.1):

1. Graduates of the Architectural Technology program will be technically proficient in manual
92-93 DTA and computer-aided drafting techniques, construction terms and techniques, as well as presentation techniques.

100% 1a. At the close of their final term 90% of the students will be able to prepare a portfolio and meet the quality control and evaluation of the Architectural Technology program faculty in the Capstone course - Portfolio (ARC 220).

2. Graduates of the Architectural Technology will be employed in the field.

83% 2a. 40% of the responding graduates of the Architectural Technology program will report employment in the field on the Graduating Student Survey administered within the first three months after graduation.

60% 2b. 60% of the responding (previous year) graduates of the Architectural Technology program will report employment in the field on the Alumni Survey distributed one year after graduation.

3. Employers of the Architectural Technology graduates will rate the technical and academic skills of the employees as average or above.

3a. The Employer Survey conducted each year will rate the graduates as above average
(1) 3.00 on the three course area performance (competency) survey questions. "Above
(2) 4.00 average" is higher than a 3.0 on a 5 point scale; however, if any of the three survey
(3) 3.00 questions has an individual rating below 3.0, that individual course area performance will be reviewed further.

100% 3b. 60% of the respondents to an employee survey will respond that they would employ future graduates of the Architectural Technology program if a position were available.

M. **Goal Accomplishment (SACS 6.2.1):** The program is fulfilling its purpose because:
  1. The majority of graduates responding (100%) stated that their goal was to obtain a degree or job skills.
  2. Of the graduates responding (83%) said that they had fully accomplished their goal while one of early leavers responding said that they fully accomplished their goal and one partially accomplished their goal.

Grads Primary Goal	Goal Accomplishment	Grads (6 of 6)	Early Leavers (2 of 6)
(6 of 6 (100%) students)	Fully	5	1
Degree 5 (83.3%)	Partially	1	1
Job Skills 1 (16.7%)	Not	0	0

N. **Student Opinion Survey (5-point scale) (SACS 3.1, 4.1.4; state law S 27 (1993)):** The opinion survey reveals that Current Students rated Instruction, Equipment, Teaching Facilities, Faculty Advising and Job Placement above average. The Early Leavers rated Instruction, Faculty Advising Teaching Facilities, Equipment and Job Placement above average. The Graduates rated Instruction, Faculty Advising, Teaching Facilities and Equipment above average; Job Placement Services average.

O. **Placement Tests (SACS 4.1.1):** Most (above 50%) of the 1992-93 students completed the ASSET placement test which is an increase over 1991-92.

P. **Curriculum Currency (SACS 4.1.3, 4.1.4):** The curriculum was modified in the last 3 years (benchmark) in order to maintain currency and relevance.

Q. **Tech Prep/Vocational Scholarships (DCC IV-c):** Four scholarships were awarded. The day enrollment increased 22%. The overall Department 3-quarter FTE decreased 20%.

R. **Instructor/Division Chair Responded To Last Years Desktop Audit Alerts (SACS 3.1):**
  No alerts, therefore, no response necessary,

IV. Program Status & Plans - Next 1 to 2 Years *(Faculty/Dept. Head/Division Chair/Dean Section)*
Status
A. **Facilities/Equipment (SACS 4.0; DCC II-d)** *(Faculty/Dept. Head/Division Chair/Dean Section)*
  Labs - computer-aided drafting lab is current with state of the art hardware and software; manual drafting lab has all new furniture and equipment;
  Classrooms - adequate
  Equipment **(DCC-II-d)** - updated manual drafting labs with all new equipment.

B. **Employment Demand -** Currently in NC there is a balance in demand for individuals in the architectural field. Local demand for architectural graduates is very good. Students regularly find jobs immediately upon graduation.

C. **Trends -** Enrollment trends are very positive for the day degree program with maximum capacity enrollment in the Freshman Fall Quarter. The evening certificate program needs improvement; perhaps revision. Anticipated growth and development in Onslow County and in Eastern North Carolina should provide for continued demand for degree-seeking students.

D. **Strengths -** A student chapter of the American Institute of Building Design (AIBD) helps in networking with potential employers.

E. **Weaknesses -** none.

Program Objectives/Action for the Next Year (SACS 4.1):
Objectives (3 to 5):
We have revised the program to run 12 months vs. 10 1/2.
1. The degree program has been revised to run the full-summer session during the Freshman year, rather than the previous half-summer session. The first full-summer session is being offered for academic year 1993/94, making the degree program run seven quarters versus the previous six and one-half quarters.
2. Research will be conducted to verify the validity of adding computer-aided-drafting (CAD) to Freshman design classes. CAD, over manual drafting techniques, is the leading technological method of drafting. Students are currently introduced to CAD in their 4th quarter.
3. The evening certificate program will be reevaluated to enhance enrollment, not to exclude the possibility of modification to create a Drafting diploma or certificate.

V. Summary Data - Architectural Tech.

A.   Operating (Dept.) Cost: Unit Cost = Total annual salaries and supplies/Annual FTE (6/30/93 financial report)

1992-93	$566.42	per annual FTE	1989-90	$280.03	per annual FTE
1991-92	352.63	per annual FTE	1988-89	364.00	per annual FTE
1990-91	366.32	per annual FTE	1987-88	349.22	per annual FTE

B.   Equipment (Dept.) Expenditures: (6/30/93 financial report)

1992-93	$13,523.00		1989-90	3,709.00
1991-92	0.00		1988-89	0.00
1990-91	0.00		1987-88	31.50

Graduation Rate/Job Placement Scale (Internal Benchmark)
Needs Improvement	Good	Excellent
0-39%..............................40-69%................................70-100%		

C.   Enrollment (Dept): *(Generated from Registrar's Office)*

Degree	# Grad	*Percent Completers	Headcount (Fa.Qtr.) FRS	State Percent Completers	T041 Student Fall FTE	Dept. 3-Quarter Avg. FTE	Dept Units
1992-93	6	33	22	13	53.06	36.27	1.66
1991-92	9	41	18	13	NA	45.19	2.07
1990-91	6	33	22		57.13	38.71	1.84
1989-90	5	28	18		NA	50.33	2.40
1988-89	4	NA	18		NA	46.65	2.22

Headcount is from a selected course.
*Percent Completers is calculated by dividing the latest year graduates by the previous year freshman (FRS) headcount.

Certificate			Night
1992-93	0	00	00
1991-92	4	25	16
1990-91	2	11	18
1989-90	4	21	19

D.   Job Placement Follow-Up Results:

Degree /Cert.	Responses	Related Employ.	Related Employ. Wages	Un-related Employ.	Un-employ.	Add Educ	Un-known	1 - Year Follow-up Related Emp.
1992-93	06	5 (83%)	$5.50	0	1	0	0	
1991-92	10	5 (50%)	6.27	2	0	3	3	6 (60%)
1990-91	08	3 (38%)	8-10	5	--	--	--	No Response
1989-90	09	9 (100%)	6.50-8.00	--	--			
1988-89	04	3 (75%)	**** 9.00		--	1	--	

****Out of area employment
Note: Employment status percents are calculated using number of responses.
Note: One Year Follow-up Surveys (Alumni Survey) were sent to students who were in unrelated fields or unemployed upon graduation only. The related employment responses to the Alumni Survey were added to related employment upon graduation.

E.   Student Opinion Survey Results:

	Excellent	Above Avg.	Average	Below Avg.	Poor
	5 ....|................. 4 ....|................. 3 ....|.............. 2.............|................. 1				

	Graduates	Early Leavers	Current Students
Overall Instruction	3.83	4.00	4.39
Faculty Advising	4.00	4.00	4.08
Teaching Facilities	4.17	4.00	4.27
Equipment	3.67	4.00	4.18
Job Placement Services	3.00	4.00	3.96

F.   Employer Survey Results: Evaluation of Students In Related Field Only

Employer Response to Survey Questions
1.	Performance of vocational or technical skills	3.00
2.	Effective communication in speaking, writing, reading and listening	4.00
3.	Demonstrates the needed math skills	3.00
4.	Uses information to analyze problems and make logical decisions	4.00
5.	Demonstrates good work habits	4.00
6.	If the need arises, would you hire a CCCC graduate in the future?	100% Yes

G.   Vocational Scholarships:

	# Granted	Withdrew	% Change in Day Enrollment	% Change in 3-Quarter Avg. FTE
1992-93	4	0	22%	<20%>
1991-92	2	0	<18%>	17%

OCCUPATIONAL EDUCATION DESKTOP AUDIT

CODE: T054	PROGRAM: DENTAL HYGIENE
	REVIEW: 1992-93 December 1993

I.   Description/Purpose
The Dental Hygiene program began in 1972 on the Georgetown Campus. It became fully accredited in 1980.

The Dental Hygiene curriculum prepares graduates to take patient histories, teach oral hygiene, clean teeth, take x-rays and apply preventive agents under the supervision of a dentist.

The program is accredited by the Commission on Dental Accreditation of the American Dental Association. The dental clinic offers cleaning, x-rays, and sealants to people of the community at a reduced fee.

II. Staffing (Full & Part-time)(SACS 4.4.2)
This program is staffed by three full-time faculty, one half time division chair, and 0.05 part-time (unit) faculty who meet SACS criteria. The half position is the Division Chair who serves half the time in the Dental Assisting program and half time in the Dental Hygiene program. The Commission on Dental Accreditation of the ADA requires a ratio of one instructor to six students during clinical hours and in certain pre-clinical labs.

III. Analysis Of Desktop Audit Summary Data
Quantitative Measurements (SACS 4.1)
A.   **Operating (Dept.) Cost:** Unit cost has remained in the fourth quartile (upper 25%) for five years. Unit cost is expected to remain in the fourth quartile because the program is operating at close to maximum enrollment.

B.   **Equipment(Dept.) Expenditures:** $125,916 was spent completely reequipping and updating the dental clinic. This total is reflected in both the Dental Hygiene and Dental Assisting programs. This equipment purchase was in response to the alert in the 1990/91 DTA.

C.   **Enrollment (1 year old Data):** Enrollment has been excellent and at the maximum capacity for five years.
     Plus the current Fall/winter FTE and Headcount provided at the Departmental final review meeting.

D.   **Demographics (1 year old Data) (DCC-IV-a,c):** The annual enrollment (1992-93) consisted of 0 males and 35 females, the majority being white female students in their twenties. Of the overall enrollment, there were no 1991-92 high school graduates

E.   **Carl Perkins-Federal Vocational Funds Eligibility (2 year old Demographic Data):** Dental Hygiene <u>does not qualify</u> to receive Carl Perkins Federal Vocational funds in 1993-94. The Special Population qualifications are listed on page 8.

(margin, rotated text: Future Planning)

Qualitative Measurements (SACS 4.1)
F.   **Graduation Rate (DCC-I-f; state law S 27 (1993)):** The graduation rate is (Degree-83%, 15 students). Graduation rate is 83% compared to the state average of 25%. Internally evaluated (benchmarked) the Coastal degree graduation rate is excellent.

G.   **Job Placement (SACS 3.1; DCC-V-d):** The related employment rate is (benchmark) excellent (100%). The One-Year Follow-up (Alumni Survey) of 91-92 graduates was not necessary since 100% found related employment which (internal benchmark) is excellent.

H.   **Employer Survey Results (SACS 3.1; DCC-V-c; state law S 27 (1993)):** The graduates working within the field of Dental Hygiene were rated above average by their employers. 100% responded that they would hire future CCCC graduates.
Note: If graduates do not give permission to contact their employer, the Research Office cannot survey the employer.

I.   **Certification/Licensure (DCC-I-e):** The State Board passing rate was excellent (100%). The National Board passing rate was excellent (100%).

J.   **Advisory Committee (SACS 6.1.3):** The Advisory Committee met in 1992-93 (benchmark) and minutes were kept.

K.   **Literacy (GED/AHS) Students Entering Curriculum Programs (DCC-I-b):** In 1992-93, no students entered.

L.   **Program/Student Outcomes at Program Completion (SACS 3.1, 4.1.4):** The student outcome measures were revised in the 1992/93 academic year. The outcome measures are used to inform students prior to entering college and during the program via handouts. *See "1992-93 Program Outcomes" booklet.*

Extract from *1992-93 Program Outcomes* booklet

Dental Hygiene
1992-93

Program/Student Outcomes/Objectives at Program Completion (SACS 3.1,4.1.1):

1.   Graduates of the Dental Hygiene program <u>will be able to demonstrate a sound grasp of</u>
92-93 DTA <u>basic skills and knowledge in the basic sciences, dental sciences, general education</u>
        <u>and dental hygiene science.</u>

100%   1a.   85% of the Dental Hygiene program graduates taking the Dental Hygiene National
                 Board will pass the exam.

2.   Graduates of the Dental Hygiene program <u>will be technically proficient</u>.

100%   2a.   At the close of their final term, 100% of the graduates will be able to demonstrate dental
                 hygiene skills with a 77% proficiency as directed by the Dental Hygiene program
                 faculty in Capstone Course - Clinical Dental Hygiene V (Den 217).

100%   2b.   85% of the Dental Hygiene Program graduates taking a State Licensure Examination
                 will pass the exam.

3.   Graduates of the Dental Hygiene program <u>will be employed in the field.</u>

100%   3a.   50% of the responding graduates of the Dental Hygiene program will report
                 employment in the field on the Graduating Student Survey administered in the first five
                 months after graduation.

100%   3b.   75% of the responding (previous year) graduates of the Dental Hygiene program will
                 report employment in the field on the Alumni Survey distributed one year after
                 graduation.

4.   Employers of the Dental Hygiene program graduates <u>will rate the technical and academic</u>
        <u>skills of the employees as average or above.</u>

                 4a.   The Employer Survey conducted each year will rate the graduates as above average
(1) 3.86   on the three course area performance (competency) survey questions. "Above
(2) 4.14   average" is higher than a 3.0 on a 5 point scale; however, if any of the three survey
(3) 3.80   questions has an individual rating below 3.0, that individual course area performance
                       will be reviewed further.

100%   4b.   75% of the respondents to an Employer Survey conducted each year will respond
                 that they would employ future graduates of the Dental Hygiene program.

Note: If graduates do not give permission to contact their employer, the Research Office cannot survey the employer.

M. **Early Leavers** *(Official, Registrar's Office)* **(state law S 27 (1993):** In 1992-93, there were no early leavers.

N. **Goal Accomplishment (SACS 6.2.1):** The program is fulfilling its purpose because:
1. The majority of graduates responding (93.3%) stated that their goal was to obtain a degree.
2. Of the graduates responding (80%) said that they had fully accomplished their goal while there were no early leavers responses to the survey.

Grads Primary Goal	Goal Accomplishment	Grads (15 of 15)	Early Leavers
(15 of 15 (100%) students)	Fully	12	0
Degree 14 (93.3%)	Partially	03	0
Per. Interest 1 (6.7%)	Not	00	0

O. **Student Opinion Survey (5-point scale) (SACS 3.1, 4.1.4; state law S 27 (1993)):** The opinion survey reveals that Current Students rated Instruction, Equipment, Teaching Facilities, Faculty Advising and Job Placement above average. There were no Early Leavers The Graduates rated Instruction, Teaching Facilities, Equipment and Job Placement Services as excellent; Faculty Advising above average.

P. **Placement Tests (SACS 4.1.1):** All students are requested to take the ASSET test prior to entry. The SAT or ACT can be substituted if it has been taken within the last five years.

Q. **Curriculum Currency (SACS 4.1.3, 4.1.4):** The curriculum was modified in the last 3 years (benchmark) in order to maintain currency and relevance.

R. **Instructor/Division Chair Responded To Last Years Desktop Audit Alerts (SACS 3.1):**
No alerts, therefore, no response necessary

IV. Program Status & Plans - Next 1 to 2 Years *(Faculty/Dept. Head/Division Chair/Dean Section)*
Status
A. **Facilities/Equipment (SACS 4.0; DCC-II-d)**
Classroom/Lab - Laboratory classroom and clinical space is adequate; *Equipment* - New dental chairs and equipment were purchased in Summer of 1992.

B. **Employment Demand** - Demand continues to be strong for our dental hygiene graduates. We continue to experience excellent placement opportunities for our graduates in Eastern North Carolina.

C. **Trends -** Continued strong demand for enrollment is projected. Computer use in dental offices has increased dramatically in the last several years. The addition of a computer system to handle patient records, recall, appointment control and clinic grading is being explored.

D. **Strengths -** There are an abundance of jobs in Eastern NC. Retention in the program has averaged 94%,100% for the past two years.

E. **Weaknesses -** The Clinical Sterilization area needs to be enlarged to meet increasing demands and OSHA standards. The secretarial work area and patient reception area need to be remodeled to provide adequate work space and efficient patient flow.

Program Objectives/Action for the Next Year (SACS 4.1):
Objectives (3 to 5)
1. A study of the admissions criteria has been conducted and the policies have been implemented.
2. In the current fiscal year, the department will analyze the new curriculum to determine relevancy and currency.

V. Summary Data - Dental Hygiene

A. Operating (Dept.) Cost: Unit Cost = Total annual salaries and supplies/Annual FTE (6/30/93 financial report)

1992-93	$1210.03	per annual FTE	1989-90	$ 858.96	per annual FTE
1991-92	1053.73	per annual FTE	1988-89	1027.12	per annual FTE
1990-91	1036.56	per annual FTE			

B. Equipment (Dept.) Expenditures: (6/30/93 financial report)

1992-93	$125,916.00	1989-90	3,528.00
1991-92	8,183.08	1988-89	3,869.09
1990-91	0.00		

Equipment is used for both Dental Hygiene and Dental Assisting Programs.

Graduation Rate/Job Placement Scale (Internal Benchmark)

Needs Improvement	Good	Excellent
0-39%.................	....40-69%.................	....70-100%

C. Enrollment (Dept): *(Generated from Registrar's Office)*

Degree	# Grad	*Percent Completers	Headcount (Fa. Qtr.) FRS	State Percent Completers	T054 Student Fall FTE	Dept. 3-Quarter Avg. FTE	Dept Units
1992-93	15	83	18	25	50.06	40.87	1.87
1991-92	17	94	18	25	NA	41.60	1.91
1990-91	16	89	18	22	50.38	40.22	1.92
1989-90	16	80	18	--	NA	42.33	2.02
1988-89	11	NA	20	--	NA	33.85	1.61

Headcount is from a selected course.
*Percent Completers is calculated by dividing the latest year graduates by the previous year freshman (FRS) headcount.

D. Job Placement Follow-Up Results:

Degree	Responses	Related Employ.	Related Employ. Wages	Unemploy.	Unknown	1 - Year Follow-up Related Emp.
1992-93	15	15 (100%)	$12.53	0	0	
1991-92	15	15 (100%)	$12.76	0	2	NA (100%)
1990-91	16	11 (69%)	12	5	--	13 (81%)
1989-90	16	16 (100%)	12	--	--	
1988-89	11	11 (100%)	9	--	--	

Note: Employment status percents are calculated using the number of responses.
Note: One Year Follow-up Surveys (Alumni Survey) were sent to students who were in unrelated fields or unemployed upon graduation only. The related employment responses to the Alumni Survey were added to related employment upon graduation.

E. Certification/Licensure Results:

	State Board:				National Board:			
	No. Tested	No. Passing	No. Failed	% Passing	No. Tested	No. Passing	No. Failed	% Passing
1992-93	15	15	0	100	15	15	0	100
1991-92	17	17	0	100	17	17	0	100
1990-91	16	16	0	100	16	16	0	100
1989-90	17	17	0	100	17	16	1	94
1988-89	11	11	0	100	11	10	1	91

F. Student Opinion Survey Results: 5 ....|..........4..........|..........3..........|..........2..........|..........1   (Excellent Above Avg Average Below Avg. Poor)

	Graduates	Early Leavers	Current Students
Overall Instruction	4.73	00	4.39
Faculty Advising	4.13	00	4.08
Teaching Facilities	4.80	00	4.27
Equipment	5.00	00	4.18
Job Placement Services	4.73	00	3.96

G. Employer Survey Results: Evaluation of Students in Related Field Only

Employer Response to Survey Questions

1.	Performance of vocational or technical skills	3.86
2.	Effective communication in speaking, writing, reading and listening	4.14
3.	Demonstrates the needed math skills	3.80
4.	Uses information to analyze problems and make logical decisions	4.00
5.	Demonstrates good work habits	4.14
6.	If the need arises, would you hire a CCCC graduate in the future?	100% Yes

Appendix E—Example Questionnaires from University of Kentucky–Lexington Campus and Coastal Carolina Community College

UNIVERSITY OF KENTUCKY
GRADUATING SENIOR SURVEY

Your answers to the following questions will help us evaluate our programs and services. Your responses will be grouped statistically and are completely confidential.

1. Social Security Number (Student ID) _____

2. Name: (Please Print)

   _____
   Last   First   MI   Unmarried Name

3. Permanent Mailing Address: (If different from above)

   _____
   Street

   _____
   City   State   Zip Code

   _____
   Area Code   Telephone Number

4. Name and address of person who will always know where you are:

   _____
   Name

   _____
   Street

   _____
   City   State   Zip Code

QUALITY OF INSTRUCTION & ADVISING

5. How would you rate the quality of each of the following aspects of the University and of your major?

	At the University?	In my Major?
	Not Applicable (0) / Poor (1) / Fair (2) / Good (3) / Excellent (4)	Not Applicable (0) / Poor (1) / Fair (2) / Good (3) / Excellent (4)
a. Quality of instruction by faculty	☐ ☐ ☐ ☐ ☐	☐ ☐ ☐ ☐ ☐
b. Knowledge and preparation of faculty in subject matter	☐ ☐ ☐ ☐ ☐	☐ ☐ ☐ ☐ ☐
c. Quality of instruction by teaching assistants	☐ ☐ ☐ ☐ ☐	☐ ☐ ☐ ☐ ☐
d. Quality of instruction in laboratories and discussion sections	☐ ☐ ☐ ☐ ☐	☐ ☐ ☐ ☐ ☐
e. Accessibility of instructors	☐ ☐ ☐ ☐ ☐	☐ ☐ ☐ ☐ ☐
f. Individual attention from instructors	☐ ☐ ☐ ☐ ☐	☐ ☐ ☐ ☐ ☐
g. Clarity of degree requirements	☐ ☐ ☐ ☐ ☐	☐ ☐ ☐ ☐ ☐
h. Availability of needed courses	☐ ☐ ☐ ☐ ☐	☐ ☐ ☐ ☐ ☐
i. Preparation for my first career job	☐ ☐ ☐ ☐ ☐	☐ ☐ ☐ ☐ ☐
j. Preparation for graduate or professional school	☐ ☐ ☐ ☐ ☐	☐ ☐ ☐ ☐ ☐
k. Quality of non-instructional services (such as computer services, library, etc.)	☐ ☐ ☐ ☐ ☐	☐ ☐ ☐ ☐ ☐

6. I would recommend UK to another student

   4. ☐ Strongly Agree
   3. ☐ Agree
   2. ☐ Disagree
   1. ☐ Strongly Disagree

169

7. To what extent do you agree or disagree with the following statements about **your major program**?

		Strongly Disagree (1)	Disagree (2)	Agree (3)	Strongly Agree (4)
a.	Faculty were genuinely interested in the welfare of departmental majors	☐	☐	☐	☐
b.	The program was academically demanding	☐	☐	☐	☐
c.	The department was characterized by mutual respect between students and professors	☐	☐	☐	☐
d.	Most faculty prepared carefully for their courses	☐	☐	☐	☐
e.	Required courses were offered regularly	☐	☐	☐	☐
f.	There were sufficient opportunities to interact with faculty	☐	☐	☐	☐
g.	Grading practices were appropriate and fair	☐	☐	☐	☐
h.	I received helpful feedback from faculty on my academic progress	☐	☐	☐	☐
i.	If I were starting over, I would major in this department again	☐	☐	☐	☐

8. To what extent do you agree or disagree with the following aspects of advising by your **major advisor**?

My major advisor . . .

		Not Applicable (0)	Strongly Disagree (1)	Disagree (2)	Agree (3)	Strongly Agree (4)
a.	Knew my name	☐	☐	☐	☐	☐
b.	Gave me feedback on my academic progress	☐	☐	☐	☐	☐
c.	Provided me with accurate information	☐	☐	☐	☐	☐
d.	Helped me with registration when asked	☐	☐	☐	☐	☐
e.	Showed an interest in me personally	☐	☐	☐	☐	☐
f.	Was on time for appointments with me	☐	☐	☐	☐	☐
g.	Spent sufficient time with me	☐	☐	☐	☐	☐
h.	Was accessible when I needed help	☐	☐	☐	☐	☐
i.	Reviewed my academic record prior to giving advice	☐	☐	☐	☐	☐
j.	Discussed what I needed to know about academic requirements and services	☐	☐	☐	☐	☐
k.	Gave me information about careers in my major	☐	☐	☐	☐	☐
l.	Referred me to appropriate resources on campus	☐	☐	☐	☐	☐
m.	Is someone I would recommend to other students	☐	☐	☐	☐	☐

SATISFACTION WITH ACADEMIC SUPPORT SERVICES

9. **ADMISSIONS AND STUDENT RECORDS**

		Did Not Use (0)	Very Dissatisfied (1)	Dissatisfied (2)	Satisfied (3)	Very Satisfied (4)
a.	Admissions Office	☐	☐	☐	☐	☐
b.	Student Records and Transcripts in the Registrar's office	☐	☐	☐	☐	☐

10. **STUDENT SERVICES**

a.	Personal Guidance and Counseling	☐	☐	☐	☐	☐
b.	Career Planning and Counseling	☐	☐	☐	☐	☐
c.	Career Placement Services	☐	☐	☐	☐	☐
d.	Financial Aid Services	☐	☐	☐	☐	☐
e.	Student Health Services	☐	☐	☐	☐	☐

11. **INFORMATION SERVICES**

a.	King Library Services overall	☐	☐	☐	☐	☐
	1. Reference desk	☐	☐	☐	☐	☐
	2. Circulation	☐	☐	☐	☐	☐
	3. Books and journals in my major	☐	☐	☐	☐	☐
	4. Hours	☐	☐	☐	☐	☐
b.	Computing Center services overall	☐	☐	☐	☐	☐
c.	PC laboratories in my department/college	☐	☐	☐	☐	☐
d.	PC laboratories at the University	☐	☐	☐	☐	☐

12. **STUDENT ACTIVITIES**

a.	Cultural Programs (lectures, concerts, etc.)	☐	☐	☐	☐	☐
b.	Recreational Programs	☐	☐	☐	☐	☐
c.	Intramural Athletic Programs	☐	☐	☐	☐	☐

PREPARATION AND TRANSFERRING TO THE UNIVERSITY

13. How effective was your high school preparation for your work at UK?

4. ☐ Very Effective
3. ☐ Effective
2. ☐ Ineffective
1. ☐ Very Ineffective

	No (1)	Yes (2)
14. Did it take you an extra semester or more to complete degree requirements at the University of Kentucky?	☐	☐

15. If YES, why did you take an extra semester or more? (Please check an answer for each item)

	No (1)	Yes (2)
a. Work obligations limited my enrollment	☐	☐
b. Family obligations limited my enrollment	☐	☐
c. Tuition and other costs of attendance limited my enrollment	☐	☐
d. A decision to change majors added to my requirements	☐	☐
e. A required course was not offered	☐	☐
f. I lost credits in my major upon transferring to UK	☐	☐
g. Some of my credits could not be applied to my general studies requirements upon transferring to UK	☐	☐
h. A double major or additional interests lengthened my studies	☐	☐
i. I failed or dropped a class I needed to graduate	☐	☐
j. I came to UK with insufficient academic preparation	☐	☐
k. Other (please indicate) _____	☐	☐

16. If you transferred from another college to UK, please answer the questions below about your experiences AFTER you transferred.

After I transferred to UK . . .	Not Applicable (0)	Strongly Disagree (1)	Disagree (2)	Agree (3)	Strongly Agree (4)
a. I felt prepared for the classes I took.	☐	☐	☐	☐	☐
b. Courses were more difficult than I expected.	☐	☐	☐	☐	☐
c. UK professors expected students to learn more on their own.	☐	☐	☐	☐	☐
d. My UK advisor expected that I would perform well.	☐	☐	☐	☐	☐
e. My UK advisor suggested I re-take a class at UK.	☐	☐	☐	☐	☐
f. It was hard to adjust to the larger classes.	☐	☐	☐	☐	☐
g. I needed more assistance to decide on a major.	☐	☐	☐	☐	☐

17. While school was in session, how many hours per week on average, did you work for pay?

1. ☐ I was not employed
2. ☐ 1-10 hours per week
3. ☐ 11-15 hours per week
4. ☐ 16-25 hours per week
5. ☐ 26-35 hours per week
6. ☐ 36 or over per week

EMPLOYMENT PLANS

18. What are your immediate employment plans?

1. ☐ I will work at the job I had before I graduated.
2. ☐ I will work at a new job I recently obtained.
3. ☐ I am currently seeking employment.
4. ☐ I do not plan to work.
5. ☐ I plan to continue my education before working.
6. ☐ I don't know.

IF YOU WILL NOT BE EMPLOYED, PLEASE SKIP TO QUESTION 25.

19. If you have accepted a position, check the box that BEST describes this position.

1. ☐ Chief Executive (Owner of business, Vice President, etc.)
2. ☐ Accountant, Loan Officer, Financial Officer
3. ☐ Engineer, Surveyor, Architect
4. ☐ Registered Nurse
5. ☐ Other Allied Health Professional
6. ☐ Pharmacist
7. ☐ Social Worker
8. ☐ Teacher
9. ☐ Therapist including Speech Pathologist
10. ☐ Administrator or other Professional Position
11. ☐ Administrative Support (administrative assistant, secretary, computer operator, etc.)
12. ☐ Sales and Sales Supervision (retail and wholesale)
13. ☐ Manager for a Service Business (retail, restaurant, hotel, etc.)
14. ☐ Graduate Teaching or Research Assistant
15. ☐ Other (please indicate) _____

20. What will you earn during your first year in this position?

1. ☐ $15,000 or less
2. ☐ $15,001 - 20,000
3. ☐ $20,001 - 25,000
4. ☐ $25,001 - 30,000
5. ☐ $30,001 - 40,000
6. ☐ $40,001 - 60,000
7. ☐ Over $60,000

21. Which BEST describes where you will be employed?
  1. ☐ Agriculture
  2. ☐ Mining and Construction
  3. ☐ Manufacturing/Industry
  4. ☐ Wholesale and Retail Trade
  5. ☐ Finance, Insurance, and Real Estate
  6. ☐ General Services/Utilities
  7. ☐ Health Services (or Health Care System)
  8. ☐ School or University
  9. ☐ Public Administration/Government
  10. ☐ Not employed

22. If employed in health care system, please indicate the specific type below . . .
  1. ☐ Hospital
  2. ☐ Nursing Home
  3. ☐ Home Health Care Agency
  4. ☐ Community Health Department
  5. ☐ Other Community Based Agency or Business (Doctor's Office, Laboratories, other)

23. To what extent is your new job related to your major at the University of Kentucky?
  1. ☐ Directly related
  2. ☐ Somewhat related
  3. ☐ Not related
  4. ☐ Not applicable

24. How important do you feel your degree was in obtaining your current position?
  1. ☐ Very important
  2. ☐ Somewhat important
  3. ☐ Not important

GRADUATE/PROFESSIONAL SCHOOL PLANS

If you plan to pursue additional education in the upcoming academic year, please complete this section.
If NO, please skip to Question 31.

25. What is the highest degree you plan to earn?
  1. ☐ No plans, undecided
  2. ☐ Masters degree
  3. ☐ Professional degree, (such as dentistry, medicine, law, theology)
  4. ☐ Doctoral degree, (such as Ph.D., D.B.A.)

26. What college or university will you attend to continue your education?
  1. ☐ Eastern Kentucky University
  2. ☐ Northern Kentucky University
  3. ☐ Western Kentucky University
  4. ☐ University of Kentucky
  5. ☐ University of Louisville
  6. ☐ Other (Please Indicate)

  _____
  College   State

27. In what general area will you pursue your degree?
  1. ☐ Agriculture and Related
  2. ☐ Arts, Visual and Performing
  3. ☐ Biological Sciences
  4. ☐ Business and Management
  5. ☐ Communications & Journalism
  6. ☐ Computer/Information Sciences
  7. ☐ Education
  8. ☐ Engineering
  9. ☐ Health Sciences (M.D., D.D.S., etc.)
  10. ☐ Allied Health Sciences (Nursing, Pharmacy, etc.)
  11. ☐ Human Environmental Sciences/Home Economics
  12. ☐ Law
  13. ☐ Letters (English, literature, classics, etc.)
  14. ☐ Physical Sciences
  15. ☐ Social & Behavioral Sciences (Psychology, Sociology, etc.)
  16. ☐ Social Work
  17. ☐ Public Affairs/Administration
  18. ☐ Other (please indicate) _____

28. To how many graduate or professional schools did you apply? _____

29. By how many graduate or professional schools were you accepted? _____

30. How will you finance your graduate/professional school education? (Check as many as apply).

	No (1)	Yes (2)
a. Scholarship	☐	☐
b. Fellowship	☐	☐
c. Teaching or Research Assistantship	☐	☐
d. Personal earnings or savings	☐	☐
e. Loans	☐	☐
f. Grants	☐	☐
g. Other (please indicate) _____		

31. We are particularly interested in what you liked best about your education at UK and what you liked least.

_____
_____
_____
_____
_____
_____
_____

Thank you for your assistance!

7049

UNIVERSITY OF KENTUCKY ALUMNI SURVEY

This survey is designed to help us learn from the experiences of our graduates. Your responses will provide an important source of information for our evaluation and planning efforts. Please answer all of the questions. If you wish to comment or qualify your answers, feel free to use the space in the margins. Your comments will be read and taken into account. All answers are confidential and will not be associated with your name. Thank you for your help.

Lexington Campus — Office of Planning and Assessment
University of Kentucky
206 Gillis Building
Lexington, KY 40506-0033

Indicate name or address below IF INCORRECT ON LABEL.

(Please Print)

Last	First	Middle Initial	Unmarried Name

Preferred Mailing Address:

Street

City	State	Zip Code

PART A.   THE UK GENERAL EDUCATION CURRICULUM

In this first section of the survey, we would like to get some feedback on the quality of courses and instruction at UK as well as the general education courses required by the University Studies Program (USP). How would you assess UK in developing your academic abilities in the following areas? Please rate only those courses you took at the University on the Lexington Campus, not those you may have transferred in from another institution or at any of the UK Community Colleges.

1. As a result of USP courses I took at the University of Kentucky I learned ...

	Not Applicable (0)	Strongly Disagree (1)	Disagree (2)	Agree (3)	Strongly Agree (4)
a. To write effectively	☐	☐	☐	☐	☐
b. To use mathematics to solve problems	☐	☐	☐	☐	☐
c. To apply the principles of logic to solve problems	☐	☐	☐	☐	☐
d. To analyze and interpret statistical data	☐	☐	☐	☐	☐
e. To convey my views orally	☐	☐	☐	☐	☐
f. To explain the basic principles which govern natural sciences and experimentation	☐	☐	☐	☐	☐
g. To apply my knowledge of science to solve simple problems	☐	☐	☐	☐	☐
h. To translate simple passages written in a foreign language	☐	☐	☐	☐	☐
i. To use a foreign language to communicate orally	☐	☐	☐	☐	☐
j. To appreciate the strengths of a culture different from my own	☐	☐	☐	☐	☐
k. To think analytically and logically	☐	☐	☐	☐	☐
l. To describe the major historical trends and conflicts in western culture	☐	☐	☐	☐	☐
m. To analyze behavior of individuals and groups	☐	☐	☐	☐	☐
n. To analyze an issue from more than one disciplinary vantage point	☐	☐	☐	☐	☐
o. To accept human differences and to be open to other viewpoints	☐	☐	☐	☐	☐

2. In thinking over your experiences at UK, how would you rate your gain or progress in each of the following areas?

	Poor (1)	Good (2)	Fair (3)	Excellent (4)
a. An increased understanding and enjoyment of art, music, and drama	☐	☐	☐	☐
b. A basic familiarity with computers	☐	☐	☐	☐
c. An ability to develop my own values and standards				
d. An understanding of the impact of new scientific and technical developments	☐	☐	☐	☐
e. An ability to put ideas together (i.e. to see relationships, similarities, and differences between ideas)	☐	☐	☐	☐
f. An ability to learn on my own	☐	☐	☐	☐
g. A conviction that I need to continue to read and learn throughout life	☐	☐	☐	☐
h. A conviction that I have some responsibility to serve the needs of others	☐	☐	☐	☐

OVERALL EVALUATION OF USP

For each of the following questions, please indicate the extent of your agreement or disagreement with the statement as it describes the University Studies Program (USP) courses you completed at the UK-Lexington Campus.

3A. The courses I took in the USP:

	Not Applicable (0)	Strongly Disagree (1)	Disagree (2)	Agree (3)	Strongly Agree (4)
a. Prepared me for upper division courses in my major	☐	☐	☐	☐	☐
b. Prepared me for my first career-related position	☐	☐	☐	☐	☐
c. Developed my ability to locate information quickly and efficiently	☐	☐	☐	☐	☐
d. Developed my ability to analyze data and draw conclusions	☐	☐	☐	☐	☐
e. Familiarized me with the major social, political, and ethical issues of our times	☐	☐	☐	☐	☐

3B. I had difficulty getting the course I wanted to fulfill my USP requirements. ☐ ☐ ☐ ☐ ☐

3C. The quality of teaching in USP courses was ☐ ☐ ☐ ☐ ☐ comparable to that I received in my major.

4. If I could eliminate one component of the University Studies Program requirements, it would be:

_____

_____

_____

_____

5. If I could require all UK students to take one USP course, it would be:

_____

6. The most valuable part of the University Studies Program Requirements for me was:

_____

_____

_____

_____

_____

_____

_____

_____

7A. How would you rate the quality of each of the following aspects of the University and your major?

	At the University?				In my major?			
	Poor (1)	Good (2)	Fair (3)	Excellent (4)	Poor (1)	Good (2)	Fair (3)	Excellent (4)
a. Overall quality of instruction by faculty	☐	☐	☐	☐	☐	☐	☐	■
b. Quality of instruction by teaching assistants	☐	☐	☐	☐	☐	☐	☐	■
c. Individual attention from instructors	☐	☐	☐	☐	☐	☐	☐	■
d. Quality of curriculum in providing job related skills and knowledge	☐	☐	☐	☐	☐	☐	☐	■
e. Quality of curriculum in preparing for further education	☐	☐	☐	☐	☐	☐	☐	■
f. Overall impression of UK/ of my department	☐	☐	☐	☐	☐	☐	☐	■

7B. Please answer the following special questions as they relate to your experiences in your major department:

	Not Applicable (0)	Strongly Disagree (1)	Disagree (2)	Agree (3)	Strongly Agree (4)
a. Grading practices and other academic policies were administered fairly	☐	☐	☐	☐	☐
b. Faculty members in my department were interested in my progress as a student	☐	☐	☐	☐	☐
c. Teachers were available for assistance outside of the classroom	☐	☐	☐	☐	☐
d. The courses required for my major were appropriate	☐	☐	☐	☐	☐
e. The content of the courses was of high quality	☐	☐	☐	☐	☐
f. Academic quality was a priority of the faculty and administration in my major department	☐	☐	☐	☐	☐
g. Compared to other courses I had at the university, my major courses were intellectually challenging	☐	☐	☐	☐	☐
h. The quality of instruction I received from my faculty in my major was uniformly high	☐	☐	☐	☐	☐

PART B: EMPLOYMENT STATUS

8. Which one of the following best describes what you are doing now?

1. ☐ Employed full-time (35 or more hours per week)
2. ☐ Employed part-time (less than 35 hours per week)
3. ☐ Not employed but seeking employment
4. ☐ Not employed and not seeking employment

9. Since graduating from UK, have you worked in a job related to your major?

1. ☐ Yes, my job is specifically related
2. ☐ Yes, my job is somewhat related
3. ☐ No, my job is not related to my major

10. Please check one statement below which best describes why you are not working in a job related to your major.

1. ☐ I found a more desirable job in another field
2. ☐ I have not seriously sought employment related to my major
3. ☐ I am continuing my college education
4. ☐ I am caring for my family
5. ☐ I am working in another field while I look for a job related to my major
6. ☐ I am unable to find a job in ANY field.
7. ☐ Other (please specify)

_____

_____

IF NOT EMPLOYED, PLEASE SKIP TO QUESTION 20 IN PART C.

11. Once you began your job search, how long did it take you to find a position related to your major?

1. ☐ Held job while attending UK
2. ☐ Secured job prior to graduation
3. ☐ Less than 30 days
4. ☐ 30 to 60 days
5. ☐ Three to four months
6. ☐ Five months to one year
7. ☐ More than a year
8. ☐ Not applicable

12. How many positions related to your college major have you held since your graduation from UK? _____

13. Please write in the space below what your current job title is: (For example: teacher, marketing representative, etc.)

_____

14. How well do you feel UK prepared you for the demands of your current position?

1. ☐ Excellent preparation
2. ☐ Good preparation
3. ☐ Fair preparation
4. ☐ Inadequate/poor preparation

15. In what state are you currently employed?

1. ☐ Kentucky
2. ☐ Other U.S. State
3. ☐ Outside the United States

16. What is your annual income from your current FULL-TIME job?

1. ☐ $ 0-15,000
2. ☐ $ 15,001-20,000
3. ☐ $ 20,001-25,000
4. ☐ $ 25,001-30,000
5. ☐ $ 30,001-40,000
6. ☐ $ 40,001-60,000
7. ☐ Over $60,000

17. Which best describes your current employer?

1. ☐ Business
2. ☐ Industry or manufacturing
3. ☐ School or University
4. ☐ Government or non-profit organization
5. ☐ Health Care System
6. ☐ Other (Please describe)

_____

18. If employed within the Health Care System, please indicate the specific type below...

1. ☐ Hospital
2. ☐ Nursing Home
3. ☐ Home Health Care Agency
4. ☐ Community Health Department
5. ☐ Other Community Based Agency or Business (Doctor's Office, Laboratories, etc.)

19A. May we contact your employer to obtain information on your performance and UK education as it relates to your position?

1. ☐ Yes
2. ☐ No

19B. Name and address of employer:

_____
Supervisor

_____
Name of company or employer

_____
Street

_____
City   State   Zip Code

PART C: GRADUATE EDUCATION

20. Where have you applied to graduate school? Were you offered support from these schools?

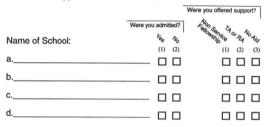

Name of School:	Were you admitted?		Were you offered support?		
	Yes	No	Non Service Fellowship	TA or RA	No Aid
	(1)	(2)	(1)	(2)	(3)
a._____	☐	☐	☐	☐	☐
b._____	☐	☐	☐	☐	☐
c._____	☐	☐	☐	☐	☐
d._____	☐	☐	☐	☐	☐

21. What is the name of the college or university you have actually attended since graduating from UK?

_____
Name   State

IF YOU HAVE NOT ATTENDED ANOTHER COLLEGE OR UNIVERSITY, PLEASE SKIP TO QUESTION 29

22. Please write in your major/program at your current college or university:

_____

23. What is your current status at your new institution?
    1. ☐ Full-time student
    2. ☐ Part-time student

24. What is your ultimate goal in attending this new institution?
    1. ☐ No degree goals
    2. ☐ Master's of Education degree
    3. ☐ Other Master's degree
    4. ☐ Law degree
    5. ☐ Medicine or Dentistry degree
    6. ☐ Ph.D.
    7. ☐ Other Doctorate (D.B.A., Ed.D., etc.)
    8. ☐ Other degree (please indicate)

_____

25. What degree have you already earned *since leaving* UK?
    1. ☐ Have not attended another university
    2. ☐ Still pursuing a degree
    3. ☐ Master's
    4. ☐ Law
    5. ☐ Other degree (please indicate)

_____

26. Please indicate your overall grade point average at the university you are now attending or have attended since graduating from UK.
    1. ☐ 3.50 - 4.00
    2. ☐ 3.00 - 3.49
    3. ☐ 2.50 - 2.99
    4. ☐ 2.00 - 2.49
    5. ☐ 1.50 - 1.99
    6. ☐ 1.00 - 1.49
    7. ☐ Below 1.00
    8. ☐ Not applicable

27. What is the name of the position you hope to obtain upon completion of your current program?

_____

28. How well did UK prepare you to pursue your graduate/professional school studies?
    1. ☐ Excellent
    2. ☐ Good
    3. ☐ Fair
    4. ☐ Poor

29. Please add any comments you may wish to below.

_____
_____
_____
_____
_____
_____
_____
_____
_____

THANK YOU FOR YOUR COOPERATION!

9075   SP94

ParSURVEY®
GENERAL SURVEY
(GST MODULE)

◀ USE NO. 2 PENCIL ONLY ▶

COASTAL CAROLINA COMMUNITY COLLEGE
Employer Survey

Happy Village Nursing Home
1111 Main Street
Jacksonville, NC 28540

Nurse Assistant

Please indicate your level of satisfaction with your employee's competencies in the following areas by using the scale below and placing your answers in the corresponding number on the right. Skip any competencies that do not apply to your employee. Use No. 2 Pencil Only.

Excellent	Average	Poor
5..............4..............3..............2..............1		

How does your new employee, Jane Doe, rate in the following areas:

How does he/she . . .

1. Perform the needed vocational or technical skills?
2. Communicate effectively in speaking, writing, reading, and listening?
3. Demonstrate the needed math skills?
4. Use information to analyze problems and make logical decisions?
5. Demonstrate good work habits such as promptness, cooperation, politeness, etc.?

6. If the need arises, would you hire a CCCC graduate from this program in the future?

   (1) Yes   (2) No

7. Please list any qualities, characteristics and/or skills that you particularly like about your Coastal graduate and his/her training.

8. ANY OTHER COMMENTS:

9. *If you do not rate all the questions above, please respond as to Why.*

ParSURVEY®
GENERAL SURVEY
(GST MODULE)

◄ ⌐ USE NO. 2 PENCIL ONLY ⌐

INSTRUCTIONS: *To the top right, please write vertically your Social Security Number using one line for each number and fill in the corresponding circle.*

Coastal Carolina Community College
Graduate Follow-Up Survey

Name:_____

(please print clearly)

Instructions: *For numbers 1-3 to the right, fill in vertically the number corresponding to your curriculum code below using one line for each number.*

College Transfer - 111	Fire Protection Technology- 133	Electrical Install & Main. - 155
Accounting - 112	Marketing/Retailing - 134	Electronic Servicing - 211
Architectural Technology- 113	Medical Laboratory - 135	Machinist - 212
Associate Degree Nursing - 114	Office Technologies- 141	Nurse Assistant - 213
Automotive Technology - 115	Paralegal Technology - 142	Practical Nurse Education - 214
Basic Law Enforcement- 121	Surveying Technology - 143	Surgical Technology- 215
Business Administration - 122	Air Cond./Heating/Refrigeration- 144	Welding - 221
Business Computer Prog. - 123	Auto Body Repair - 145	College Special Studies - 222
Criminal Justice Technolgy - 124	Child Care - 151	Technical Special Studies - 223
Dental Hygiene - 125	Cosmetology - 152	Vocational Special Studies - 224
Electronic Engineering - 131	Dental Assisting - 153	Micro-Computer Systems-225
Emergency Medical Science-132	Diesel Vehicle Maintenance- 154	

INSTRUCTIONS: *For numbers 4-9 below, after considering each of the following items, fill in the most appropriate response by using a #2 pencil:*

4.   What was your primary objective/reason for attending CCCC?
   (1)   Obtain Associate Degree, Diploma, or Certificate
   (2)   Enhance my job skills in my present field of study
   (3)   Enhance my job skills for a new line of work
   (4)   Take courses to transfer to another college
   (5)   Take courses for personal interest
5.   To what extent do you feel you accomplished your objective while attending CCCC? (Select one)
   (1)   Fully accomplished
   (2)   Partially accomplished
   (3)   Not accomplished
6.   What is your current employment status (since graduation)?
   (1)   Retired
   (2)   Unemployed-not seeking employment
   (3)   Unemployed-seeking employment
   (4)   Employed part-time
   (5)   Employed full-time
6a.   If you are working, what is your job title? _____
   Company name: _____
   Supervisor's Name: _____
   Address: _____
   Phone Number: _____
7.   Is your job (job skills) related to your studies at CCCC?
   (1)   Yes
   (2)   No
   (3)   Somewhat
7a.   What is your approximate Gross Monthly Salary? $_____ or
        Hourly Wage? $_____
   (This information will only be used to calculate an average entry salary for this occupation.)
8.   To improve the Coastal curriculum, we would like to contact your employer for input. May we contact your employer?
   (1)   Yes
   (2)   No
9.   After graduation from CCCC, did you transfer your college credits to another curriculum at CCCC?
   (1)   Yes
   (2)   No
   If yes, what curriculum? _____

(Please Continue on Back)

© SCANTRON CORPORATION 1989 ALL RIGHTS RESERVED.

SCANTRON® FORM NO. F-414-ERI

(Note: This page begins with #51)

51. OR did you transfer your credits to another two or four year college?
    (1) Yes
    (2) No
    If yes, what college? _____
    Where is it located? _____
52. If #51 was yes, then you received accurate information about transferability of transfer courses.
    (1) Strongly Agree   (2) Agree   (3) Do not Agree
53. If you did not transfer credits into another curriculum at CCCC or another college, have you enrolled in any CCCC classes since graduation in Curriculum?
    (1) Yes
    (2) No
54. In Continuing Education?
    (1) Yes
    (2) No
55. If no, would you consider taking any courses at Coastal in the future?
    (1) Yes
    (2) No

INSTRUCTIONS: *For numbers 56-72 below, please indicate your rating of the following services by filling in the most appropriate response from the following options. Answer only those questions that aply to you. If the item is not applicable or you have no opinion, please leave the response BLANK:*

(5) Excellent	**(2) Below Average**
(4) Above Average	**(1) Poor**
(3) Average	

56. Overall Instruction
57. Faculty Advising
58. Teaching Facilities
59. Equipment
60. Job Placement Services
61. Library Services
62. Admissions Procedures
63. Counseling
64. Financial Aid
65. Veterans Affairs
66. Registration Procedures
67. Student Activities
68. Business Office
69. Bookstore (Student Emporium)
70. Cafeteria
71. Security
72. Overall CCCC experience

Please provide us with your permanent mailing address. This information will be used for college survey purposes only and will be kept strictly confidential.

Name: _____

Address: _____

_____

Phone : _____

51 ⑤ ④ ③ ② ①
52 ⑤ ④ ③ ② ①
53 ⑤ ④ ③ ② ①
54 ⑤ ④ ③ ② ①
55 ⑤ ④ ③ ② ①
56 ⑤ ④ ③ ② ①
57 ⑤ ④ ③ ② ①
58 ⑤ ④ ③ ② ①
59 ⑤ ④ ③ ② ①
60 ⑤ ④ ③ ② ①
61 ⑤ ④ ③ ② ①
62 ⑤ ④ ③ ② ①
63 ⑤ ④ ③ ② ①
64 ⑤ ④ ③ ② ①
65 ⑤ ④ ③ ② ①
66 ⑤ ④ ③ ② ①
67 ⑤ ④ ③ ② ①
68 ⑤ ④ ③ ② ①
69 ⑤ ④ ③ ② ①
70 ⑤ ④ ③ ② ①
71 ⑤ ④ ③ ② ①
72 ⑤ ④ ③ ② ①
73 ⑤ ④ ③ ② ①
74 ⑤ ④ ③ ② ①
75 ⑤ ④ ③ ② ①
76 ⑤ ④ ③ ② ①
77 ⑤ ④ ③ ② ①
78 ⑤ ④ ③ ② ①
79 ⑤ ④ ③ ② ①
80 ⑤ ④ ③ ② ①
81 ⑤ ④ ③ ② ①
82 ⑤ ④ ③ ② ①
83 ⑤ ④ ③ ② ①
84 ⑤ ④ ③ ② ①
85 ⑤ ④ ③ ② ①
86 ⑤ ④ ③ ② ①
87 ⑤ ④ ③ ② ①
88 ⑤ ④ ③ ② ①
89 ⑤ ④ ③ ② ①
90 ⑤ ④ ③ ② ①
91 ⑤ ④ ③ ② ①
92 ⑤ ④ ③ ② ①
93 ⑤ ④ ③ ② ①
94 ⑤ ④ ③ ② ①
95 ⑤ ④ ③ ② ①
96 ⑤ ④ ③ ② ①
97 ⑤ ④ ③ ② ①
98 ⑤ ④ ③ ② ①
99 ⑤ ④ ③ ② ①
100 ⑤ ④ ③ ② ①
101 ⑤ ④ ③ ② ①
102 ⑤ ④ ③ ② ①
103 ⑤ ④ ③ ② ①
104 ⑤ ④ ③ ② ①
105 ⑤ ④ ③ ② ①
106 ⑤ ④ ③ ② ①
107 ⑤ ④ ③ ② ①
108 ⑤ ④ ③ ② ①
109 ⑤ ④ ③ ② ①
110 ⑤ ④ ③ ② ①

ParSURVEY®
GENERAL SURVEY
(GST MODULE)

◄ USE NO. 2 PENCIL ONLY

INSTRUCTIONS: To the top right, please write vertically your Social Security Number using one line for each number and fill in the corresponding circle.

Coastal Carolina Community College
Leaver/Withdrawal Follow-Up Survey

Name: _____
(Please print clearly)

Instructions: For numbers 1-3 to the right, fill in vertically the number corresponding to your curriculum code below using one line for each number.

College Transfer - 111	Fire Protection Technology- 133	Electrical Install & Main. - 155
Accounting - 112	Marketing/Retailing - 134	Electronic Servicing - 211
Architectural Technology- 113	Medical Laboratory - 135	Machinist - 212
Associate Degree Nursing - 114	Office Technologies- 141	Nurse Assistant - 213
Automotive Technology - 115	Paralegal Technology - 142	Practical Nurse Education - 214
Basic Law Enforcement- 121	Surveying Technology - 143	Surgical Technology- 215
Business Administration - 122	Air Cond./Heating/Refrigeration- 144	Welding - 221
Business Computer Prog. - 123	Auto Body Repair - 145	College Special Studies - 222
Criminal Justice Technolgy - 124	Child Care - 151	Technical Special Studies - 223
Dental Hygiene - 125	Cosmetology - 152	Vocational Special Studies - 224
Electronic Engineering - 131	Dental Assisting - 153	Micro-Computer Systems-225
Emergency Medical Science-132	Diesel Vehicle Maintenance- 154	

INSTRUCTIONS: For numbers 4-9 below, after considering each of the following items, fill in the most appropriate response by using a #2 pencil:

4. What was your primary objective/reason for attending CCCC?
   (1) Graduate with an Associate Degree, Diploma, or Certificate to get or advance my job skills or continue on at a University
   (2) Enhance my job skills in my present field of study but not to graduate from Coastal
   (3) Enhance my job skills for a new line of work but not to graduate from Coastal
   (4) To take courses to transfer to another college but not to graduate from Coastal
   (5) Take courses for personal interest only

5. To what extent do you feel you accomplished your objective while attending CCCC? (Select one)
   (1) Fully accomplished
   (2) Partially accomplished
   (3) Not accomplished

Fill in one item only out of Questions 6, 7, 8, or 9.

6. Which **best** describes your reason for withdrawing from CCCC?
   (1) Academic
   (2) Child Care
   (3) Death of Family Member
   (4) Dissatisfaction with Class

7. (1) Dissatisfaction with Instructor
   (2) Dissatisfaction with Services
   (3) Employment
   (4) Family Problems

8. (1) Financial
   (2) Health
   (3) Left Area
   (4) Marriage

9. (1) Military
   (2) Separated or Divorced
   (3) Transportation
   (4) Transferred to another College
       Other_____

(Please continue on back)

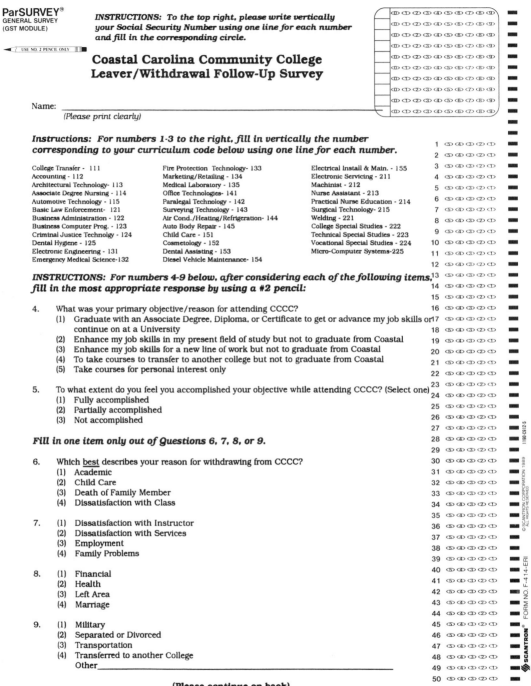

(Note: This page begins with #51)

INSTRUCTIONS: *For numbers 51-67 below, please indicate your rating of the following services by filling in the most appropriate response from the following options:*

(5)	**Excellent**	**(2)**	**Below Average**
(4)	**Above Average**	**(1)**	**Poor**
(3)	**Average**		

51. Overall Instruction
52. Faculty Advising
53. Teaching Facilities
54. Equipment
55. Job Placement Services
56. Library Services
57. Admissions Procedures
58. Counseling
59. Financial Aid
60. Veterans Affairs
61. Registration Procedures
62. Student Activities
63. Business Office
64. Bookstore (Student Emporium)
65. Cafeteria
66. Security
67. Overall CCCC experience

INSTRUCTIONS: *For numbers 68-73 below, fill in the most appropriate response to this question, "Could we have done anything differently that may have helped you remain in college?"*

68. Provided you help in getting a job?
   (1) Yes   (2)   No
69. Provided you help in obtaining financial aid?
   (1) Yes   (2)   No
70. Provided you child care?
   (1) Yes   (2)   No
71. Provided you tutoring:
   (1) Yes   (2)   No
72. Provided you personal counseling?
   (1) Yes   (2)   No
73. Provided you help with reading, writing, math or study skills (if yes, circle the area/areas with which you need help)?
   (1) Yes   (2)   No

51 (5) (4) (3) (2) (1)
52 (5) (4) (3) (2) (1)
53 (5) (4) (3) (2) (1)
54 (5) (4) (3) (2) (1)
55 (5) (4) (3) (2) (1)
56 (5) (4) (3) (2) (1)
57 (5) (4) (3) (2) (1)
58 (5) (4) (3) (2) (1)
59 (5) (4) (3) (2) (1)
60 (5) (4) (3) (2) (1)
61 (5) (4) (3) (2) (1)
62 (5) (4) (3) (2) (1)
63 (5) (4) (3) (2) (1)
64 (5) (4) (3) (2) (1)
65 (5) (4) (3) (2) (1)
66 (5) (4) (3) (2) (1)
67 (5) (4) (3) (2) (1)
68 (5) (4) (3) (2) (1)
69 (5) (4) (3) (2) (1)
70 (5) (4) (3) (2) (1)
71 (5) (4) (3) (2) (1)
72 (5) (4) (3) (2) (1)
73 (5) (4) (3) (2) (1)
74 (5) (4) (3) (2) (1)
75 (5) (4) (3) (2) (1)
76 (5) (4) (3) (2) (1)
77 (5) (4) (3) (2) (1)
78 (5) (4) (3) (2) (1)
79 (5) (4) (3) (2) (1)
80 (5) (4) (3) (2) (1)
81 (5) (4) (3) (2) (1)
82 (5) (4) (3) (2) (1)
83 (5) (4) (3) (2) (1)
84 (5) (4) (3) (2) (1)
85 (5) (4) (3) (2) (1)
86 (5) (4) (3) (2) (1)
87 (5) (4) (3) (2) (1)
88 (5) (4) (3) (2) (1)
89 (5) (4) (3) (2) (1)
90 (5) (4) (3) (2) (1)
91 (5) (4) (3) (2) (1)
92 (5) (4) (3) (2) (1)
93 (5) (4) (3) (2) (1)
94 (5) (4) (3) (2) (1)
95 (5) (4) (3) (2) (1)
96 (5) (4) (3) (2) (1)
97 (5) (4) (3) (2) (1)
98 (5) (4) (3) (2) (1)
99 (5) (4) (3) (2) (1)
100 (5) (4) (3) (2) (1)
101 (5) (4) (3) (2) (1)
102 (5) (4) (3) (2) (1)
103 (5) (4) (3) (2) (1)
104 (5) (4) (3) (2) (1)
105 (5) (4) (3) (2) (1)
106 (5) (4) (3) (2) (1)
107 (5) (4) (3) (2) (1)
108 (5) (4) (3) (2) (1)
109 (5) (4) (3) (2) (1)
110 (5) (4) (3) (2) (1)

APPENDIX F—Summary of Department Assessment Plans in the Major, State University of New York at Albany

Senior Thesis or Research Project

Africana Studies* (within senior seminar)
Latin American & Caribbean Studies
Women's Studies*
Political Science & Public Affairs*
French Studies (honors)

Performance Experience

Theater (ACT festival)
Music* (performance)
Public Affairs (internship)
Social Welfare (field internship with seminar)

Capstone Course

Africana Studies*
French Studies
Judaic Studies*
Linguistic & Cognitive Science*
Mathematics*
Philosophy
Religious Studies Program
Women's Studies*
Business Administration*
Social Welfare (seminar with internship)

Comprehensive Examination

Accounting* (CPA exam)
Chemistry
Computer Science
German Language & Literature*
Hispanic & Italian*
Social Studies (NTE)
Music (theory)
Physics
Psychology*
Slavic Languages & Literature*
Sociology*

Student Portfolio of Learning Experiences

Art (portfolio of artistic works)
English (writing portfolio)

Senior Essay (or Survey) and Interview

Anthropology*
Atmospheric Science*
Biology*
Classics (joint faculty review)
Communication
East Asian Studies (with faculty retreat)
Geological Sciences & Earth Sciences
German Language & Literature*
Hispanic & Italian*
History
Judaic Studies*
Slavic Languages & Literature*
Sociology*
Women's Studies*
Criminal Justice*
Psychology*

Alumni Studies and Use of Departmental and Placement Data

Anthropology*
Atmospheric Science*
Economics*
French Studies*
Geological Sciences*
Hispanic & Italian*
Linguistic & Cognitive Science*
Psychology*
Sociology*
Business Administration*
Accounting*

Multi-method Combination

APPENDIX G—Extract from *Reflections of a University: Some Questions Clemson Has Asked*

Table of Contents

2. How good are the reasoning skills of our students?

The College BASE examination, given to freshmen and upper-level students in the Fall semester of 1989, included items assessing reasoning skills. Three-quarters of the items on that exam address reasoning abilities. The other one-quarter of the items test recall of facts. Three levels of reasoning are examined. A brief description of each is shown in Table 2.1.

Table 2.1. Description of the types of reasoning abilities measured by the College Base examination

---

Interpretive Reasoning
The ability to translate information into one's own words. Includes the ability to paraphrase and summarize information.

Strategic Reasoning
The ability to go beyond interpretive reasoning and compare and contrast information. Includes the ability to infer deductively.

Adaptive Reasoning
The ability to synthesize new rules or theories and to predict outcomes of causal relationships. Includes the ability to infer inductively.

The College BASE examination provides data on each level of reasoning competency and classifies performance of students into thirds. The thirds are based on the expected competency for students who would have completed two years of a college general education curriculum. Data for each of the reasoning levels are shown in Figure 2.1.

The top graph shows that the majority of freshmen already are doing well regarding Interpretive Reasoning, the lowest level of reasoning ability tested. By the Junior year, approximately 75% of our students, demonstrate an interpretive reasoning ability that would put them in the top-third of a national sample.

Regarding Strategic Reasoning, shown in the middle graph, most of the freshmen are found in the middle bracket. By the junior year, a shift occurs such that the majority have moved into the top third with the remaining students in the middle third. No shift is evident for Adaptive Reasoning, the highest reasoning level. The majority of freshmen and upper-level students are in the mid levels.

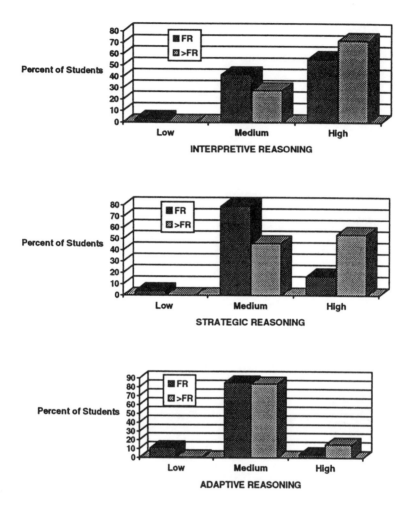

FIGURE 2.1   PERCENTAGE OF STUDENTS CLASSIFIED BY
                  PERFORMANCE AND REASONING SKILLS.

While these data are based on one theoretical approach to "critical
thinking" and on one test of that theory, they suggest the following about
our students' reasoning skills:

*   Incoming students use interpretive reasoning skills. They can
    summarize information and recast it in their own words. They are

11

less able to reason at the higher levels requiring inferential processing.

- During the first two years at Clemson, students learn to use strategic reasoning. Many of them acquire the ability to compare and contrast information and to use deduction.

- The first two years at Clemson do not appear to contribute greatly to our students' ability to use adaptive reasoning. Most of the freshmen and upper-level students remain at the mid-level of performance when it comes to synthesizing information, predicting relationships or using induction.

- While we should be pleased that few of our students fall into the bottom third of students regarding reasoning skills, we could make significant strides by exposing students to material and tasks that require the use of strategic and adaptive reasoning.

3. Can our students write?

As part of the Matrix version of the College BASE examination that was administered in the Fall semester of 1989, 72 freshmen and 79 upper-level students wrote an essay. The exam is designed to "measure writing proficiency through both indirect (multiple-choice items) and direct (writing exercise) assessment." As for the writing assignment, the "examinees are presented with a realistic campus issue and are instructed to take a position and defend it. This mode was chosen because, according to experts, it represents the kind of writing that examinees are most likely to encounter in their college courses."

The results indicate that our students can write better than the "typical college student" upon which the mean of the examination was based. The troubling aspect of the assessment of writing skills was the lack of increase in writing ability when freshman scores were compared to those of upper-level students. The mean score actually decreased slightly which is not significant and well within expected random fluctuation. However, after two or more years of additional college level education, the expectation was to find upperclassmen scoring several points higher than entering freshmen.

In terms of scoring by the College BASE examiner, "the writing exercise is scored on a scale of 1 to 6 by holistic rating method which is guided by a detailed rubric for each score point possible. Each essay is scored by at least two raters. In addition, raters are selected only after they meet stringent criteria regarding their experience with teaching and evaluating college-level writing and only after they participate in a College BASE training session."

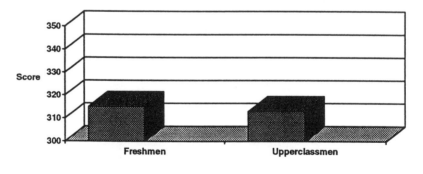

FIGURE 3.1.   WRITING PERFORMANCE BASED ON ESSAY
                SCORING BY COLLEGE BASE.

Prior to the results being reported from College BASE, members of the English department scored the writing samples. English department members also used a prescribed scoring method with multiple raters.

The raters had no knowledge of the sex, classification, or any other variable associated with the student taking the exam. As a result of their scoring, a significant gender difference was found, indicating that females performed better than males. Also, a significant difference was found due to classification, indicating that non-freshmen performed better than freshmen. In all fairness however, it must be noted that these differences although statistically significant, was of little practical significance since the greatest difference was only .49 points between the means of the two most divergent groups; leaving both means between 3 and 4 on the 1 to 6 scale.

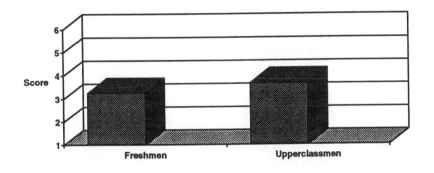

FIGURE 3.2.   WRITING PERFORMANCE BASED ON ESSAY
                   SCORING BY THE ENGLISH DEPARTMENT.

Members of the English department are working together to identify some other method which may be used in the future to assess writing skills. Discussions have ranged from using the College BASE again, and asking the English department to score the writing sample, to using a portfolio method.

The portfolio method has been used successfully at other schools to provide an indication of growth during the college experience. Basically, the portfolio method requires the student to keep a record (portfolio) of samples of work across the college years. The portfolio can be reviewed by members of the English department, by outside reviewers, or by a combination of these to add credibility to the rating which is given. This method has the advantage of allowing flexibility in the choice of materials which make up the portfolio, thereby not restricting the student to one examination which could vary due to outside influences. A concern with using the portfolio method is the difficulty associated with the administrative aspects of keeping up with the portfolio and assuring the appropriate materials are included. A major advantage in using a properly designed student portfolio system is that it allows one to evaluate writing performance as it applies to specific needs within the major discipline (e.g., creative, scientific, business, or technical).

Two other techniques used on many campuses are also designed to answer the question of how well students can write and provide documentation which can be considered non-subjective. One is capstone courses. Several universities use capstone courses in majors or concentrations as a way to determine how well the student has been able to synthesize the various courses related to the major or concentration. Out of this same idea can spring the other technique which seems to have merit, the senior thesis. The senior thesis can be graded by members of the department as well as an outside review team. The thesis can be read with an eye toward not only how well the student has mastered the necessary concepts but also, how well the student is able to express those concepts in writing. In other words, it can be graded for composition as well as content.

Whatever is determined to be the best method for this university, it is important to keep the focus on the intended use of the results. We intend for the results to be used as a general indicator which can guide us to look more closely at areas which turn up unexpected results, not to immediately make changes as a result of a single examination score. As such, the test does not need to have the same level of rigor as one which is being used to make decisions about students or programs. There is no disagreement that the test should be as good as we can possibly obtain or develop. However, consideration must also be given to ease of administration and cost since we are interested in obtaining information on a university level. It is unfair for the University community to point fingers at the English department for little growth in the area of writing ability. Unless the student is an English major, they will likely have few hours in English writing courses beyond those at the beginning of the college career. Writing is an important skill which should be reinforced and expected in many courses regardless of the department.

The answer to the initial question appears to be "yes." The disturbing finding is that writing does not improve between the freshman and senior years. As a response to the current concerns for speaking and writing a question will be continued on future surveys and will give us an indication of whether we are requiring more oral and formal written communication over the next few years. Figure 3.3 illustrates the findings based on the survey of 1990 alums.

16

As the figure illustrates, 79% of the 1990 students made fewer than 11
oral presentation during their undergraduate experience. Likewise, 68%
report making it through their undergraduate experience having
produced fewer than 11 formal papers. Forty percent report writing 5 or
fewer papers.

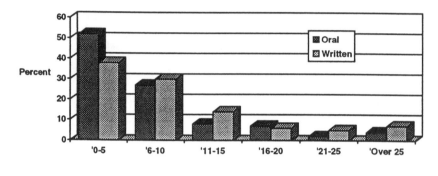

FIGURE 3.3   ORAL AND WRITTEN PRESENTATIONS MADE BY
                 STUDENTS WHO GRADUATED IN 1990.

APPENDIX H—*Review of Educational Units Regulations and Instructions*, University of Kentucky–Lexington Campus

*Text in italics has been added to explain more completely Lexington Campus guidelines to be used in the review.

The purpose of program/unit review is to improve the quality of teaching and learning, research, and public service by systematically reviewing mission, goals, priorities, activities and outcomes. Continuous program/unit improvement requires a planning process which integrates current goals and priorities with the basic mission. Continual improvement also requires a review process which evaluates progress toward goal achievement and provides feedback which assists in refinement of plans and direction for the unit. The planning and review processes used by each unit should be appropriate to that unit, but all such processes will include three basic elements: (I) strategic planning; (II) annual review; and (III) periodic review.

The primary concern is the degree of progress of the educational unit. Thus, the chief administrative officers of the educational units will be evaluated in terms of the unit(s) and program(s) for which they are responsible and not in isolation from these, in relation to the contributions of their units to the broader goals of the University and the Commonwealth, in relation to available resources and support, in relation to established University priorities, and in terms of the responsibilities defined in the Governing Regulations.

(I) STRATEGIC PLANNING. The University's Strategic Plan establishes the broad framework for planning at all levels of the institution. Within this framework, each unit must engage in a continuous planning process which involves faculty, staff and students. Clear goals and expected outcomes should be developed for the unit overall as well as for each of its instructional, research and service programs.

(II) ANNUAL REVIEW. The performance of each educational unit (including any college, community college, school, department, graduate center, research center/institute, and interdisciplinary instructional program) should be reviewed annually by the administrator to whom the unit reports. The annual review should be utilized to assess progress toward goals and to modify where deemed appropriate the unit's goals, priorities, and expected outcomes.

(III) PERIODIC REVIEW. The unit's performance will be comprehensively evaluated periodically. The primary purpose of both annual review and periodic review is improvement in the quality and effectiveness of the units and their programs.

(I) STRATEGIC PLAN

Each unit shall have a strategic plan which includes, but is not necessarily limited to, the following:

A. MISSION STATEMENT. Statement of the unit's mission, a description of each of the unit's instructional, research, and public service programs, and an explanation of how each supports the University's mission.

B. ENVIRONMENTAL/SELF-ASSESSMENT. An assessment of the unit's strengths and weaknesses, and an assessment of external environmental trends influencing the unit at the present and in the future (e.g. quality and quantity of faculty, students, and staff; support provided to the University and to the public; quality of facilities and equipment; demand by majors and by non-majors; demand for graduates; etc.).

C. CURRENT PRIORITIES AND OBJECTIVES. Statement of the unit's current goals and priorities in instruction, research, and service. For each of the priorities identified, the unit should designate:

1. EXPECTED RESULTS, STANDARDS OF PROGRESS, & EVALUATION METHODS. Description of the criteria or standards used to determine progress toward goals of the unit along with a description of evaluation techniques and methods (qualitative and/or quantitative) used to assess goal attainment.

2. USE OF RESULTS. Description of how the results of assessment and evaluation activities are used both to improve program quality and the overall effectiveness of the unit and to refine unit goals, priorities, and expected outcomes in the unit's plans.

D. EDUCATIONAL OUTCOMES FOR DEGREE PROGRAMS. Statement of each degree program's goals and expected educational outcomes for students who complete the program. For each educational outcome, the unit should designate:

1. STANDARDS OF PROGRESS & EVALUATION METHODS. Description of the standards used to determine progress toward goals of each degree program in the unit along with a description of evaluation techniques and methods (qualitative and/or quantitative) used to assess goal attainment.

2. USE OF RESULTS. Description of how the results of assessment and evaluation activities are used to improve program quality and the overall effectiveness of the unit and to refine unit goals, priorities, and expected outcomes as it relates to degree programs.

E. IMPLEMENTATION PLAN. A copy of the unit's plan which identifies actions to be taken and a time frame for accomplishment of goals.

The Lexington Campus Planning forms 1 and 2 can be used as a blueprint to format information required by this section.

The planning cycle for departments and other units below the college and vice presidential level will normally be determined by the dean of the college, or president in the Community Colleges, in consultation with the appropriate chancellor/vice president. Plans must be completed at least once during a unit's review period, typically in the self-study year as preparation for the periodic review. In each planning cycle, the unit's plan must be reviewed by the administrator to whom the unit reports. Resource allocation requests should be included in the deliberations of the unit's administrator's subsequent plans when budget matters are considered.

(II) ANNUAL REVIEW

The purpose of the annual review is to assess progress in accomplishing goals and objectives during the year based upon the resources available and to identify objectives for the next academic year. Objectives would be based on the goals and priorities of the unit's plan.

The annual review will consist of a concise report to the unit's administrative superior which summarizes: (1) accomplishments during the past year; (2) adjustments made to the unit's strategic plan, objectives, or programs; and, (3) goals and priorities for the next year.

(III) PERIODIC REVIEW

The purpose of periodic review is to provide the unit with the opportunity for an in-depth analysis of itself, a review of its strategic plan, and a review by a committee external to the unit, regarding effectiveness in meeting goals in instruction, research, and public service. Specifically, the periodic review phase of the planning and review cycle includes the following three components: (1) preparation of a self-study report by the unit, (2) evaluation by a review team external to the unit, and (3) revision of the unit's strategic plan, as based on recommendations from the self-study process and the periodic review team.

Review schedule: The Chancellors for the Lexington Campus, the Medical Center, and the Community College System and the Vice President for Research and Graduate

3

Studies shall conduct reviews of all colleges and educational units under their administrative authority according to a set schedule. This formal, structured review of each educational unit is usually scheduled every four to six years.

In the case of a community college, periodic review will occur at least once in each five-year period and usually during the decennial institutional self-study related to accreditation or during the fifth year after such a study.

Notification that the periodic review process is about to begin shall be provided to the unit by the appropriate administrative superior approximately three months prior to the formal appointment of the review team. This notification shall signal the initial development of the self-study report. The focus of the unit's internal review and the resultant self-study should be the quality of the unit's programs. Areas of special interest to the unit shall be identified at the beginning of the periodic review by the unit administrator and its administrative superior, usually a dean, for educational units and by the dean and chancellor/vice president for college and center/institute reviews.

To avoid duplication of effort, the periodic review should be coordinated with accreditation or other external reviews whenever possible. Any information gathered for accreditation self-study or other evaluation reports completed within the past three years, including the unit's annual reports, should serve as the core of the periodic review.

<u>Changing a periodic review schedule:</u> The periodic review of any educational unit at other than the regularly scheduled time may be requested by a majority of the members of the unit, the chief administrative officer of the unit, or the administrative officer to whom the chief administrator reports. Such requests must be in writing, must include a rationale for the "off-schedule" review, and must be submitted to the appropriate chancellor/vice president. "Off-schedule" reviews may also be initiated by the appropriate chancellor/vice president or by the President. Any change in schedule must be approved by the appropriate chancellor/vice president who communicates such changes to the President and the Senate Council or Community College Council whichever is appropriate. Extension of a regularly scheduled periodic review shall not exceed two years.

The outcome of program review should be a well-designed and agreed-upon plan for enhancement of the programs and the unit. Plans should be explicit, realistic, and viable, and should reflect the aspirations of each unit. **The program review process as well as the strategic plan should focus on improvements that can be made using resources that currently are available to the program.** *Consideration can also be given, however, to proposed program improvements and expansions that would require additional resources. In such cases, the need and priority for additional resources must be clearly justified and supported by the dean(s).*

4

Responsibilities For Conducting The Review

The primary responsibility for overseeing the review of an academic program lies with the college dean who has administrative responsibility for the department. In the case of a college review, the Chancellor has responsibility for appointing the committee and performing other duties associated with the review.

The unit being reviewed is responsible for preparing a self-study source document. It is anticipated the dean who administers the department will assign to the relevant department chair the responsibility of seeing that the self-study is completed in a timely manner and that the dean insure that the self-study is adequately prepared for the review team. Faculty associated with the program should be involved in the preparation of the self-study and should have an opportunity to review and comment upon the self-study report before it is submitted to the dean.

While the dean has the primary responsibility for overseeing the review of the academic programs within the college, the Deans of Undergraduate Studies and the Graduate School and other administrators also should be involved in the review process as appropriate.

Support for Data Analysis & Collection of Data

Much of the data requested in the self-study source report can be provided by the Lexington Campus Office of Planning and Assessment and the Graduate School. Where centralized data is available, it should be used to ensure comparable definitions and time frames. A package of reports for the review period which can be used in the self-study process will be provided by the Chancellor's office to the Dean of the College early in the academic year of the review. Assistance can be provided in collecting additional data, presenting, analyzing, and interpreting relevant data by the Office of Lexington Campus Planning and Assessment.

A.   UNIT SELF-STUDY REPORT

In the first step of the periodic review, the unit prepares a self-study report. The report shall provide background data and other information needed by the periodic review team. The unit's strategic plan and the results of the annual reviews shall serve as an important source of information for this report. In addition, the report shall include information on at least the following points relating to the unit:

(1) CURRENT PLANS. A copy of the unit's current strategic plan and annual reports since the last self-study shall be provided. The plans should include those items outlined in the strategic plan section of this regulation (See Section I.) including statements of the unit's current goals, objectives, priorities, expected results and criteria used to

5

evaluate success in meeting the unit's goals for instruction, research, and service. *Lexington Campus Planning forms 1 and 2 may be used.*

> *a. Specify clearly the primary mission of the academic unit.*
> *b. Specify the intermediate and long-range goals for instruction, research, and public service.*
> *c. List the specific objectives of the department for the next six years. (Example: increase baccalaureate graduates by fifty percent over the next four years.)*
> *d. Specify briefly the plans which have been formulated in the unit to achieve its goals and identify procedures used in formulating program plans and establishing priorities.*

(2) EVALUATION OF PLANNING & DECISION MAKING. A description and evaluation of the effectiveness of the unit's planning process along with the appropriateness of faculty and others' participation in the planning process shall be provided. Description of the extent to which the unit's strategic plan is appropriate given resources available and whether the plan is being implemented should be provided.

(3) QUALITY OF DEGREE PROGRAMS & EDUCATIONAL OUTCOMES. Evidence of quality instruction, research and public service shall be provided including statements of each degree program's goals and expected educational accomplishments and outcomes for students who complete each program in the unit.

> *a. **General Information.** Student enrollment and degrees awarded information has been provided to the Dean's office for each program under review. Request for other data may be made to the Lexington Campus Planning and Assessment Office.*
>
> *b. **Quality of Degree Programs and Student Learning Outcomes.** For each degree program included in the unit's review, list the student learning objectives as well as provide evidence to demonstrate that these objectives are being met. Assess the quality of the curriculum, admissions and recruitment efforts, undergraduate and graduate classroom instruction, advising and other student activities and support services provided by the unit. (Lexington Campus Planning forms 3 and 4 may be used as the basis for this section).*
>
> *c. **Quality of Research and Service Programs.** Assess the quality of the research and service programs. Provide information where possible to show how this program compares with the best programs of its type in the United States.*
>
> *d. **Faculty Quality and Accomplishments.** Provide evidence of the quality of*

6

faculty, staff, and programs, including brief copies of faculty vita.

Attach a brief vita for each faculty member. The vita should include the following information from the past three years:

1. Special awards received, journals edited, etc.
2. Publications in refereed journals
3. Books, book chapters, monographs
4. Extension publications where applicable
5. Other significant publications, creative activities, works and performances (excluding any in the above categories)
6. Grants and contracts applied for and received.

*e. **Quality of Management, Adherence to Policies, & Collegial Environment.** Describe the environment in the unit and how effective management of the unit's available resources is in maximizing program effectiveness. Provide a copy of the unit's relevant policies and procedures.*

Materials, Information, and Questions Provided to the Review Team

Upon appointment of the review team, the dean should provide the following to each member of the review team. A copy of this material should be available to the unit undergoing the review.

1. *A copy of the university program review policy document*

2. *The unit's self-study report with appendices, accreditation reports, or other reviews conducted since the last review. The team may request additional information.*

Appendices to Self-Study

A. *Tables, charts, and graphs that are referred to in the body of the report*
B. *Roster of current faculty and staff; part time faculty and adjunct faculty should be included along with their qualifications and vitae.*
C. *Summary curriculum vitae for each faculty member.*
D. *Relevant catalog materials.*

7

E.   *Copies of the unit's strategic and implementation plans, annual reports, past reviews and reports, policy documents, student recruiting brochures, and other items. appropriate to the self-study*

F.   *Brief description of the self-study process.*

3.   *A list of specific questions the review team is asked to address. This list should be developed by the dean after receiving suggestions from appropriate sources including the unit undergoing review, the faculty Senate Council, and the dean or chancellor responsible for the review.*

4.   *A schedule for submission of the team's preliminary, the final report and timetable for the completion of the implementation plan by the unit.*

The Lexington Campus Planning and Assessment Office can be used as a central place to make available bulky documents to the review team which do not warrant copying.

(4) RECOMMENDATIONS. Recommendations for modifications in the structure, programs, or goals of the programs of this unit shall be included as well as recommendations for eliminating functions which cannot be adequately supported.

To facilitate the review process, the unit's self-study should conclude with a summary and recommendation section which includes: (1) summary of major strengths of the unit, (2) summary of major problems facing it; and (3) summary of recommendations regarding the unit.

The nature of the unit and/or any special focus given the periodic review may require that additional issues be addressed in the unit's self-study report.

B. TEAM REVIEW

The purpose of the team review is to provide the unit with an external perspective. This includes a judgement of program quality and assessment of the effectiveness of the instruction, research, and public service programs.

After consultation with the unit's administrative officer, the administrative officer, the administrative office to which the unit reports will appoint and charge an ad hoc Review Team. Review teams for departments shall be appointed by the college dean after consultation with the appropriate college council. The Chancellor/Vice President shall consult with the Senate Council to seek nominations prior to appointment of review teams for colleges. The appropriate dean(s) shall also be consulted prior to appointment of the review team.

The review team for instructional units shall be formed principally from faculty members and shall include faculty members from within and without the unit being reviewed. (Individuals from within the unit will be expected to not participate in matters which will prevent members of the unit from being candid.) The team shall also include undergraduate and graduate student representation as appropriate and may include alumni and practicing professionals. The review team for research units shall include faculty members in the field and may include researchers knowledgeable in the field from outside the University.

Each review team should collect information it deems most appropriate, but certain information shall be incorporated in all reviews. However, systematic assessment and evaluation will involve all unit faculty, staff, and students (where appropriate) regarding the operation and progress of the unit.

The review team should focus its review and recommendations on the following major areas:

(1) **Quality of the Degree Programs & Student Learning**
a. Quality and appropriateness of the curriculum, instruction, advising, and other student activities and support services of the unit.

b. Quality of students, admissions requirements, and recruitment efforts.

c. Effectiveness of the unit and program in promoting student learning and achievement.

9

(2)   Quality of Research & Service Programs
a. Quality, range, and focus of research, scholarship, or creative activities of the unit.

b. National and international standing and reputation of the program.

c. Quality and appropriateness of continuing education and service programs and activities.

(3)   Quality of Faculty/Staff and Unit Productivity
a. Quality of instruction and advising at the undergraduate and graduate level by faculty in the department.

b. Quality of teaching and orientation programs for teaching assistants in the unit.

c. Faculty honors and accomplishments.

d. Quality of personnel policies and practices (faculty recruiting, affirmative action, mentoring, development, and evaluation).

(4)   Quality of Recruitment and Retention of a Diverse Faculty, Staff and Student Body
Describe progress in recruiting and retaining a diverse faculty, staff, and student body. Describe awards and honors have faculty received and their roles in national professional associations.

(5)   Quality of Management, Adherence to Policies and Collegial Environment
a. The collegial environment within the unit and with other units of the college and university (i.e., among and between faculty, staff, and students.

b. The on-going relationship between the unit and relevant constituencies external to the university (e.g., alumni, employers, and special interest groups).

(6)   Quality of Planning, Evaluation, and Resource Maximizing Program Effectiveness in Terms of

10

Allocation
a. Evaluation of whether the unit's planning activities are participatory and lead to a consensus on goals for the department, its faculty, and its students.

b. Evaluation criteria are clearly delineated and evaluation processes lead to the improvement of faculty and the unit's programs.

c. Data on the achievements of faculty, students, and the program are collected and used in the planning process.

d. Resources and support services available to the unit are adequate and/or managed to achieve goals set by the department.

(7)   **Recommendations.** *The recommendations should focus on improvements that can be made using resources that currently are available to the program. If recommendations are made for changes that would require additional resources, the need and priority for additional resources should be clearly specified.*

Upon completion of this phase of the periodic review, the review team should meet with the unit faculty, staff, and chairperson/director and with the unit's immediate administrative supervisor, to discuss the findings.

The substance of the review team's report is to be shared with the administrative officer of the unit being evaluated, and the full report is to be forwarded to the next levels of administration, including the appropriate chancellor/vice president. An executive summary of the report is to be prepared by the chancellor/vice president and forwarded to the President.

In the case of unit reviews, the administrative officer receiving the review team's report shall provide a preliminary copy of it to each faculty/professional staff member in the unit and shall make a preliminary copy available to students and staff. Before distribution, the preliminary report may be edited by the administrator to whom the report is submitted to eliminate material clearly invasive of personal privacy and material which may be libelous.

In the case of college reviews, the chancellor/vice president shall provide each faculty member/professional staff in the college with a summary of the review team's final report. This summary shall include all major findings and conclusions and all recommendations. In addition, copies of the full, final report shall be distributed to each department/division in the college and to the University library for access by faculty, staff, and students. Before providing access, copies of the final report may be edited by the chancellor/vice president to whom the report is submitted to eliminate material clearly invasive of personal privacy and material which may be libelous.

In the case of both reviews, the administrative officer receiving the reports will work cooperatively with the unit leadership to address issues and recommendations raised throughout the review process. A brief report addressing the activities planned to respond to the recommendations will be prepared by the administrative officer, filed with the unit evaluated, and forwarded through appropriate administrative channels to the chancellor/vice president.

C. REVISION OF THE STRATEGIC PLAN & IMPLEMENTATION

Upon completion of the periodic review phase of the planning cycle, the unit will revise and refine its strategic plan based on the recommendations from the unit's self-study as well as those of the periodic review team. In addition, the unit will prepare as part of the regular annual review process an implementation plan which designates responsibility and sets a schedule for activities to achieve goals based on agreed upon recommendations.

In the concluding step of the periodic review, the unit assimilates the recommendations from the periodic review to refine its strategic, thus completing one planning and review cycle and beginning another.

The revised strategic plan and departmental response should (1) identify and prioritize the goals of the unit over the next six years, (2) identify the strategies which will be used to accomplish those goals, e.g., what actions are to be taken by whom and by what deadlines, and (3) the expected outcome or results of the implementation plan. Each college may design their own planning format, however, information included in the Lexington Campus Strategic Planning forms 1 and 2 may be used.

Where appropriate, a budget recommendation will be made by the dean for funds to remedy problems identified in the program review process, to support unit goals which should be addressed, and to strengthen the program. Where additional funds are required to implement a plan, the appropriate dean(s) will involve the chancellor prior to finalizing the plan to ensure that necessary support will be available. Where recommendations from the review committee are not accepted by the dean(s) or chancellor or the institution is not able to implement them, the reasons should be discussed with the department and other relevant parties. Budget adjustments and recommendations should involve and be coordinated by all academic sectors of the University.

12

D.   PREPARATION OF THE CHE PROGRAM REVIEW DOCUMENTS

Because the goals of the University's unit review and the program assessment review required by the Kentucky Council on Higher Education are compatible, the report prepared under this administrative regulation may be used as the basis for the review required by the Kentucky Council on Higher Education. Since the University's schedule for programs does not coincide with the Council on Higher Education's, a summary of the findings of the most recent internal unit review may be used unless deemed otherwise by the Chancellor/Vice President of that sector/area. Because the academic structure varies by sector/area, the Chancellor/Vice President in each sector/area will assign responsibility for completion of these reports. The reports will be submitted to the Council on Higher Education by the President. (See Appendix I.)

The Lexington Campus requires only a 2-3 page executive summary of the review and a complete listing of all recommendations of the review team. The CHE documents will be finalized the year the program is to be reviewed by CHE.

1001a-93.

APPENDIX I—Assessment Cycles at Sam Houston State College/Jefferson State Community College/Collin County Community College

Sam Houston State University Assessment Cycle

Each summer the Institutional Effectiveness Committee identifies approximately 15 (or 20% of the total) academic and administrative departments for participating in assessment activities with the assistance of the Committee. These departments are notified and asked to appoint an "assessment liaison" to work with the Committee on behalf of their department. Over the next two years, departments work with the Committee to complete a schedule of assessment activities. During workshops held in the fall, departments are given an overview of what is expected and an orientation to the methods of assessment they might choose to use. During the first two years of the cycle listed below, departments received considerable support from the Committee and Institutional Research. During this period, departments are encouraged to assess those outcomes that are more difficult, require more effort or that may be more expensive. Not all intended outcomes are assessed simultaneously. Departments continue to assess outcomes over the next three years with minimal assistance from the Committee, although they are still given both technical and clerical support through the Office of Institutional Research.

First Fall Semester
    1. Write drafts of goals and intended outcomes.
        A. Goals are written or revised so that they are stated in measurable terms.
        B. Intended outcomes are stated in measurable terms.
    2. Draft of goals and outcomes are submitted to the Institutional Effectiveness Committee for review. (Committee certifies goals and outcomes as measurable or recommends revision.)
    3. By end of semester, goals and outcomes are adopted by department and approved by the Committee.

First Spring Semester
    1. Assessment Plans are designed for each department.
        A. Assessment liaisons work with Committee to identify potential means of assessing each outcome.
        B. Assessment liaisons present assessment methods to department for selection and adoption.
        C. Committee reviews draft of department assessment plans and develops recommends schedules and funds to support assessment efforts during the next year.
        D. Departments submit final assessment plans which include goals, intended outcomes, assessment techniques, and schedule of activities.
        E. Development of assessment instruments may commence.
        F. Nature of support to be provided by the Office of Institutional Research is established.

Second Fall Semester
    1. Assessment instruments are finalized, some may be administered.

Second Spring Semester
    1. Assessment instruments are administered and other assessment data are gathered.
    2. Assessment data are analyzed and first run is given to department. Additional analyses may be performed.
    3. Departments review findings submit report.

Third, Fourth and Fifth Fall Semesters
    1. Departments continue assessment of outcomes.

Third, Fourth and Fifth Spring Semesters
    1. Departments continue to use results of assessment.
    2. Departments submit annual report of assessment activities, findings, and use of the results to the Committee.

Sixth Fall Semester—Cycle begins anew.

Jefferson State Community College Assessment Cycle

INSTITUTIONAL EFFECTIVENESS AT JEFFERSON STATE: AN OVERVIEW

The philosophy underlying Jefferson State's efforts related to institutional effectiveness is exemplified by Peter Ewell's "self-regarding" institution. Like the institution described by Ewell and Lisensky, Jefferson State's goals are to clearly understand its commitments to its students and the community that it serves, to have informed discussions based on explicit information at all levels, and to willingly change as needed to fulfill those commitments. Additionally, Jefferson State as a public institution, recognizes and accepts its responsibility to respond to legitimate requests for accountability from external constituencies and agencies by providing accurate and appropriate data on its educational efforts.

In its effort to attain these goals Jefferson State has developed an institutional effectiveness model comprised of three components—purposes, plans, and results—which are refined and modified continuously through the processes of planning, implementation, and evaluation. Each of these is an integral part of efforts to achieve effectiveness, and although each has been developed and implemented separately, it is only when all are fully integrated that Jefferson State emerges as a truly effective institution.

Numerous attempts to develop a flowchart that accurately illustrates the interrelationships and dynamics existing among the various components and processes in Jefferson State's model have led to the realization that efforts to achieve effectiveness can neither be described as a series of discrete events nor organized in a linear sequence, no matter how many lines and arrows are used. The model used in physics to represent light and its component wavelengths provides a more accurate representation. Separated, the wavelengths may be red or blue or green or a number of other colors; however, when all of the wavelengths are focused together, the individual colors merge, and white light appears. Just as with light, any part of Jefferson State's model may take precedence for a time with the college's efforts focused primarily on that part as needed. Efforts may focus on planning and plans for awhile and then move to the implementation of plans; at other times, the focus may shift to evaluating the results of implementation, to modifying plans, or to refining expected results.

Even as the focus shifts from one component to another, however, the other components of the model remain ongoing, and, just as white light emerges only when all of the wavelengths are focused on one point, Jefferson State emerges as an effective institution only when all of the components/processes are fully integrated. The following sections provide an overview of each of the components and processes in Jefferson State's model, and briefly describe the interrelations among them.

PURPOSES/COMMITMENTS

Effectiveness is viewed in many difference ways, and one of the first tasks facing an institution in implementing effectiveness measures is to decide how effectiveness is to be defined at that institution. At Jefferson State effectiveness is defined as how well the institution is doing what it says it is doing— how well the results achieved match the results expected or outcomes intended.

For an institution to know what it is about requires explicitly stated purposes which are clearly understood and supported at all levels. Jefferson State's *Statement of Philosophy and Purpose* identifies three very broad institutional purposes. In order to operationalize the institutional purposes, each operational unit of the college has defined its purposes and commitments in relation to those of the college, thus, linking its operations to the college purposes and accepting responsibility for contributing to the achievement of one or more of them.

PLANS/PLANNING

It is not enough for an institution to merely identify its purposes and hope for the best. An institution must work at developing and implementing plans which can realistically be expected to yield the outcomes intended when the purposes were adopted. Our regional accrediting agency, the Southern Association of Colleges and Schools (SACS), mandates "...an obligation to all constituents to evaluate effectiveness and to use the results in a broad-based, continuous planning and evaluation process." Jefferson State's planning processes occur within the context of long-range goals derived from the *Statement of Philosophy and Purpose*. The process begins each year with an evaluation of the past year's accomplishments and identification of action priorities for the coming year. These action priorities provide the basis for planning at the operational unit level. The operational unit plans are integrated at the dean's level. The culmination of this process is the formulation of the Annual College Plan.

RESULTS/EVALUATION

The effective institution does not stop with planning and the implementation of these plans. Results must be evaluated, held up against some intended or expected standard, and critically examined in light of what should be. Only then can the institution clearly perceive the directions in which it is going and make realistic plans for proceeding in those directions or for changing course. Jefferson State's evaluation plan requires evaluation at four levels, thus obtaining valuable insights about the effectiveness of the institution from four different perspectives, that of the institution, the operational units, the college personnel making up those units, and the students.

At the operational unit level, evaluation occurs through annual reviews used to establish trends and identify problems severe enough to require further evaluation and a more in-depth analysis at less frequent but regular intervals. Assessment at the institutional level involves the compilation and analysis of data from the appropriate units for selected performance measures. At both the institutional level and the operational unit level the intent of evaluation is to compare the results achieved with those expected or intended and to provide information which can be used to improve programs and services by reducing the disparity between the two.

College personnel are evaluated annually. Student evaluation begins with assessment of their basic skills in writing, reading and mathematics. Tests scores on the evaluation instruments are used to place students in appropriate ability-level courses. After their initial course placement, student progress is evaluated using primarily traditional in-class measurements. Some students in specialized fields are also evaluated through state and national licensure/certification examinations.

Collin County Community College Institutional Effectiveness Cycle

In January 1992 the Strategic Planning Task Force merged with the Council on Institutional Effectiveness to form the Council on Planning and Institutional Effectiveness (CPIE). The Council has as its mission, "To develop, implement and monitor planning and evaluation processes which are designed to ensure the effectiveness of the educational programs, services and operations of the institution." Implementing this mission, CPIE has established a two-year institutional effectiveness cycle to correspond with the State of Texas' biennial funding cycle. The chart below illustrates this cycle.

Date	*Activity*
Fall '92	Planning/Evaluation Workshop
	Evaluation of '91-'92 plan
	Improvement for '92-'93
	Implementation of '92-'93 plan
Spring '93	'93-'95 plans developed
Fall '93	All-Staff Retreat
Fall '93-Spring '94	Implementation of '93-'94 plan
Fall '94	Planning/Evaluation Workshop
	Evaluation of '93-'94 plan
	Improvement for '94-'95
	Implementation of '94-'95 plan

For example, at the Fall '92 planning/evaluation workshop the president, vice presidents, deans and directors evaluated their success in meeting the goals/objectives and budgetary allotments articulated in the plan for the immediately preceding fiscal year and presented key goals they established for the following year. Regarding the published strategic plan, in Fall '92 every instructional and non-instructional department head assessed the achievement status of every objective set the preceding year and indicated what modifications, if any, would be made to that objective for the ensuing year. This evaluation also facilitated the college-wide planning process for the 1993-'95 biennium undertaken in the Spring of '93. The All-Staff Retreat in Fall '93 had as a key objective the review of and suggestions for revision in the college-wide goal statements.

INDEX